Who put the ball in the net?
How Bolton Wanderers joined Europe's elite

Chris Flanagan

VERTICAL EDITIONS
www.verticaleditions.com

First published in the United Kingdom in 2014 by Vertical Editions, Unit 4a, Snaygill Industrial Estate, Skipton, North Yorkshire BD23 2QR

www.verticaleditions.com

ISBN 978-1-904091-87-5

A CIP catalogue record for this book is available from the British Library

Cover design by HBA, York

Printed and bound by CMP (uk) Ltd, Poole, Dorset

In memory of grandad

Contents

Foreword by Kevin Davies

I never expected that I'd get the chance to play in Europe when I first came to Bolton Wanderers, particularly as I only arrived on trial after being released by Southampton. But I'm proud now to have been involved in part of Bolton's history, the first time the club were involved in the UEFA Cup.

It was just fantastic to be involved in that squad and what we achieved. For a club like Bolton Wanderers to be playing in the UEFA Cup and finishing so high up in the Premier League, people said we were punching above our weight. But we had a really good set of players and manager, with a fantastic backroom staff. We had a good spirit and a real belief. The Reebok was rocking at times, and it pushed us on and on. We were even pushing for the Champions League.

Looking back now at some of the clubs we played, those years in the UEFA Cup were fantastic. I've still got the black and white shirt of Lokomotiv Plovdiv from our first tie in the UEFA Cup in 2005, which I got from their number 3. Another of my favourite memories is the match at Marseille. Even though we went out, there was a fantastic picture on display at the Reebok of that game, of me standing and looking at the arched stands they had at the Stade Velodrome. I just loved that match, and the atmosphere there. That picture is still one of my favourites.

The whole club loved that first season in Europe and when you get a taste for it you want more, so to qualify again in 2007 was fantastic. To qualify twice is an incredibly hard thing for a club like Bolton to do.

In that second season in the UEFA Cup, of course, was the Bayern Munich game. I can remember the excitement when we heard during training that we'd been drawn against them, and that night at the Allianz Arena was just incredible. It's something that is part of the club's history now – that we went there and got a 2-2 draw. It was a fantastic achievement, I'm proud to have been a part of that and to score the equaliser was an amazing feeling. Over the 10 years I spent playing for Bolton there are a lot of great memories for me personally, but that's probably the one that stands out.

After that we went on to knock out Atletico Madrid. What a result that was. The 1-0 win in the home leg has to down as one of the great nights at the Reebok. The Sporting Lisbon tie was an anti-climax and of course those of us who didn't travel to the away leg were gutted to miss out. But in all our games in Europe over the two seasons, I don't think we ever embarrassed ourselves against some really big clubs. We held our own.

The supporters travelled everywhere with us, too. I remember how family and friends used to look forward to those little European trips away to places that you'd never even heard of sometimes! The fans always supported us home and away, so although we wanted to be playing in those sorts of competitions for ourselves as players, we also wanted to do something for them. It was great for them and for us to be playing in stadiums like Marseille, Munich and Madrid. Us, little old Bolton!

They loved it, we as players loved it, everyone involved loved it. They were great times.

Prologue

When a journalist approaches a high-profile footballer for an interview, it is not unusual for their first answer to be no. But ask many of Bolton Wanderers' former stars if they are willing to share their memories of the club's two seasons in the UEFA Cup, and the answer is an immediate yes.

They speak with smiles on their faces, the happy memories flooding back. They are only too pleased to talk about some of the most remarkable moments of their career. That tells you everything about how special Wanderers' UEFA Cup adventure was – not just for the supporters but for the players who helped to make it all happen.

As a lifelong supporter, I was fortunate enough to be at all 18 of the club's games in the UEFA Cup, the highlight of 25 years watching Bolton Wanderers. It has been a pleasure and a privilege to speak to so many of those who were involved in that incredible journey around the continent.

I travelled to clubs such as West Ham, Preston, Wigan and Accrington to speak to those who have since departed Wanderers. El-Hadji Diouf kindly offered to meet me at the Whites Hotel at the Reebok Stadium, while Henrik Pedersen spoke to me over the phone from behind the bar of his pub in Denmark. All were generous with their time, enjoying recounting tales of a wonderful era.

Speak to Ricardo Vaz Te about his wonder goal in Guimaraes or Ali Al Habsi about his incredible save from Franck Ribery at Bayern Munich, to name just two examples, and you can sense the genuine affection they still have for those moments. I would like to thank Bolton Wanderers for their help and thank everyone who has contributed to this book, including Russell Byrne-Fraser and Simon Marland for providing additional information.

I would also like to take this opportunity to remember Gary Speed, a hugely popular and important figure in Wanderers' UEFA Cup team who tragically died in 2011. His role in the club's success will never be forgotten.

Finally, I and the rest of my family would like to dedicate this book to my grandfather. From the very start, I was writing this for him. It was with my grandfather and my father that I first started to visit Burnden Park as a child. We travelled around the country together supporting Bolton Wanderers. He was a season ticket holder until Bolton's final season in the Premier League, aged 91.

I wanted to write something that would make him proud. I told him I would bring him the manuscript for the book as soon as it was finished.

At midnight on the evening I was completing that manuscript, he passed away. He was loved by everyone, and he loved Bolton Wanderers. He will always be missed.

Introduction

The European Dream

On August 29, 1987, Bolton Wanderers were in action in the Fourth Division of English football at the old Athletic Ground at Scarborough. Months earlier, in the original version of the Football League play-offs, they had humiliatingly lost to Aldershot to be relegated to the domestic game's bottom tier for the first time in their history.

That day at the Athletic Ground, Wanderers faced a Scarborough side playing only the third Football League game of their long existence, after promotion from the Conference under Neil Warnock in the previous season. In front of a crowd of little more than 4,000, Bolton were thrashed 4-0.

It was very early in the 1987/88 season, but those Wanderers fans who had made the trip to Yorkshire realised they were witnessing a new low for the club. It left Bolton 16th in the Fourth Division table. The era of Nat Lofthouse and FA Cup glory had long gone.

Even the existence of the club was no longer certain. Under threat of closure during the 1980s as cash problems took hold, the club were saved by the launch of the Lifeline lottery scheme, spearheaded by the great Lofthouse himself. Controversially, more funds were raised by selling off a large chunk of the famous Embankment at Burnden Park to Normid, who built a superstore on the site. An ugly presence in one corner of the ground, it seemed like Wanderers had sold part of their soul. But the club felt they had little choice. Things had got that bad.

In those dark moments, playing in one of Europe's biggest competitions seemed like an impossible dream. But 18 years after that Scarborough game, almost to the day, Bolton officials were in Monaco for the first round draw of the UEFA Cup. The club were playing in a major European competition for the first time in their history. Wanderers had been born again, and now they were coming of age.

Two days after the Scarborough defeat, Bolton took on Peterborough at Burnden Park in front of a crowd of only 3,746. On occasions, greater numbers than that would travel thousands of miles across the continent to watch Wanderers play in the UEFA Cup. Rarely before had Bolton supporters felt more proud.

The club had played in Europe before, if not in quite the same fashion, back in the 1993/94 season. In the end, they recovered from the nightmare at the Athletic Ground to gain promotion back to the Third Division at the first attempt in 1987/88, going up on the last day of the season at Wrexham. They went up once more in 1993, again on the final day of the campaign thanks to a John McGinlay penalty at home to Preston.

Their arrival back into the second tier of English football earned them a place in the Anglo-Italian Cup. Technically, their first game in European competition was against the exotic opposition of Tranmere Rovers. Wanderers won 2-1 at Prenton Park thanks to goals from McGinlay and Owen Coyle in a preliminary round fixture witnessed by less than 3,000 people. There were not many more at Burnden Park a week later when Coyle scored twice to give Bolton a 2-0 triumph over Sunderland, confirming that they would top their three-club preliminary round group and progress to play some actual foreign opponents.

Playing against sides from the Italian Serie B, Wanderers were drawn in Group A, where they would face Ancona, Brescia, Pisa and Ascoli. They thrashed Ancona 5-0 in their first match at Burnden with the aid of a double from McGinlay and further goals from Jason McAteer, Alan Thompson and Jimmy Phillips. The fixture drew a crowd of only 3,500.

Even less were present when Wanderers drew 3-3 at home to Brescia, despite the presence of Gheorghe Hagi in the visitors' line-up. Months later the Romanian would star at the 1994 World Cup and earn a move to Barcelona. He scored at Burnden that night with a low free kick that slipped through the grasp of Aidan Davison. Coyle, McGinlay and Scott Green netted for Bolton but perhaps more notable was the man in the middle, who stood out even in such a low key fixture. With a bald head and noticeably sharp and cacophonous blasts on the whistle, he seemed different from the referees that fans were used to seeing in England. His name was Pierluigi Collina, unknown then but now regarded by many as possibly the greatest referee of the modern era.

After that Wanderers travelled to Italy for their first away fixture, taking 500 supporters to Pisa in Tuscany. Fans spent the day under the famous Leaning Tower of Pisa, then undergoing restoration work, with popular club commentator Dave Higson interviewing supporters for the official video of the trip.

Directors and dignitaries, including club legend Lofthouse, also visited the nearby city of Florence.

Wanderers supporters made up nearly half of the crowd at the ramshackle Arena Garibaldi, which was probably named more in honour of the famous Italian general and politician than the biscuit. They sang incessantly and saw Phillips score in a 1-1 draw. Some Bolton supporters made the 70-mile trip on to England's World Cup qualifier against San Marino in Bologna a day later – the match when Graham Taylor's side infamously trailed after eight seconds but went on to win 7-1 in the manager's last game in charge.

Wanderers' Anglo-Italian Cup campaign ended at Ascoli when Mark

Seagraves netted in another 1-1 draw, which finished dramatically as Italian players aimed kicks at English referee Peter Foakes in disgust at his handling of the game. German striker Oliver Bierhoff – the scorer of the winner in the final of Euro 96 – saw a goal disallowed for Ascoli, but the match was played just before Christmas and only a handful of supporters travelled.

In a somewhat convoluted format, only the English team with the best record from their four matches progressed. Even though they were unbeaten throughout the competition, Bolton's six points from four games were not enough. Notts County qualified from Wanderers' group, together with Italian side Brescia. In Group B, Southend progressed as well as Pescara, who had edged out Gabriel Batistuta's Fiorentina. After the semi finals, Notts County faced Brescia in the final at Wembley, losing 1-0. The crowd was just 17,000.

A revised format for the competition in 1994/95 meant Wanderers were not invited to take part, having finished in the bottom half of the First Division league table a season earlier. But the experience had given some, including club secretary Simon Marland, a taste for European football.

"I was the club accountant then and we organised the team's travel and the supporters' travel," he says. "We went to Pisa for the first game and there were about 500 fans there. There was a photograph of all the Bolton fans around the Leaning Tower. It was closed at the time, I don't think you could go up it.

"At that time we were probably getting crowds of 14,000 at home, and for the fans who went to Italy it was an opportunity. They were thinking, 'This is Europe, because we aren't going to get into any of the big competitions. These are going to be our trips to Europe.'

"Like a lot of the stadiums in Italy, it didn't belong to the club, I think it belonged to the town so the maintenance wasn't great, it was just a stadium, there was nothing special about it whatsoever. The atmosphere was poor too because of the number of people there, Bolton fans made more noise than the Italians. But it was a good experience.

"In comparison to the UEFA Cup it was a lot more low key because they were competitive games but these days they'd be seen as a hindrance. There was no money in it, financially you could forget it. I think in both games in Italy the crowd was around 1,000, and the gates at Burnden for the two home games weren't great either. But it was just the prestige of it, and I remember the game against Brescia when Gheorghe Hagi played, that was magnificent just to be able to see that.

"The very last game we played in it was in Ascoli and from 500 people going to Pisa, I think there were 10! It was three days before Christmas, and I think Notts County and Stoke were going out to Italy as well, so we shared a plane with them to cut costs. There was a big fracas at the end of that game with all the players and the referee, although it was handbags. The games in England were refereed by an Italian, and the games in Italy had an

English official refereeing. You could imagine then that when things didn't go the Italians' way and we looked like we were going to get a point, they weren't happy.

"We just missed out as Notts County went to the final that year at Wembley. It was disappointing, we hadn't lost a game but hadn't quite made the final. That would have been nice, a game at Wembley. But they were happy days. You looked at that and thought what it would be like in a proper game, in proper European football?"

It would be another 12 years before Bolton would face European opposition in a competitive match, this time for real.

Wanderers returned to the top flight for the first time in 15 years in 1995, with a dramatic victory over Reading in the play-off final at Wembley, before a spell yo-yo-ing between the top two divisions. Qualifying for Europe was still far from the horizon when Sam Allardyce was appointed as manager in October 1999, two years after the club's move to the altogether more modern Reebok Stadium, with Bolton mid-table in the second tier. Phil Brown, caretaker boss before Allardyce's arrival, became assistant manager.

During Allardyce's tenure, Europe started to edge ever closer. First promotion to the Premier League in 2001, then narrow survival in consecutive seasons. More and more top quality players were beginning to arrive. Bruno N'Gotty was followed by Youri Djorkaeff, Jay-Jay Okocha, Ivan Campo and Stelios Giannakopoulos.

Many were free transfers, considered past their best. But Allardyce recognised their ability and persuaded them to sign for a previously unfancied club who had spent almost all of the past 40 years outside the top division of English football. It was the start of a remarkable era.

Allardyce changed things off the field as well as on it, focusing on areas such as statistical analysis and sports science. The club's Euxton training ground was transformed from a social club that the Wanderers squad shared with local bowls enthusiasts, into a state-of-the-art facility with virtually everything that players could ever need – including a cryotherapy fridge, where temperatures could dip to minus 150 degrees. Instigated by performance director Mike Forde, who would later move on to Chelsea, staff would have regular away days where they would lock themselves in a hotel room and brainstorm new ways to steal a march on their rivals.

With such blue sky thinking, Wanderers were beginning to compete with the best. In 2004 they came within just one game of qualifying for the UEFA Cup. Facing Aston Villa in the semi finals of the Carling Cup, they raced into an incredible 3-0 lead in the first 17 minutes of the first leg at the Reebok Stadium thanks to a free kick from Okocha, a strike from Kevin Nolan and a stunning overhead kick from Stelios. Villa responded with two goals but N'Gotty scored before Okocha netted arguably the best goal the stadium has ever seen – spotting a tiny gap between wall and near post from an angled free kick, before bending a thunderous shot into the net with the outside of his right boot. Even Roberto Carlos would have been proud of that one.

"You'll never see a free kick like that again," says Nicky Hunt, who played at right back that night. "It went the wrong side of the wall and came back in, it was unbelievable."

It gave Wanderers a 5-2 lead for the second leg at Villa Park. The home side pulled a goal back through Thomas Hitzlsperger and then overcame the dismissal of future Bolton player Gavin McCann – shown his second yellow card for a foul on Jussi Jaaskelainen – to score again late on through Jlloyd Samuel. The defender was another who would later go on to play for Wanderers. But Villa could not find the third goal they needed and Bolton progressed to the final 5-4 on aggregate.

"The scenes in the changing room afterwards were brilliant, we were going to the Carling Cup final," Hunt remembers. "It was a surreal moment, Djorkaeff with next to nothing on, Okocha, everyone was naked celebrating. It was a really random moment!

"Playing in Europe was a big motivation for us, without a shadow of a doubt, and we were thinking we could really do it. We were playing Middlesbrough and we had nothing to fear."

Wanderers had also been within one game of the UEFA Cup when they reached the League Cup final in 1995, but back then they were still in the second tier and were probably not ready for major European competition. Expected to lose in the final, they were beaten 2-1 by heavy favourites Liverpool.

Fast forward nine years and this time it was Bolton themselves who were slight favourites to defeat Middlesbrough at Cardiff's Millennium Stadium, going into the game a place higher than Steve McClaren's side in the Premier League table. But they succumbed to a nightmare start to the match, played in an ear-splitting atmosphere under the stadium's closed roof.

Joseph-Desire Job scored on the counter attack after two minutes, and Boudewijn Zenden made it 2-0 from the penalty spot five minutes later – after referee Mike Riley failed to spot that the Dutch winger had slipped and illegally kicked the ball against his standing leg, wrong-footing Jaaskelainen.

Bolton halved the deficit soon afterwards when Mark Schwarzer fumbled Kevin Davies' shot in the net, but an equaliser never came. Not only had Wanderers missed the chance to claim their first major trophy since 1958, but the place in the UEFA Cup would go to Middlesbrough. No-one knew if Bolton would ever get that close to Europe again, although Hunt believes that disappointment gave them even greater desire to qualify in the future.

"Everything leading up to that final was perfect but on the day we got hit by two sucker punches," he said. "The penalty shouldn't have been allowed, it was a double touch by Zenden. At the final whistle everyone was just deflated, lying on the pitch, watching them celebrate and pick up the trophy. It was so disheartening for everyone because we knew how hard we'd worked to get there, what performances we'd put in.

"We had a party afterwards, we were going to have one anyway whether we won it or not with friends and family at the hotel, but a lot of the lads were deflated. I was in bed for about 12.30am, which is not like me when there's a party going on!

"We were inches away from Europe, a goal away basically and it made you think what if it had been different. I wanted that feeling again. I wanted to go into a game knowing that if we got a result then we were in Europe."

In the final months of that season, Wanderers responded by climbing to a hugely impressive eighth place in the table. Now they were starting to establish themselves as a top half side. Only a season after missing out on Europe in the Carling Cup final, they would secure qualification for the UEFA Cup via the league – finishing sixth during the 2004/05 campaign.

Gary Speed and Real Madrid great Fernando Hierro had joined the club at the start of that season, which they began in lightning quick fashion – thrashing Charlton 4-1 on the opening day, after another thunderbolt free kick from Okocha. Djorkaeff had departed by that stage but he was swiftly replaced by El-Hadji Diouf on a season-long loan from Liverpool.

"To be sure in my life I never thought before that I was going to play for Bolton Wanderers," Diouf admits. "But after I had a meeting with Sam Allardyce, I knew he was my man. He is one of the best managers I've seen. After I talked to Jay-Jay Okocha who was asking me to come to Bolton, I knew we were going to have fun."

A highly controversial figure after spitting at Celtic fans during a UEFA Cup tie in his time at Anfield, the expectorator extraordinaire earned a three-match ban early in his Wanderers career after old habits returned. During a home defeat to Portsmouth, Diouf had been caught on camera spitting at Dutch defender Arjan de Zeeuw. Not helped by his absence, Wanderers lost six consecutive league games to slip to 13th in the table.

But Diouf's return and the decision to switch Hierro from centre back to midfield saw Wanderers go on a stunning run in the second half of the season. Hierro was imperious in the holding role, hardly ever giving the ball away. Fans knew they were privileged to watch such a player.

Bolton won seven in a row in all competitions early in the New Year, with Stelios scoring the goal in a 1-0 triumph at home to Arsenal. Diouf netted the winner at the second attempt after earning a controversial penalty at Blackburn. Now Wanderers were seventh and catching Everton, Liverpool and Middlesbrough above them.

With Chelsea winning the Carling Cup that season and the FA Cup final contested between fellow Champions League regulars Arsenal and Manchester United, the sides finishing fifth, sixth and seventh in the league would all earn places in the UEFA Cup. Wanderers just had to hang on where they were, but Allardyce and his side sensed they could achieve something even more incredible. Continuing their fine form, they moved up to fifth and to within two points of Everton in the final Champions League spot with five games of the season remaining. Could Bolton really climb into the top four and qualify for the Champions League? For years and years, no club anywhere near as small had represented England in the competition.

It said a lot about how far the club had come since 1987 that there were slightly mixed emotions at the end of that season. After Jose Mourinho's Chelsea won 2-0 at the Reebok to seal their first league title in 50 years, Wanderers travelled to Portsmouth for their penultimate game of the season on May 7, 2005.

Bolton went into the match sixth – one point behind Liverpool and four points behind Everton, who also had a game in hand. Anything but victory would end Wanderers' hopes of qualifying for the Champions League, but even a draw might be enough to seal a place in the UEFA Cup with a game to spare.

It was a massive match in the club's history, but Diouf was informed that he would not be travelling to the south coast. This was the first time Bolton had faced Portsmouth since the De Zeeuw spitting incident earlier in the season, and Allardyce feared the reaction from Pompey players and fans would be detrimental to Wanderers' chances of getting a result.

"I was not supposed to play in that game because of the incident I had with Arjan De Zeeuw," recalls Diouf, as we meet up to discuss his memories of those days. "Sam Allardyce called me into his office on the Thursday to tell me that I wasn't playing. He said, 'I'm not taking you because I don't want any problems, they're waiting for you and I don't want to take you.'

"I didn't say anything, I knew what Sam was like. When he says something he doesn't want someone to say something back. So I went to see Phil Brown and I said, 'Phil, listen, I love pressure like that, this game is too important for us, if we draw we go to the UEFA Cup. Please, I want to play this game, go to tell him that I want to play this game. If I don't play this game I'm not going to feel good. I have to go because I know they're waiting for me, it is my game, let me take that pressure off the team.'

"Phil went to talk to him and Sam just called me to his office on the Friday morning to ask me if I was sure I wanted to play. So I told him there was nothing to worry about, it's only a football game, I want to play and I know I can win the game. He said, 'Okay, let's go'."

It was a significant turn of events. Eleven minutes into the game, Diouf raced clear of the Portsmouth defence and scored – to the ire of the Pompey fans amassed behind the goal.

"I scored the goal to take Bolton to the UEFA Cup," he says. "The Portsmouth fans were not happy but my job was not to make them happy. I didn't play for Portsmouth, I played for Bolton."

Wanderers wondered briefly whether that goal could also revive their Champions League hopes. But Everton took a 2-0 lead at home to Newcastle, and Yakubu equalised for Portsmouth with 18 minutes left at Fratton Park.

A top four spot would be mathematically out of reach by the final whistle, but a draw would be enough to confirm UEFA Cup qualification – providing the match between eighth-placed Middlesbrough and seventh-placed Tottenham did not also end in a draw.

Fans able to check on their mobile phones discovered that Middlesbrough were winning 1-0, although many supporters did not seem to know that Wanderers were now minutes away from confirming their place in Europe. As injury time ticked down and Hierro was helping to stem the Portsmouth tide, an argument broke out between a couple of fans around me about standing up, or some equally trivial issue. It seemed a curious moment to have a row. Bolton were about to qualify for the UEFA Cup.

Finally, the whistle blew. Wanderers had drawn 1-1 and Middlesbrough had beaten Tottenham. Bolton had done it. They were in the UEFA Cup.

Still hardly anyone realised. Players applauded fans like any other match and trudged off, faintly disappointed that they had not been able to win the game and continue their Champions League challenge.

Only minutes later did they receive confirmation that Bolton had qualified for Europe. There was champagne in the cramped Fratton Park dressing room delivered by jubilant chairman Phil Gartside.

"It was like we won the championship," Diouf says. "We finished sixth in the Premier League. People never thought in their life that a club like Bolton were going to finish sixth in the Premier League.

"But Sam always used to say it was about making the fans dream. With the players we had, with the quality we had on the pitch, we could do it and we used to do it. That's the best memory I have from my time at Bolton."

"Four years earlier we were still in the First Division and we were all sat in the cinema room at the club where we used to watch videos," Kevin Nolan remembers. "The manager laid out a plan of qualifying for Europe in five years, and I remember everyone chuckling because of where we were at the time. I was only a young pup of 17 then, but it was about big dreams and taking the club in the right direction.

"We did it in four years, we were fantastic that season. I thought I can't believe we have done it, and a year earlier than what he said. It was just elation. We had a great party, knowing we were going to be in the UEFA Cup against some of the top clubs. It was little old Bolton in Europe, we had put them on the map and done the club very proud."

Stelios had played in the Champions League previously with Olympiakos, but the size of Wanderers' achievement was not lost on him.

"I think it was the best thing that Bolton achieved in their modern history," he says. "The size of Olympiakos in Greece and Bolton in England is not the same. Olympiakos is like Manchester United who are regularly playing in the Champions League. Nobody expected Bolton to qualify for Europe, but we made it."

Shortly after the final whistle, Allardyce made a swift exit from Fratton Park to catch a flight. Mission accomplished, he was already starting his scouting for the summer ahead. Bolton had a European campaign to prepare for.

Brown, who had joined Bolton as a player in the Third Division in 1988, was the man to face the media. "To qualify for Europe is probably the biggest goal we could have set out to achieve and we've done it," he said after the match.

As it turned out, Brown would not take part in Wanderers' ventures into Europe. That summer he received an offer he felt he could not refuse and became a manager in his own right at Derby.

Before his departure, though, Brown clubbed together with Allardyce and four players – Nolan, Davies, Speed and Jaaskelainen – to form the 'You Trotters' syndicate and buy a horse. To celebrate qualification for the UEFA Cup, they named it 'European Dream.'

Allardyce reflects now with real pride on becoming the manager to guide Wanderers into Europe.

"One of my childhood dreams was to play professional football when I left school, so to actually go back and manage the club you started with, and realised your dreams with, was a bit special," said Allardyce, who hails from Dudley in the West Midlands but came through the youth ranks at Bolton in the 1970s.

"I always said to people at the time to make sure you enjoy it while it's happening, don't kick yourself however many years down the line if Bolton aren't where they are now, because you'll look back and say 'Wow, what a team that was.'

"We sold out most weeks because of the entertainment value we gave with the team we had. We'd accumulated seven, eight, maybe 10 players who had either World Cup experience or were European Championship winners, World Cup winners, Champions League winners, UEFA Cup winners or league winners in their own league before they joined us. That made the international flavour of the team and people like Kevin Nolan, Gary Speed, Joey O'Brien and Nicky Hunt fitted into that. They grew better with those types of players.

"Kevin Nolan got better because he was playing with Jay-Jay Okocha, Ivan Campo, Fernando Hierro and Gary Speed. Then Stelios, Dioufy, Bruno N'Gotty and later with Nicolas Anelka, it became a constant growth for us with top international players who wanted to experience the Premier League but couldn't get to the big clubs for whatever reason.

"Ours became the next best option. We had a fantastic stadium – 28,000, not too big, not too small, so it was always full and created a great atmosphere – and with those players our best football could beat anybody in the league. That's why it was such a great era for me.

"We grew into a team that was well established in the Premier League, that was always finishing in the top eight or better, and we started to get to cup finals and to Europe. To clinch qualification for the UEFA Cup at Portsmouth and take the club into Europe for the first time in their history was a fantastic feeling for me, rewriting the history books if you like.

"It wasn't us qualifying via the Carling Cup or the FA Cup, it was by our consistent high level of performance in the biggest league in the world, something you achieve at the end of a season of 38 games. A lot of hard work paid off."

"I've been a fan since I was six years old and from the early 1960s we'd not had a lot to shout about as Bolton fans," Gartside says. "I can remember going to Gillingham on a wet Tuesday night in what was the Third Division, or Newport County. It was awful.

"It was never my intention to get involved full time with the club originally. But then qualifying for Europe, to actually be around for something like that to happen was a big achievement, and a big personal thing for me. It's one of my fondest memories. I always said as long as I was chairman, if 50 per cent of that time was spent in the Premier League I would be chuffed to bits."

If players and fans had not been able to celebrate European qualification together at Portsmouth, they made sure they did so on the last day of the season. Wanderers beat Everton 3-2 at the Reebok and Hierro played the final game of his distinguished career after deciding to retire.

When substituted late on he received a standing ovation from all corners of the ground, including from a significant number of Real Madrid fans who had travelled to bid him farewell. As Hierro paused on his way off to hug team-mates and acknowledge the crowd, Duncan Ferguson was less generous – forcibly shoving the Spaniard towards the touchline. Everton may have already secured their Champions League place, but they were keen to get on with the game.

Wanderers were losing one of the most accomplished players of an already remarkable team, but they had plenty to look forward to now.

Just as the season ended, the anticipation started. The 18-year journey from Scarborough to European qualification was complete. Bolton were going into the UEFA Cup, into uncharted territory.

Fans did not yet know where across the continent their European tour would take them, but a new journey was about to begin.

1

Going Loko Down in Monaco

Bolton 2 Lokomotiv Plovdiv 1 – September 15, 2005

From the very start, Wanderers' UEFA Cup adventure was never going to be boring. Even before their dramatic opening match, events had taken an unexpected and deadly turn.

Many Bolton supporters, relishing the opportunity to see their side play in major European competition for the first time, spent the summer pondering exactly where Wanderers might travel for their first ever UEFA Cup tie. Fans saved money and days off work to make sure they would be able to follow their team wherever they went.

The possibilities were endless and exciting. A total of 52 countries had representation in European competition that season. Wanderers' first UEFA Cup trip could take them anywhere from Iceland to Kazakhstan, from Malta to Moldova.

Bolton fans who wanted the latest news on potential opponents came to appreciate the tireless work of a chap called Bert Kassies – a middle aged IT man from the small city of Meppel in the Netherlands who ran a quaint, no frills website giving every minor detail of which clubs had qualified for Europe and how likely it was that they would progress through the qualifying rounds to reach the first round of the UEFA Cup.

Wanderers knew they would enter the competition at that stage, in a two-legged tie in late September. Many intriguing opponents fell by the wayside during two qualifying rounds, from Atlantas Klaipeda and Khazar Lenkoran to Wisla Plock and MTZ-Ripo Minsk. A final list of 40 potential opponents emerged after the results of the second qualifying round, the night before the first round draw on August 26. By virtue of the previous success of English clubs in Europe, Wanderers had been seeded in the draw and would avoid big names such as Roma, Bayer Leverkusen, Galatasaray, AEK Athens and holders CSKA Moscow.

The 40 unseeded teams in the draw came from 25 different countries and ranged in difficulty from Russian team Zenit St Petersburg to Irish side Cork City. Other options included a Battle of Britain with Hibernian, or maybe a trip to Maccabi Petah Tikva in Israel and all the logistical issues that would bring.

By the morning of the draw, UEFA divided up the clubs into sections, whittling down Wanderers' list of 40 possibilities to just five. They were

Zenit, Debrecen of Hungary, Polish side Groclin, Norwegians Tromso and Lokomotiv Plovdiv of Bulgaria.

Zenit, starting to emerge as the Russian powerhouses that have since gone on to compete in the Champions League on a regular basis, were the highest ranked of the unseeded teams. As interesting as the trip to Saint Petersburg would have been, there was a real risk that Wanderers could have gone out in the first round.

Groclin had shocked Manchester City previously, while Debrecen had just lost a Champions League qualifier to Manchester United. Tromso, in the Arctic Circle in the far north of Norway, was an intriguing option after coming to the attention of the English public in 1997, when they defeated Chelsea in the Cup Winners' Cup in just about the worst blizzard you could imagine. Precious little was known about Plovdiv, the lowest ranked of the five options.

Officials from every club involved in the first round of the UEFA Cup were required to travel to Monaco for the draw, which took place at the Grimaldi Forum as part of a major UEFA gathering. Delegations from the continent's biggest clubs were also in Monte Carlo for the Champions League group stage draw a day earlier. Hours after the UEFA Cup draw, the nearby Stade Louis II was playing host to the UEFA Super Cup final between Liverpool and CSKA Moscow.

Everyone who was anyone in European football was in Monaco for those couple of days, and now Wanderers were taking their place alongside them. Chairman Phil Gartside and secretary Simon Marland were among those who made the trip to Monaco to represent Bolton.

Looking back, Gartside still regards being present for Wanderers' first UEFA Cup draw as his personal highlight from the club's whole European experience.

"That first draw I went to and the fact that our name was in the hat was probably the most emotional bit for me," he says. "To go to Monaco to represent the club with the Real Madrids, the Barcelonas and everyone else was unbelievable. That was as good for me as the games were. It was amazing to sit in UEFA's headquarters with the European elite of football and see our name in that pot.

"There was a dinner the night before and then there was all the build-up to the draw. Then at the draw you have to go and meet the club you're going to play. We were at the top table for the first time ever in the history of the club, we were actually there. The games are great memories, of course they are, but that moment of sitting there as a representative of the club at that forum, that was the pinnacle for me."

"I went, the chairman went and I think the chief executive at the time, Allan Duckworth," says Marland. "It was exciting because we'd never been there before. You're seeing clubs there that you just automatically assume are in Europe every year. They do this all the time, the Liverpools, Manchester Uniteds, Arsenals who are there for the Champions League draw. It's the norm, they have it in the diary. But here we were with them thinking, 'Blooming heck, we're going to have start giving this some thought now!'

"Monaco was a nice place, although you didn't get any time to really enjoy it, which was no problem because you were there to do a job. I had a little bit of time to have a look around Monaco's stadium, thinking it would be nice to play there."

The UEFA Cup draw was beamed back live to England via Eurosport. It was a very formal affair held in a dimly lit theatre, conducted by UEFA officials usually armed with a baffling array of big balls and little balls. Rather unfortunately, the ceremonies were often presented by a grey-haired, bespectacled Italian gentleman who struggled badly with the pronunciation of the English word 'draw', the one word he needed to say quite a lot. Eventually, a piece of card bearing Wanderers' name was drawn out of one of the little yellow balls. 'BOL-TON WAN-DER-ERS FC', the UEFA official announced, in some strange European way that the club's name had never been pronounced before.

Officials from each club were lined up in rows and placed behind placards bearing their side's name, ready for television cutaways to gauge their reaction to the draw. Thankfully there was never any need for Greg Dyke-esque cut-throat gestures from Gartside or Marland when Bolton discovered their opponents.

Out of another little ball came the name PFC LOKOMOTIV PLOVDIV. Even in Monaco, Gartside could probably hear the townsfolk back in Bolton exclaiming 'Who?' and 'Where?' Before knowing anything about the Bulgarian club, somehow the name Lokomotiv Plovdiv did not exude glamour and prestige. This was not one of the great romantic names of European football.

Things were about to get even more complicated than Wanderers had anticipated. The expected post-draw meeting with officials from their opponents would prove a little tricky.

"We drew Plovdiv and they didn't have any representatives there at the draw because their club president had been shot the night before, after their qualifying game," says Marland.

"It was a bizarre set of circumstances," Gartside added. "The president gets shot and when we go to the draw the guy's not there because he'd been shot, and we didn't know where we were going to be playing or what was happening. It was very strange."

Reports were emerging in the media that Lokomotiv Plovdiv president Georgi Iliev had been murdered only an hour after the club's second qualifying round victory over Serbian side OFK Belgrade. The 39-year-old businessman had been in a bar celebrating his team's triumph when he was hit by a bullet in the chest as he spoke on the phone.

Iliev was reported to have had links to the Bulgarian underworld, and his death was not thought to be related to football. The sniper was not found but a body was found in the sea further up the coast a week later, with reports suggesting it might have been the man responsible for Iliev's murder.

The Bulgarian government announced an investigation into organised crime gangs. It certainly seemed a world away from the Premier League. Wanderers must have wondered quite what sort of situation they would be travelling into. In English football, club officials don't tend to get shot. "You'd hope not!" Gartside said.

While Plovdiv were in mourning for their president, Wanderers had to somehow sort out the arrangements for the tie, which was only weeks away. Bolton had been drawn to play at home on September 15, and away a fortnight later. After searching for Lokomotiv officials at the Grimaldi Forum without success, Marland had to ask representatives of another Bulgarian club to help them contact Plovdiv.

"I had a look to see if there was anyone there, and then there was another Bulgarian team who had a representative," he says. "She took all my details and said she would get someone back in Bulgaria to get in contact with us. Fortunately they did, but it took a lot longer than I anticipated.

"We were already going into something we'd never been involved in before, dealing with clubs we had not dealt with before. You were thinking the whole idea of the draw was representatives from clubs were there to organise the games. Then finally we managed to get in touch with them and found out that we couldn't actually play at their ground because it didn't have the certificate for European football.

"We ended up playing Plovdiv in Burgas about 150 miles away, or something like that, which was an experience dealing with. I wouldn't call it a backwater, but it was off the beaten track.

"If we'd been lucky we could have played maybe a French or a German lower team and that would have made life a little bit easier for our first game. When we played some of the bigger teams later on, Munich, Marseille, it was so much easier to organise because of the infrastructure they had compared to Plovdiv. You could contact somebody straight away. But that first draw certainly set the stall out for the rest of the European games."

If Wanderers fans were wondering who on earth Lokomotiv Plovdiv were, and quite why they were known locally as 'the Smurfs', maybe those Bulgarians who had not followed the Premier League so closely in recent years were saying the same about Bolton. While Wanderers were UEFA Cup debutants, Plovdiv had played in Europe in 13 previous seasons during their history – albeit without much success.

They did reach the quarter finals of the Fairs Cup in 1965, however, where they finished all square with Juventus after two matches. They lost a third play-off game 2-1 in Turin, eliminated only by two goals from Omar Sivori, once the world's most expensive player. Plovdiv's own star of that era was Hristo Bonev, one of Bulgaria's greatest ever players who would later return to Lokomotiv as manager and then chairman.

From the second largest city in Bulgaria, Lokomotiv Plovdiv were the product of a forced merger of a number of clubs in the area during the early Communist days after World War II. Only a few clubs were allowed in each area in a bid to strengthen the performance of the best teams. Like fellow Communist era clubs Lokomotiv Moscow, Lokomotiv Sofia and Lokomotiv Leipzig, they took their name because of a connection with the national railways company who provided funding and employed the players.

Lokomotiv Plovdiv, however, watched city rivals Botev Plovdiv and Spartak Plovdiv win domestic trophies while they flitted in and out of the division's top flight. They were relegated again in 1998 before Iliev bought the club and merged it with another team he owned, Velbazhd Kyustendil, who were based 100 miles away but had finished third in the Bulgarian league for the past three seasons. The club remained based in Plovdiv – retaining the Lokomotiv name and their black and white stripes – but soon consisted mostly of Kyustendil's players, who again finished third in the top flight. A year later, in 2004, Lokomotiv Plovdiv won the league title for the first time in their history.

Eduard Eranosyan – a respected former Plovdiv star with playing experience in Greece and Portugal, as well as with the national team – was Lokomotiv's manager then and he was still in charge when they faced Wanderers a year later.

Plovdiv had gone out of Champions League qualifying at the first hurdle to Bruges in 2004/05, before finishing third in the domestic league to qualify for the UEFA Cup.

In the second qualifying round against OFK Belgrade, Metodi Stoynev's goal had given Plovdiv a 1-0 win in the second leg in Burgas to put them through on away goals. Star striker Martin Kamburov had scored in the 2-1 first leg defeat in Serbia but had then been sent off for spitting – earning himself a three-match ban that would rule him out of both legs of the tie against Bolton.

Little was known about the rest of their squad, although it did contain Bulgarian internationals such as defensive trio Kiril Kotev, Aleksandar Tunchev and Vladimir Ivanov as well as midfielder Georgi Iliev, who was no relation to the now deceased president. Robert Petrov and Boban Jancevski had arrived from Macedonia, while Ivan Krizmanic had come in from Serbia.

In some senses though, the fact that Wanderers fans knew little about their opponents was part of what they expected the UEFA Cup experience to be about. Europe was a journey into the unknown.

"I had never heard of them before," admits El-Hadji Diouf about Plovdiv.

"But we had a professional team and we used to play every game the same." Wanderers had done their research, sending chief scout Jack Chapman to watch Plovdiv play before the Bulgarians arrived in England for the first leg.

Wanderers had beaten Manchester City and the Thailand national team to win the Premier League Asia Trophy in Bangkok that summer and started the new season in encouraging fashion. They sat seventh in the table after a 0-0 draw at home to Blackburn when the big day finally arrived – the club's first ever game in major European competition.

Plovdiv brought around 500 supporters to the Reebok, a respectable number boosted largely by Bulgarians already based in the UK. Bulgaria, not one of Europe's wealthiest countries, were still two years away from joining the EU and the cost of making the trip to England was prohibitive for many Lokomotiv fans.

The Bulgarian side arrived in England a day beforehand, and ahead of the game officials from both clubs would meet for a pre-match briefing that was part of normal UEFA procedure for every European fixture. UEFA had a number of requirements that were alien to Wanderers, many because of exclusive sponsorship agreements the governing body had.

"We would have a pre-match meeting with the officials, the clubs, the officials from the game and the UEFA delegate to iron everything out, things like what colours you're playing in," says Marland. "You had to take your kit so the officials had them on the desk and could see there were no colour clashes. You'd talk about how many tickets have been sold, all the information on the game."

"Simon and myself used to go to these meetings and they were like pulling teeth," says Russell Byrne-Fraser, a former Blackpool apprentice who had left a coaching role in the Bloomfield Road youth set-up to become Wanderers' kit man in 2001. "You'd have to sit there and listen to the security arrangements about the car parking and everything the match delegate wanted to know. Have you got a pitch? Have you got the ball?

"Jussi used to wear these Uhlsport gloves and they'd have the logo on the back of the palm and the name written down the index finger of the gloves. But they tried to tell me he couldn't wear them because there were too many logos. I said, 'Well you tell him he can't wear them.' So you just used to put a bit of tape over it.

"The shirts couldn't have the Premier League branding on – UEFA had their own badges – and neither could the footballs.

"It's an almost dictatorial way that UEFA treat you when you take part in these competitions. Even at home your ground isn't your own, it belongs to UEFA that night. They used to dictate that your dressing room had to be ready by something stupid like 3pm. You had to have all the kit out by that time. I think it was a media thing so someone could film it and then walk out again.

"You couldn't follow your own routine. Sometimes you were having to fight with officials to get into your own office!"

It was also a UEFA regulation for both managers to hold press conferences a day before the game. Plovdiv boss Eranosyan admitted that his side would face an almighty task to progress. "Bolton are the favourites," he said. "I'm a realist and can confess that our rivals are a much better side."

His Wanderers counterpart Sam Allardyce had warned that he would make some changes to his starting line-up as he attempted to juggle a busy fixture list, although he stressed that he was determined to get a result from the game. He had not spent years trying to qualify for Europe only to throw it away in the first match.

Gary Speed and Tal Ben Haim did not feature, while Kevin Davies and Kevin Nolan started from the bench. But seven players remained from the side that faced Blackburn and one of those introduced to the line-up was Hidetoshi Nakata, not exactly an inadequate replacement considering he was regarded as one of Asia's finest ever players.

Wanderers had an experienced and cosmopolitan squad, and Nakata was one of several in the starting line-up who had played in European competition before – together with Diouf, Jay-Jay Okocha, Ivan Campo, Stelios Giannakopoulos, Bruno N'Gotty and Henrik Pedersen. Ricardo Gardner, Radhi Jaidi and Jussi Jaaskelainen had no European experience but had played senior international football for their countries, while Nicky Hunt had represented England under 21s.

Nevertheless, Stelios felt the nerves of the club's first game in Europe in the dressing room before kick-off.

"It was a very special night for everybody," he remembers. "It was a new experience for the staff and the fans. We had players who were very experienced in European games, but for the club itself it was something new and it was unbelievable the anxiety that you could feel in the dressing room.

"Some players were playing for the first time in Europe, and some other players were playing in Europe for the first time for Bolton, so in that way it was the first time for everyone. We wanted to do well and make a good start, make a good impression."

"We were a bit nervous and edgy, certainly from a staff point of view, but I put the responsibility on the players who'd played in Europe so many times before," Allardyce says. "Probably 70 per cent of the team had all played in European competition on a pretty regular basis. In many ways that helped me in my first experience of managing in Europe. I had players who were Champions League winners, so I put the responsibility on them. I said that as they had all been there before, they knew what they had to do, so help the young lads and the lads who haven't been there before."

Stelios tried to use his experience of Champions League football with Olympiakos to settle any nerves his team-mates felt.

"The general idea was that we were not playing the Premier League clubs that we played week in week out, so the hard game would be for our opponents, not for us," he said. "In the back of your head a normal level of anxiety was expected, especially for the English players who had not played in Europe before. That was the key thing to try to avoid, to get rid of those nerves. The main thing was to transfer the nerves to our opponents.

"I had some great moments in Europe with Olympiakos. I played in their first game in the Champions League. It was a fantastic atmosphere with an unbelievable crowd at home against Porto. We won 1-0, I scored a fantastic goal from 40 metres with a volley and that year it was voted the goal of the season in the Champions League. It was a great memory."

Perhaps the most surprising thing about that was not the incredible goal that Stelios scored in that game in 1997, given the obvious talent he displayed during his time at Bolton, but the fact that video footage showed he still had a full head of hair when he scored it.

Wanderers had reduced ticket prices for the game and it attracted a crowd of 19,723 – even if that was 5,000 down on the league attendance four days earlier. Those who were there contributed to a special atmosphere on a very special night for the club.

With no centralised television deal for the UEFA Cup in those days, it was Wanderers' responsibility to agree TV rights with a UK broadcaster. A deal was struck for Channel Five to televise both legs of the Plovdiv tie. 'Thursday night, Channel Five', may have been a somewhat derisory terrace chant over the years, aimed at clubs who had ambitions to be in the Champions League rather than the UEFA Cup. But for Wanderers and their fans, Thursday nights on Channel Five were something they were more than happy with.

Many of the club's UEFA Cup games would be on Five and that meant commentator John Helm would provide the sound bites to accompany a number of Wanderers' biggest moments in Europe. A Yorkshireman and avid Bradford Park Avenue fan, Helm had vast experience after commentating for many years for the BBC and for ITV, at World Cups and virtually every tournament or competition you could name, in virtually every country you could name.

"I did an A to Z of every country I've visited to commentate on football and I think I've just about done every letter of the alphabet!" he laughed. "What I found about Bolton is for many people it's become a bit of a joke, the Thursday night football on Channel Five, which was not the competition they wanted to be in. But Bolton were exactly the opposite.

"Even though the first game was against Lokomotiv Plovdiv, which does not sound very romantic, they were thrilled to be in Europe and I thought it reflected in the atmosphere between the players and the supporters.

"I was very lucky because I had some great co-commentators with me following Bolton in the UEFA Cup – Joe Royle, Terry Butcher and Pat Nevin –

and we had an absolute ball. It put the town on the map and I like to think that Channel Five did it justice."

Just before kick-off, Wanderers lined up for a team photo to mark the historic moment. It was a special night for Hunt, the one local lad in the team. "European football was something I hadn't experienced before and because it was the first time in the club's history, it was exciting," he says.

Hunt grew up in Westhoughton and had emerged through the youth ranks at Bolton. A few years ago I dug out the programme from my own first match as a Bolton supporter, a Third Division fixture against Bradford in 1990. By complete accident I stumbled across the page detailing the mascot that day, a certain Nicholas Hunt. "Nicholas will be seven on Monday," it said. "He has been a member of the Junior Whites since he was three years old and his favourite player is Tony Philliskirk."

On Hunt's first league start for the club in 2003 he had the rather tricky task of marking Cristiano Ronaldo, who was making his debut for Manchester United. Against Plovdiv he would have to keep an eye on the raids of the slightly lesser known Robert Petrov.

Jaidi headed wide early in the game and N'Gotty had an effort cleared off the line but Plovdiv, wearing all black, were proving a tougher nut to crack than Bolton had hoped. They had played in Europe before and knew what they needed to do away from home in the first leg. Their first half strategy of defending in numbers and looking for a crucial away goal on the counter attack worked perfectly.

Pedersen, a striker when he arrived from Silkeborg in his native Denmark four years earlier, had been asked to play in an unfamiliar left back position in recent matches. He was a reluctant full back but, perhaps known more for his endeavour than for silky skills, he had adapted surprisingly well in the absence of the injured Gardner. Although Gardner was fit again, Allardyce had opted to stick with Pedersen at left back and play the Jamaican on the left wing.

"To be honest I didn't enjoy playing left back as much as playing as a striker but I always thought it was better to be in the team than on the bench," Pedersen says now. "At that time there were some quality players in the striker positions and if I could play left back it was better than being on the bench.

"Eventually I played nearly 40 games there, so it got easier and easier, I was learning to protect our own goal instead of scoring goals. It's just a part of who I am, always trying to do the best and of course I played with some great players and that made it a little bit easier. Sometimes players don't want to play in different positions but I was up for it and that's the first thing, if you're up for it it's easier to have success with it.

"It was a special atmosphere that night for fans and players. I know not all of the players had played in Europe before, although a few had done in different countries. But it was special for Bolton because you could feel the atmosphere from the fans, it was a bit more special than in a Premier League game.

"A lot of the games in Europe were difficult though because you don't know the opponents as well as you do in the Premier League. It was bound to be difficult."

Plovdiv were indeed making it difficult both for Wanderers and Pedersen. The Dane was no slouch, but Lokomotiv's right wing back Vladimir Ivanov was proving to be seriously rapid.

In the 28th minute, not for the first time, Pedersen was outpaced after a neat one-two on the right flank. Ivanov advanced and whipped a low cross into the area. There were gasps of shock from the crowd as Macedonian forward Jancevski arrived ahead of Hunt and hammered his shot past Jaaskelainen into the top corner.

That was not supposed to happen. Bolton were a top Premier League side playing unknown Bulgarian opposition. It was supposed to be straightforward, a comfortable victory. Plovdiv were supposed to be inferior, not up to the task in hand. But they had just scored the sort of incisive goal that any Premier League team would have been proud of.

Now Wanderers were losing, and in trouble. No-one wanted Bolton's first ever game in Europe to end in embarrassment. Even a draw in the home leg would leave the Whites with a tricky task going into unknown territory for the second game.

"I think we underestimated our opposition a little bit," Hunt admits. "We'd never heard of them, we'd watched videos but the videos were against amateurish teams, it wasn't the Premier League. I think we could have taken that game comfortably but a few of the lads had never played in Europe before, myself included. Even though we had experienced players, it was a difficult night."

The travelling Plovdiv fans, who had celebrated their goal with real joy, sensed the chance of an upset. Their team knew how to play this, too. Time wasting is not exactly uncommon in England, but as soon as they went in front Plovdiv took it to new levels. It was an education in just what teams are prepared to do to steal an advantage in Europe.

By the middle of the second half, with Slovenian referee Darko Ceferin doing nothing to counteract the issue, it was becoming beyond a joke. Plovdiv players were going down injured virtually every two minutes, allowing the physio to come on and break up the play. It seemed to be a well-honed routine.

Allardyce made changes to try to find a goal. On came 32-year-old striker Jared Borgetti – recently signed from Pachuca in his native Mexico but yet to score for the club – in place of Pedersen. Gardner reverted to left back, with Diouf moving to the wing after originally starting the game up front. Soon afterwards Nolan and French midfielder Fabrice Fernandes were introduced.

Nolan had observed Plovdiv's time-wasting from the bench and decided he was having none of it. The clock was ticking down and Bolton badly needed a goal.

Plovdiv's worst time-wasting culprit had been talented midfielder Iliev. On 72 minutes, boos rang around the ground as Iliev went to ground once more. Gardner seemed unsure about whether to kick the ball out or play on until Nolan raced across and took the ball from him.

"They had been diving a lot," Nolan says. "It was something we hadn't really seen much, playing in the physical Premier League week in week you didn't see people going down just off a touch and staying down. But once they went 1-0 up all that happened – the diving, the staying down for a couple of minutes, time wasting, everything. It opened your eyes to the European aspect of football and what you've got to deal with.

"I came on and there was a tackle and their player went down. Ricardo didn't know what to do and I just demanded the ball off him because I knew the player wasn't injured. At that time there was the rule where it was up to you whether you kicked it out or not and I decided to carry on playing."

There was an instant cheer from the crowd as Nolan turned and started a Bolton attack to Plovdiv's visible disapproval. The ball went from Jaidi to Hunt, who crossed the halfway line and then arrowed a trademark diagonal ball into the area from deep.

It was inch perfect. Escaping his marker, Diouf raced in from the left flank and met the cross with the most sumptuous of diving headers. It beat keeper Stoyan Kolev and found the far corner.

There was jubilation around the Reebok, followed by sounds of Tony Christie's 'Is This The Way To Amarillo' over the speaker system. The song had been revived by Bolton comedian Peter Kay and had been specially adapted by Wanderers fans into a chant for Diouf. Every time he scored, the music would be played.

'Sha la la, la la, la la la, DIOUF DIOUF! Sha la la, la la, la la la, DIOUF DIOUF! Sha la la, la la, la la la, El-Hadji Diouf will spit on you!'

Perhaps a chant celebrating Diouf's habit of spitting at people was not big or clever, but it was quite amusing. Widely reviled by much of English football, Diouf had become a cult hero at Bolton. He may have been a bad boy, but fans regarded him as their bad boy, and a superbly talented player on his day. It seemed fitting that Diouf should score Bolton's first ever goal in Europe.

"I scored the goal to take Bolton to the UEFA Cup against Portsmouth and I scored the first goal ever for Bolton in Europe as well," Diouf says proudly. "People used to tell me that I scored the first goal for Bolton in Europe. I realised after the game because they came to ask me for my shirt to sign it, put the date on it and they put it up at the training ground. I asked them, 'Why do they want the shirt? Can't I keep my shirt? It's my first UEFA Cup shirt for Bolton'. But they told me, 'No, we need it because you scored the first goal for Bolton ever in Europe'.

"For me I think that's massive for a club like Bolton, who no-one thought before were going to be in Europe one day. If you ask people, I know a lot of people have passed away, if you had woken them up right then, people who used to watch the Bolton games at that stadium, Burnden Park, and told them that Bolton were playing in Europe, no-one would have believed you.

"It was a good header, we were losing 1-0 and it was a good cross from Nicky Hunt. The stadium was crazy, I remember when we used to play at home, it was always full and people were always happy to come and see us.

"I don't play football only to win, winning is important but you have to make the fans happy and that's what we used to do. We used to mix a winning mentality and champagne football, as Jay-Jay Okocha used to call it. We had to make the fans happy, Jay-Jay had to do his tricks, I had to do something, Ivan Campo, everyone had something special."

Wanderers suddenly had a lifeline. They were back in the tie, to Plovdiv's great anger. The visiting players felt Nolan had been disrespectful by playing on while Iliev lay injured, and were not shy in telling him so.

"The lad jumped up and wanted to fight!" Nolan chuckles. "After the game they didn't forgive me either. They thought he was injured but obviously he was play-acting. But with them only having broken English and me talking to them in my Scouse accent, it was all going off. They weren't a happy bunch, to say the least!"

But 1-1 was still not enough for Bolton. Plovdiv's away goal meant that, if things stayed the same, Bolton would have to score in Bulgaria. They had 18 minutes left to give themselves a crucial advantage to take into the second leg.

Now pushing forward, Fernandes fired a shot narrowly wide but injury time had arrived and Plovdiv were still hanging on. It reached the final seconds of the game when Fernandes – a former Fulham and Southampton midfielder who made only five appearances during his brief spell at Bolton – chipped the ball across the face of the area. Nakata nodded the ball on and there stood Borgetti at the far post, completely unmarked.

Plovdiv players stopped, appealing for offside, but Borgetti controlled the ball and scuffed an angled shot that bobbled beautifully into the far corner. The keeper probably would have saved it had Borgetti made a better contact on the ball, but the Mexican had a knack of finding the net.

A predator in the penalty area who was nicknamed El Zorro del Desierto, or 'the Desert Fox', it was felt that he did not contribute enough in general play to justify being a regular starter in the Premier League. But Borgetti scored a record 46 goals in 89 games for Mexico during his career, notably netting against Italy at the 2002 World Cup. His fame in Central America was such that when he initially arrived at Wanderers, the club were left bewildered by the myriad of people claiming to be his agent. Give him a chance in front of goal, and he would put it away.

"He was a Mexican international, he'd been there and done that," says Hunt. "The manager had a knack for drafting in really experienced players when you thought he could never get them in. Borgetti was a total box player, he wouldn't run the channels or anything like that but if you got it into the box he'd be in the right place at the right time, swivel and knock it in the bottom corner. He didn't really feature too much in the league but he was on fire in Europe for us."

"I got to know Jared Borgetti because I speak Spanish," says commentator Helm. "Coming from Mexico there weren't too many people here who spoke Spanish and he was delighted to speak Spanish with someone. I don't think Sam's Spanish was up to very much!

"He was always very courteous with me and I was able to chat to him about different places in Mexico because I had an uncle who lived there in a place called Cuernavaca. I mentioned these places to him and he said, 'Oh yes, I was there!'. I did the World Cup there in 1986 so I was able to talk to him about places like Puebla, Monterrey and Guadalajara, and he appreciated that I think.

"His goalscoring record for Mexico stood up against anybody. More recently it's been Javier Hernandez, but Borgetti was up there with his ratio."

The Reebok erupted when Borgetti found the net, before racing to celebrate with fans. Plovdiv players stood distraught, having come so close to a very notable result.

Scoring a last minute winner in any game is memorable. Scoring a last minute winner in the club's first ever game in Europe was special – even if it was against Lokomotiv Plovdiv. Borgetti's first goal for Bolton would go down in history.

There would still be work to do in Bulgaria, but the momentum had shifted massively in Bolton's favour. Right then, the slenderest of victories felt like one of the club's finest moments.

Elsewhere in the UEFA Cup that night, Everton were thrashed 5-1 in their first round first leg at Dinamo Bucharest – having missed out on the Champions League group stage with a defeat to Villarreal in qualifying.

Their European campaign was virtually over. For Wanderers, it was only just beginning.

Bolton: Jussi Jaaskelainen; Nicky Hunt, Bruno N'Gotty, Radhi Jaidi, Henrik Pedersen (Jared Borgetti 57); Hidetoshi Nakata, Ivan Campo, Jay-Jay Okocha (Kevin Nolan 67); Stelios Giannakopoulos (Fabrice Fernandes 67), El-Hadji-Diouf, Ricardo Gardner. Subs not used: Ian Walker, Joey O'Brien, Abdoulaye Faye, Kevin Davies.

Booked: Nakata, Gardner.
Goals: Diouf 72, Borgetti 90.

Lokomotiv Plovdiv: Stoyan Kolev; Vladimir Ivanov, Kiril Kotev, Vlademir Giordani, Aleksandar Tunchev, Robert Petrov; Georgi Iliev (Yavor Vandev 81), Ivan Krizmanic, Krasimir Dimitrov; Ilami Halimi (Daniel Georgiev 45); Boban Jancevski (Metodi Stoynev 90). Subs not used: Vasil Kamburov, Hristo Zlatinski, Ivo Mihaylov, Velko Hristev.
Booked: Jancevski, Iliev, Giordani.
Goal: Jancevski 28.

Attendance: 19,723.
Referee: Darko Ceferin (Slovenia).

2

Sleeping with the Jellyfishes

Lokomotiv Plovdiv 1 Bolton 2 – September 29, 2005

Wanderers did not know quite what to expect when they departed for their first ever away game in the UEFA Cup. By the time they returned to England, they had diced with jellyfish, the Bulgarian mafia and embarrassing elimination from the UEFA Cup. Despite it all, they had been part of the one of the most special nights in the club's history.

Even the most basic details of the away leg had been a headache for Wanderers. For several days after the first round draw in Monaco, Bolton could only be sure that they would be playing somewhere in Bulgaria – in one of three cities spanning more than 200 miles.

It was looking unlikely that they would actually be going to Plovdiv, with the club's decaying Lokomotiv Stadium deemed unfit by UEFA to host matches in European competition. The stadium, known locally as the Lauta, had only been opened in 1982 but was already looking decidedly shambolic. The running track around the pitch was cracked and the uncovered stands were little more than 1920s-style terraces, with uninviting seats bolted on. The Lauta held 24,000 people but that figure was halved in 2004 when parts of a stand collapsed – miraculously without any casualties.

It seemed a pity that Wanderers and their supporters might not be able to visit the city where their opponents actually came from, particularly for the club's first European trip.

A city of close to 400,000 people in the centre of the country, Plovdiv is surrounded by the Sredna Gora and Rhodope mountains where tourists visit to ski during the winter. It was a key city in the ancient region of Thrace before being taken over by the Greeks, the Romans, the Byzantines, the Ottomans, the Russians and eventually the Bulgarians. The settlement was named Philippopolis by the Greeks, after King Philip II of Macedon, and was still referred to by that name in Western Europe until well into the 20th century – despite being renamed as the slightly less appealing Plovdiv by the Bulgarians well before then.

Bulgarian legend Hristo Stoichkov, a hero of the 1994 World Cup, had grown up in the area but played for Lokomotiv's city rivals Maritsa before moving further afield – eventually ending up at Barcelona.

Wanderers fans who were eager to start making travel plans waited for four frustrating days before Lokomotiv Plovdiv – pre-occupied with grieving for their murdered club president – officially confirmed that the game would definitely not take place in their own city. It was money down the drain for those Bolton supporters who had jumped the gun by booking travel and accommodation within minutes of the first round draw.

The options then were the Bulgarian capital of Sofia 80 miles to the north west, or the Black Sea resort of Burgas more than 150 miles to the east. CSKA Sofia and Levski Sofia were both due to host UEFA Cup games themselves on September 29, so the capital was out unless there was a fixture change. There was even brief talk of Wanderers' two legs against Plovdiv being reversed, although that was quickly dismissed.

In the end Sofia was indeed ruled out, and a whole five days after the first round draw it was announced that Wanderers' away match against Plovdiv would be held in Burgas. It was a city of 200,000 people in the south east of Bulgaria, but within range of the burgeoning Black Sea tourist resorts 20 miles north, most notably Sunny Beach.

Wanderers officials soon flew out to Burgas for a fact-finding mission, ahead of the squad's arrival weeks later.

"Once the draw had been carried out we always made plans to travel to wherever we were playing for a recce," says secretary Simon Marland. "There was myself, the safety officer, someone from the police and even Brian the chef in the majority of cases. We would go to the ground, meet the local police and the safety people from the home club, and then we would go around the hotels – deciding not just where the team were going to stay but the supporters and corporate people too. You had maybe a day and a half, just being taken from place to place to place."

Wanderers were initially awarded only 910 tickets for the match at the 18,000-capacity Naftex Stadium – then the home of mid-table Bulgarian side Naftex Burgas. UEFA rules stated that away supporters must be offered a minimum of five per cent of the capacity. The allocation was never going to be sufficient, though. Despite the less than glamorous location, many Bolton fans had decided to travel to the club's first ever European away game.

Wanderers warned fans not to travel without tickets, but later secured an extra allocation of 1,000. Some still made the trip without tickets, and found no trouble gaining admission as more seats were made available.

Tickets were printed on the flimsiest scrap of paper, with the match details written in indecipherable Cyrillic. This really did pass for a football ticket in Bulgaria. Already, it seemed a world away.

Supporters travelling independently found that flights to Burgas were available, if not exactly frequent. Summer had just officially ended but some like Carl Crook, a lifelong Wanderers fan and former British and Commonwealth lightweight boxing champion, arrived days before the game and made a week of it at Sunny Beach.

"There were four of us who went on the Monday and we met the lads we knew from Blackpool, who we always met up with at games," Crook said. "To get in Europe was fantastic, so we couldn't miss the first away game. We watched the game and stayed until the next Monday. By then there was nobody in Sunny Beach, because the holiday season had finished and all the bars were empty. We had no money left anyway!"

The bars were full in the lead-up to the Wanderers match though, as more and more fans arrived at the resort. Sunny Beach's construction began during the Communist era in 1958, when Russians would make the trip to sun themselves beside the Black Sea, which was actually more of an idyllic crystal clear blue. Later it would become popular with Western Europeans too, as high rise hotel after high rise hotel sprung up. This though had been the place where Plovdiv president Georgi Iliev had been shot dead.

Wanderers fans had been warned to be on their best behaviour – particularly after Liverpool supporter Michael Shields had been jailed months earlier for attempted murder in the resort of Varna further up the coast. Shields continued to plead his innocence, and was later pardoned by the British Government and released from prison. In Sunny Beach, though, Bolton supporters had thoughts only of having fun as they relished the start of their European adventure.

"It was great, there were loads of Bolton fans," says Crook. "There was this pub, the Happy Duck, and people all tended to go there. It was a big wooden hut on the beach. One night everyone was eating their food there and this lady was singing. All of a sudden all the fans just jumped up, all singing Amarillo. This lady couldn't carry on singing, everyone was so loud. She didn't know it was a Bolton song. Then as soon as we stopped singing, everyone sat down and started eating their meals again as if nothing had happened!"

The Wanderers squad arrived in Bulgaria on the day before the game and were also staying in Sunny Beach.

"It was like being on holiday!" laughs Henrik Pedersen, part of the travelling party. "We went outside the hotel and there were people on holiday all over the place. It was a funny place to play."

"There were massive tower blocks everywhere, think of Cold War Russia and it was tower blocks with big numbers on the side," remembers Russell Byrne-Fraser, Wanderers' kit man at the time. "But 500 yards either side of our hotel it was like Las Vegas, it was unbelievable.

"We went for a meal the night before the game and there was some Bulgarian equivalent of the Spice Girls or the Pussycat Dolls making a video, it was so surreal. All you needed to do was lift your head and all you could see were these grey depressing concrete tower blocks. Then there were these four or five gorgeous women dancing on this little manufactured strip of beach. It was crazy stuff.

"But there was an overriding feeling of being somewhere darker than you were used to. I had an incident with what I thought might be the Bulgaria mafia while I was there. I went to the airport early when we were going home so we could check all the gear in, all our metal boxes. They said everything was fine and then I asked for receipts. He said, 'No, you don't need any receipts'. I kicked up a bit of a stink and said, 'I'm not going until I get a receipt'.

"The guy gets on the radio, and another guy walks over. He said, 'You don't need receipts', and then he opens his jacket and he's got a gun there. I don't think he was threatening me, he was just trying to make a point. I'm saying, 'Listen, shoot me, but I need receipts!' I got them but it was obviously some guy who thought they could have it away with all this gear had I not made a fuss."

An impressive 2,000 supporters in total made the trip to this far-flung part of Bulgaria – more than had followed Wanderers to places as close as Everton and Liverpool at times. Some had flown to Sofia before making the journey to Burgas via rail or road, but more than 1,000 had opted to travel officially with the club.

Wanderers had linked up with a travel company to charter flights that would depart from Manchester Airport early on Thursday morning before returning in the early hours of the following day. It would become the norm for away fixtures in Europe, and the transport of choice for the inexperienced traveller. Coaches and a full itinerary were planned out for them once they arrived in Bulgaria. All they had to do was turn up at Manchester Airport.

The charter flights were also useful for those who could only afford one day off work, although supporters who were back at the office on Friday were generally rather bleary-eyed after an arduous 24 hours of much travelling and precious little sleep. Just staying awake throughout matchday could be a challenge. On this occasion, some parents took their children out of school for a day so they could witness Wanderers' historic first away match in Europe.

Flights departed for Bulgaria at 7am, meaning many left Bolton as early as 4am, when it was still dark. Some did not even bother going to bed. The excitement was too great for the trip they had been looking forward to ever since qualification for the UEFA Cup in May.

Even the sight of an airport lounge full of Bolton fans was a new experience. After a three-hour journey across Europe, the official charter planes touched down at Burgas Airport at noon local time.

It was a small, basic airport much different to the one that fans had departed in England. Seven years later, in 2012, six people were killed outside Burgas Airport by a suicide bomber targeting a bus full of Israeli tourists. On this day it seemed the calmest place in the world as the sun beat down on the Eastern European tarmac.

Fans boarded coaches to be taken to nearby Nessebar, a sleepy coastal town known as Bulgaria's Dubrovnik. The route took them on ramshackle roads that Communist era cars shared with horses and carts. Houses looked altogether shabbier than in England. Straight away it was apparent that there was a humbler way of life here. It was a place different to anywhere many Wanderers fans had seen before, either in England or in their conventional western holiday destinations.

Supporters travelling officially with the club were being taken to Nessebar for the afternoon to keep them away from the city of Burgas, where Plovdiv fans were arriving by rail. Police feared the Bulgarian supporters may look for trouble. A handful of Wanderers fans travelling independently experienced that first hand, with one supporter suffering a black eye when he was punched and kicked by Plovdiv hooligans.

Nessebar, packed with historic buildings and ruins from as far back as 400 BC, had been made a UNESCO World Heritage Site and supporters whiled away the afternoon in the many restaurants and bars overlooking the Black Sea.

Many independent travellers were still a few miles north in Sunny Beach, where the Wanderers squad were starting to gear up for the match that night. The players would often go for a walk in the afternoon, and this time their amble would take them towards the Bolton fans enjoying the afternoon in the resort's bars.

"You take the players for a walk before they go for a game at night, just to stretch their legs," Sam Allardyce says. "I remember Mike Forde was saying, 'Don't walk down there, that's where all the Bolton fans are'. But I said, 'No, let's walk down there'.

"I said to the players, 'This is what it means to the fans'. There were thousands of Bolton fans, and they'd all had a few too many lagers!"

It was a smart move by Allardyce, a simple way of stressing the importance of the game they were about to play. The message was not lost on El-Hadji Diouf.

"When we used to travel I was saying, 'We're never going to have fans over there'," Diouf remembers. "But from the first game I saw lots of fans travelling, that was my first impression. Before the game we would wake up at one o'clock and go to walk for 10 or 15 minutes, and I saw a lot of people with Bolton shirts, a lot of fans at the bars singing. I realised how important the UEFA Cup was for the fans."

Allardyce's time in Sunny Beach was not without incident though, as he had a brush with some Black Sea jellyfish during the trip.

"The players were in the gym with the fitness staff and Sam, myself, Sammy Lee and Jimmy Phillips were waiting for them to finish," says Byrne-Fraser. "It was boiling and we said, 'Let's go for a wade'. We went for a paddle with T-shirts and shorts on, and we were chatting away in the water. Then all of a sudden we looked and thought, 'What's that? Is it a plastic bag?'

"We were surrounded by jellyfish. They'd all just drifted in. We were all just stood there for 15 minutes, we couldn't move! Thankfully they all just floated off again. Sam was just stood there laughing, as he did. He was bullet proof, Sam was, unbelievable!"

If they had been a little apprehensive about their encounter with the mafia, this time it was not so much sleeping with the fishes, as sleeping with the jellyfishes.

By late afternoon on matchday the squad made their way to Burgas for the game, which kicked off at 5.55pm local time – as early as 3.55pm in the UK.

Fans who had travelled with the club's official travel got back on their coaches in Nessebar and headed for the Naftex Stadium. There was a comical interlude halfway to Burgas as some supporters urged bus drivers to stop so they could have a comfort break after an afternoon in the bars. That was followed by the sight of rows of Wanderers fans lining the edge of highway relieving themselves. It was like some bizarre Eastern European Benny Hill sketch. Heaven knows what the passing locals thought.

The journey continued into Burgas, past line after line of Communist tower blocks, growing ever more daunting. This was the gloom that once sat behind the Iron Curtain. The Red Army of the USSR had occupied Burgas in 1944, moving on to take control of the whole of Bulgaria. It paved the way for the country to become a repressive left-wing state following the end of World War II.

Fans eventually reached their destination, the Naftex, where Lokomotiv Plovdiv had faced OFK Belgrade in their previous UEFA Cup home match. The stadium perhaps could have been worse, by Eastern European standards at least, but it was far from Premier League quality.

Covered stands of green and yellow seats lined both sides of the pitch, while open ends curved around the outside of the running track that surrounded the playing surface. As seemed to be the case in many grounds on that side of Europe, a fire engine was stationed behind the goal, ready and waiting should anything go awry.

Around 10,000 Plovdiv fans had made the four-hour train journey to Burgas for the OFK Belgrade game and a similar number were in attendance for this game – most in the stand on the other side of the pitch. Looming over it was a tower of flats, from which curious residents peered out.

The 2,000 Wanderers supporters were housed in the main stand, spilling over into the uncovered bowl of seating behind the goal.

"The English fans are very special, they follow their team all over the world," Pedersen says. "It was unbelievable to see all the fans who went to the away games. They gave us massive support."

"It wasn't a great stadium but we weren't that bothered because it was the first game in Europe," says Crook. "We were behind the goal, I had a big

Chorley flag that I'd taken over there.

"There was one lad sat with us who only paid £3 on the door to get in. He was a lad from Chorley who said to his wife, 'Oh, let's go to Bulgaria, Bulgaria looks good.' Then when he got there he said, 'Oh look, Bolton are playing!' That was his way to get over there to watch Wanderers!"

Crook was not the only boxer in the away section that day. Another to have travelled was fellow Wanderers fan Amir Khan, the famous Boltonian who had won a silver medal at the Olympics in Athens a year earlier and would later become a world champion in the professional ranks. Bulgaria was a strong amateur boxing country and Khan had fond memories of his previous visit. He actually fought in Plovdiv itself in 2004, winning the Strandja Cup to earn qualification for the Olympics. At only 17, it had made him Great Britain's youngest boxing Olympian since 1976.

John Helm was at the Naftex Stadium to commentate for Channel Five, although his memories of past visits to Bulgaria were less fond.

"The first time I went to Bulgaria I wouldn't say I liked it!" he laughed. "I went there with England on a pre-season tour when I was working for the BBC. The food was absolutely dreadful.

"I went again in 1990 straight after the World Cup in Italy. I had a message when I got home saying, 'You're going to Bulgaria on Friday with Hull City on a pre-season tour. I thought, 'What?' I remember treating Stan Ternent, the manager of Hull, to a meal on behalf of Yorkshire Television. We had a four-course slap up meal with God knows how many bottles of wine and it didn't come to £20 for six of us, which was ridiculous!

"But by the time I went to Burgas with Bolton, Bulgaria had improved tremendously, although the commentary position at the stadium was very low down and behind glass. The stadium wasn't really up to it. Then Sam sprang one on me by naming someone I'd never heard of called Fojut on the bench."

Jaroslaw Fojut was a young Polish defender who had emerged from Wanderers' reserve team. With an adequate, if not exactly decisive, 2-1 lead from the first leg against Plovdiv, Allardyce had fielded a weaker team for the second match – making seven changes. It was a calculated gamble as he tried to balance UEFA Cup progress with the fact that Wanderers would have to travel back across Europe for an away game at Wigan in the Premier League three days later.

Wanderers were going into the game on the back of two victories in the Premier League. After beating Plovdiv 2-1 at the Reebok in their first ever European game, they had rounded off a fine few days for the club by winning 1-0 at Manchester City that weekend in extraordinary fashion. City had hit the woodwork FIVE times, before Richard Dunne handled in injury time and Bolton completed the king of all smash-and-grabs with a Gary Speed winner from the penalty spot. A week later, Kevin Nolan's bicycle kick gave them a

1-0 win at home to Portsmouth.

Speed and Nicky Hunt were ruled out of the Plovdiv game through injury, while Nolan, Kevin Davies, Ricardo Gardner, Hidetoshi Nakata and Jussi Jaaskelainen were rested but placed on the bench in case of emergencies.

Despite the changes, Wanderers still fielded an experienced line-up with the likes of Bruno N'Gotty and Jay-Jay Okocha retaining their places. Internationals El-Hadji Diouf, Stelios Giannakopoulos, Jared Borgetti, Ian Walker and Abdoulaye Faye all came into the team – together with Fabrice Fernandes and 19-year-old Joey O'Brien employed in a holding midfield role.

The former reserve team captain had gained experience on loan at Sheffield Wednesday the season beforehand, when he also made two substitute appearances for the Wanderers first team. Five days before the match in Plovdiv he had come on as a 10th-minute substitute for the injured Speed against Portsmouth, but this was new territory for O'Brien in more ways than one.

"It was my first start for the club," remembers the Irishman. "I'd gone over to Bolton at 15 or 16 and I made my debut in the Carling Cup against Yeovil – I replaced Fernando Hierro. There's not many people who can say that, and that's a picture I'm still trying to chase down!

"I was a young player coming through at Bolton trying to get that chance and the manager gave it to me. At the time we had a great squad and I'll always remember that game in Bulgaria. It was a hostile atmosphere but it was a great night for me and for the club."

In the away section before kick-off, a plethora of beach balls bounced around – having been cunningly transported from England by a chap who would imaginatively become known to some as 'beach ball man'.

As the game got underway in the late afternoon sun, Plovdiv supporters were doing their best to generate noise in their adopted UEFA Cup home, chanting 'Lo-ko-mo-tiv!' enthusiastically.

Before kick-off, back in Burgas for the first time since Iliev's murder, they had marked the death of their president by holding up placards bearing his image.

"They had this big emotional tribute for him," Wanderers chairman Phil Gartside remembers. "They were the sort of things you didn't know were going to happen before you got there on these European trips.

"They were the sort of moments that stood out, the things you remember from the away games."

Plovdiv knew one goal would put them ahead in the tie on away goals. A goalless draw would put Wanderers through, however, and the first half was not a classic. It might have left some Thursday afternoon Channel Five viewers back in England reaching for the remote.

Bolton were not particularly fluent with a much changed line-up and created little, with Borgetti struggling to get into the game this time – having netted the winner in the first leg at the Reebok.

With no standard UEFA Cup ball in those days, Wanderers prepared for European games thoroughly by flying in footballs from the relevant country, allowing the squad to practise with them during training ahead of away matches.

That practice was not making much difference early in this game though, as Diouf fired a shot over the bar. Similarly, Plovdiv's Serbian midfielder Ivan Krizmanic headed off target as the hosts made few inroads in their attempts to level the tie on aggregate.

The start of the second half was briefly delayed as Plovdiv fans greeted their team back on to the pitch by lighting a long row of flares at the front of the stand they were occupying on the far side of the pitch. It sent smoke drifting across the playing surface, with Finnish referee Jouni Hyytia patiently waiting until it cleared.

A Wanderers supporter in the away section responded by lighting a flare of his own, something that was rarely seen in English stadiums. Another fan did the same at the end of the game, but they later faced bans from European matches after being identified by video footage. Bolton also faced a fine from UEFA, together with their opponents.

Plovdiv flares were being lit again just six minutes into the second half, as the match took a dramatic turn. The deceased president's namesake Georgi Iliev had been at the centre of the play-acting row in the first leg. But he was a clever midfielder with a powerful right foot, and he used it to put Lokomotiv on the verge of what would have been a major shock.

Striding forward in midfield, Iliev unleashed a stunning 25-yard effort that arrowed into the top corner. Walker, a 33-year-old who had played at the top level with Tottenham and England, could get nowhere near it. Even two goalkeepers would have struggled to save it.

Lokomotiv fans went into raptures, chanting 'Loko, Loko', believing they could be about to secure their biggest result in Europe since the 1960s.

Wanderers fans feared the worst. All of a sudden, what had been a dream day looked like it may be about to turn into a nightmare. The tie was now 2-2 on aggregate, and Plovdiv were set to progress by virtue of their away goal at the Reebok. Bolton had 39 minutes to score, or their UEFA Cup adventure would end virtually as soon as it had begun.

After all the hard work and many years to get to this point, it could be one tie, one trip, all over. No guarantees that Wanderers would ever be back in Europe again, just the memories of a defeat to the curiously named Lokomotiv Plovdiv.

Ask Blackburn Rovers fans how humiliating it felt to crash out of Europe in their first ever tie against Swedish minnows Trelleborgs. They were never allowed to forget it. Bolton did not want that embarrassment.

"When we went 1-0 down I was thinking, 'Come on lads, we've got to pull this through'," Allardyce remembers. "We were desperate not to go out in the first round."

The manager wasted no time. He called for the main men. On came Davies and Nolan, the latter still unpopular with the Plovdiv players following his actions in the first leg. Off went the ineffective Fernandes and Borgetti, with O'Brien also soon withdrawn – replaced by Nakata.

Bolton pressed, but for a long time it did not look like the goal would come. Wanderers fans prayed for a goal. Some might have traded every result for the rest of the season for just one goal in the final minutes in Burgas, so significant had this game become.

Thankfully, in the closing minutes Wanderers got not just one goal but two. The crucial equaliser came with only 11 minutes left. Henrik Pedersen, again starting at left back, was being encouraged to get forward at every opportunity. The Dane darted forward and curled a not particularly impressive cross towards the six-yard box.

It seemed to be the simplest of tasks for goalkeeper Stoyan Kolev to collect, but suddenly there was a mix-up. There were no Wanderers strikers in the vicinity but defender Aleksandar Tunchev did not know whether to leave the ball or clear it. In the end he did neither.

To the relief, glee and laughter of the Bolton fans stationed at that end of the ground, the ball comically bounced off Tunchev's knee, past Kolev and into the net. Wanderers could not believe their luck. Saved by a moment of high farce.

To this day, Wanderers owe a debt of gratitude to that little known Bulgarian defender, who would go on to have an unremarkable spell in English football with Leicester and then Crystal Palace. Without his blundering and entirely needless intervention, all of Bolton's incredible European experiences – certainly that season, and maybe those later on too – might never have happened.

He had probably cost Plovdiv one of the most famous victories in their history. But if you are reading this Aleksandar – and let's face it, you probably aren't – Wanderers salute you.

First time around at least, Channel Five unfortunately weren't able to capture the goal in all its glory. For reasons puzzling to most, the Bulgarian live feed had instead opted to focus on a close up of Pedersen's rear end as his cross made his way into the area. Henrik's a lovely guy, but no-one really wanted to see that. That's Bulgarian television directors for you, I guess.

"When you're in the hands of other people in another country like Bulgaria the coverage is a lot more dodgy," Helm admits. "The cameras are supplied by the local company but people at home don't realise. They think, 'Oh Channel Five, their cameras are useless'."

At that point, Bolton led 3-2 on aggregate and even a Plovdiv goal would only take the game into extra time.

But seven of the most memorable minutes in Bolton's recent history were completed with a second goal for Wanderers. Davies advanced down the left and pulled the ball back for Nolan on the edge of the area. The midfielder, always a goal threat throughout his career, brilliantly struck the ball first time into the bottom corner.

If the first goal brought with it a mixture of joy and relief, now there was sheer euphoria. Wanderers knew they were through. In nail-biting and dramatic fashion, they had won in Bulgaria. Nolan raced over to celebrate with Bolton fans in the corner of the stadium, joined by team-mates and even substitutes including young Portuguese forward Ricardo Vaz Te. Fans jokingly chanted, 'Easy, easy.' A number of players, delirious at the turnaround in the game, joined in the chant from the pitch.

"I remember me and Davo came on and caused a bit of carnage in that game," Nolan says. "I was expecting a backlash from the Plovdiv players from the first leg and when I came on I could see they were still very angry and they didn't like me, although after that second game they were all fine, there was no problem. There were sportsman's handshakes.

"We got the goal back to make it 1-1 and then I remember the ball coming across and me just putting it into the far corner. My dad was there, he travelled everywhere. I remember seeing him afterwards and him being all drunk and emotional. He'd obviously had a good day with all the fans and he had a great evening with the fans after it! I stayed away from him on the flight home because he was that bad! But he was on good form and it was great that he was able to share those nights with me.

"It was great too because we had so many fans there, so we really enjoyed it at the end of the game. The first away game in Europe was just brilliant and to score my first European goal is something I'll always treasure."

Nolan's goal meant Plovdiv needed three goals in the final five minutes to progress, which was never going to happen. A week later, their boss Eduard Eranosyan was sacked. His managerial career eventually took him to Angola with Kabuscorp, after a four-year ban for giving players pills containing an anabolic steroid during a spell in charge at Cypriot club APOP Kinyras. In the months after facing Bolton, Plovdiv sold many of their stars, as they started to suffer financially following the death of their benefactor Iliev.

If there were hard times ahead for Plovdiv, Wanderers' celebrations could really start when the final whistle blew at the Naftex Stadium. They'd had a narrow escape, but they were in the group stage of the UEFA Cup. They would now be guaranteed four more matches, and two more European trips. The entire Bolton team made a special effort to go over and applaud the fans. The joy on the faces of the players – even someone like Okocha, who had achieved so much in the game – was obvious.

"It was a big relief because we didn't want to lose in the first game," Stelios says.

"The rapport between the players and the supporters was unusual," Helm adds. "I've been abroad with 20 English teams – Manchester United, Liverpool, Leeds, Arsenal, Tottenham, I've been abroad with all of them. There was a better camaraderie between the Bolton players and their supporters than any other club I think. Even at airports the players would mingle with the supporters, which you don't often get these days. I think the rapport was partly down to the fact that it was a romantic journey for them. They'd never played in Europe before.

"Bolton were behind and it would have been so embarrassing and disappointing to have gone out to a team called Lokomotiv Plovdiv! But the drama was great for us, Channel Five loved it. We had a heck of a good time in Bulgaria."

UEFA procedures meant that away supporters were kept in the stadium for a long period of time for safety reasons after all European matches, while the home fans departed. It simply gave Wanderers fans more time to celebrate together, as they held a party never to be forgotten inside the Naftex – before heading for the exits half an hour later.

Celebrations continued that night for those staying in Sunny Beach. "After the game we got back to Sunny Beach and it was full of Bolton fans in the bars," says Crook. "It was a real party. The first game in Europe and winning like that, it was superb."

Like the Wanderers squad, another Bolton player was celebrating in Europe too – although not in Bulgaria.

"I broke my fibula in the game before that so I was out for about three months and missed the second leg," says defender Hunt. "But the gaffer was brilliant with me. Because I couldn't do anything and was in a cast he said, 'Why don't you go away?'. So I went to Cyprus for a week with my girlfriend Louise and I watched the game in a nice little boozer on the beach. We had a big screen TV and there were a few Bolton fans there, older couples. I just wanted the lads to get the job done and then hopefully I'd be back and could play later on in the competition. When we won I texted all the lads, and we had a few beers that night celebrating."

Fans travelling officially with the club returned briefly to Nessebar after the game, where the bars reopened, sensing profits to be made. Supporters swapped shirts with Plovdiv fans, before heading on to the small and by now overcrowded airport. Tired but proud, Wanderers fans on chartered flights touched down back in Manchester at 3am, ready to tell the tales of one of the most incredible days of their lives.

Wanderers had come from behind to win with two late goals in a pivotal moment in their history in 1993, on a Friday night against Hull City at Boothferry Park. That victory paved the way for automatic promotion a week later, as the club finally escaped the bottom two divisions of English football for the first time in a decade. Many Bolton fans who were there that night still regard it as one of the best games they have ever witnessed.

Just as at Hull, the opposition in Bulgaria was not the finest Bolton had ever faced. The result itself may not stand out as the finest in the club's history. But to be there in Burgas was to understand just how special it felt. This time, it had paved the way for Wanderers to firmly establish themselves on the European stage. Over two seasons in the UEFA Cup, it was an opportunity they would not pass up.

Bolton: Ian Walker; Tal Ben Haim, Bruno N'Gotty, Abdoulaye Faye, Henrik Pedersen; Jay-Jay Okocha, Joey O'Brien (Hidetoshi Nakata 66), Fabrice Fernandes (Kevin Nolan 56); Stelios Giannakopoulos, Jared Borgetti (Kevin Davies 56), El-Hadji Diouf. Subs not used: Jussi Jaaskelainen, Ricardo Gardner, Jaroslaw Fojut, Ricardo Vaz Te.
Booked: Nakata.
Goals: Tunchev 79 og, Nolan 86.

Lokomotiv Plovdiv: Stoyan Kolev; Vladimir Ivanov, Kirl Kotev, Vlademir Giordani, Aleksandar Tunchev, Robert Petrov; Georgi Iliev, Ivan Krizmanic (Ilami Halimi 80), Krasimir Dimitrov; Yavor Vandev (Metodi Stoynev 63), Boban Jancevski. Subs not used: Vasil Kamburov, Ivo Mihaylov, Daniel Georgiev, Vladislav Zlatinov, Velko Hristev.
Goal: Iliev 51.

Attendance: 14,000.
Referee: Jouni Hyytia (Finland).

3

Playing with Fire

Besiktas 1 Bolton 1 – October 20, 2005

The opening to the group stage could not have been more daunting. A visit to one of the most intimidating places in world football – the city where east meets west, and where rioting fans would eventually meet police.

Five days after the club's victory in Bulgaria, Wanderers officials were in UEFA headquarters in the Swiss town of Nyon to find out their four opponents for the round robin stage of the competition. In those times, a curious format saw clubs drawn into groups of five, meaning that on each of the five matchdays one team would be left twiddling their thumbs. Bolton would play two of their opponents only at home, and the other two only away. The top three teams in the group would progress to the last 32 after Christmas. Quite who came up with such a puzzling mish-mash of a group phase is unclear, but it was scrapped in 2009 when the UEFA Cup was rebranded as the Europa League, taking the same format as the Champions League.

The 40 clubs in the draw were split into first, second, third, fourth and fifth seeds according to UEFA rankings. Only Wanderers and Middlesbrough remained to fly the English flag in the competition, with Everton's disastrous European campaign already over after their first round exit to Dinamo Bucharest.

Bolton, because of the success of English clubs in previous years, were among the third seeds for the draw. It meant they would be handed a glamour tie against one of the first seeds – CSKA Moscow, Roma, Stuttgart, Monaco, Hertha Berlin, Lokomotiv Moscow, Besiktas and AZ Alkmaar.

Of the second seeds they could not face fellow English side Middlesbrough, so their options were Sevilla, Marseille, PAOK Salonika, Slavia Prague, Basel, Espanyol and Lens.

The fourth seeds, who Bolton would be expected to finish above, were Steaua Bucharest, Brondby, Grasshoppers Zurich, Zenit St Petersburg, Levski Sofia, Strasbourg, Rennes and CSKA Sofia.

Rounding off the draw, the fifth seeds were Vitoria Guimaraes, Litex Lovech, Halmstads, Viking Stavanger, Dinamo Bucharest, Rapid Bucharest, Maccabi Petah Tikva and Tromso.

As it turned out, Bolton did not get the easiest of draws. They were matched with the highest ranked of the fifth seeds, Vitoria Guimaraes of Portugal. Then came Zenit St Petersburg, the Russian club they had been fortunate to narrowly avoid in the first round but would now pose a real danger to Bolton's hopes of reaching the last 16. Bolton were also drawn to face the highest ranked of the second seeds, Sevilla, the side that would ultimately win the UEFA Cup that season.

Besiktas were not the strongest of the first seeds, but much would depend on whether Bolton would face them at the Reebok or in Istanbul. That was decided by UEFA in the minutes after the draw, when news emerged that Bolton would have to make the fear-inducing trip to Turkey for their first match in Group H. Then came a home fixture against Zenit and a visit to Vitoria Guimaraes, before Wanderers rounded off the group by facing Sevilla at the Reebok.

The match at Besiktas would give Bolton a taste of European football at its most vivid and vibrant, and give supporters an intriguing window into a world that most had never previously experienced. But there were real concerns about the game in Istanbul, too. The city perhaps had the reputation as the most dangerous place in Europe for visiting football fans, and with good reason. Only five years earlier, two Leeds United fans had been stabbed to death in Taksim Square, in the very centre of Istanbul, the night before a UEFA Cup semi final with Galatasaray.

Istanbul had already been known to be a particularly volatile place for football. Famously, ahead of a Champions League tie in 1993, Manchester United were greeted at the airport by 'Welcome To Hell' banners. All manner of problems then ensued as they were eliminated from the competition. Eric Cantona was attacked by a truncheon-wielding policeman, and bricks were put through the windows of the team coach. A total of 164 United fans were arrested, many on flimsy pretexts. Some were beaten and had their possessions stolen.

There were other problems in Istanbul too. In 2003, terrorists detonated four truck bombs in the city, killing 57 and injuring 700. The British Consulate was one of four places targeted. As a result of the bombings, a match Besiktas and Chelsea was moved halfway across Europe to the German city of Gelsenkirchen – where the Turkish expat population is large.

Wanderers fans not used to travelling across Europe to watch football were understandably wary of the risks they may face. For both safety and financial reasons, many instead decided to make Vitoria Guimaraes, and the more western venue of Portugal, their one and only destination during the group phase. That match was a month further down the line.

There were little more than two weeks between the group stage draw and Wanderers flying out to Istanbul, and ticket sales were modest. Take-up was so slow that some travel packages had to be cancelled. In the end, around 450 supporters made the journey, most opting for the safer option of the one-day round trip officially organised by the club.

"I think when you're going to a lot of the Eastern European places there are always safety concerns because the atmosphere in those sorts of places is totally different to what we're used to," says club secretary Simon Marland. "Not many fans travelled and that was a knock-on from what had happened when Leeds went out there, and people had heard as well about Galatasaray, Welcome to Hell and this, that and the other."

Istanbul had been the scene of happier times for an English club months earlier, when Liverpool had come from 3-0 down to defeat AC Milan on penalties in the Champions League final. Wanderers midfielder Kevin Nolan, a lifelong Liverpool supporter, had been among the 69,000 crowd at the Ataturk Stadium – built for Istanbul's failed bid for the 2008 Olympics and situated more than 10 miles west of the centre of the city.

Istanbul, in the far west of Turkey, was not the capital of the country – that honour is held by the more geographically central Ankara. But with a metropolitan population of more than 14 million people, it comfortably dwarfed Moscow as the biggest city in Europe and was a place with a rich history.

Its strategic position next to the Bosphorus strait, on the isthmus connecting Europe with the Middle East, had long made it an important location for rampaging empires. The Greeks settled on the western side of the Bosphorus in 660 BC, naming the location Byzantium. They had to recapture it from the Persians 200 years later but the city later gained independence before becoming part of the Roman Empire.

Constantine the Great laid out plans for a new Christian city to replace Byzantium and it became known as Constantinople. In the year 330 it was declared as the capital of the Byzantine Empire, the eastern part of the Roman Empire. During the Middle Ages, Constantinople was the wealthiest city in Europe and at times the largest city in the world. As the Byzantine Empire crumbled, the Ottoman Turks from the east captured the city after an eight-week siege in 1453.

Constantinople was quickly transformed into a symbol of Islamic culture with a number of mosques and iconic buildings constructed during the reign of Suleiman the Magnificent. But the Ottoman Empire waned and World War I resulted in the city being occupied by British, French and Italian troops – despite Allied defeat at nearby Gallipoli earlier in the conflict. In 1922, the occupation of the city ended with the declaration of the Republic of Turkey by Mustafa Kemal Ataturk. Istanbul became the city's official name in 1930.

That incredible history gave rise to an incredible city, a vast sprawling mass that by now had expanded into huge areas on both sides of the Bosphorus. Today the strait, which connects the Black Sea in the north with the Sea of Marmara and the Mediterranean in the south, is the official border between Europe and Asia. The three footballing giants of Istanbul are not technically all from the same continent. Galatasaray and Besiktas hail from the European side of the city on the west bank of the Bosphorus, the historical centre of

Istanbul. On the east bank, connected to the rest of the city by the huge Bosphorus Bridge, stand Fenerbahce in Asia.

Fenerbahce would host German club Schalke at the Sukru Saracoglu Stadium in the Champions League on the night before Wanderers' UEFA Cup match at Besiktas, in a fervoured atmosphere that gave Bolton fans watching on television an indication of what they were about to travel into.

Earlier that day Wanderers' squad had already arrived at Istanbul airport, which like the Olympic stadium and many places in the city was named after national hero Ataturk. As soon as they got on the roads, they realised they were in a very different place to anything most had experienced before. Fourteen million people were all trying to get somewhere in a hurry, and basics such as lanes were ignored by most drivers. It was a free for all more reminiscent of south east Asia than a major European city.

"Traffic was the first thing we noticed, it was absolutely mental," remembers Russell Byrne-Fraser. "The squad got picked up by coach but I used to have a flat-backed lorry because of all the gear we used to take for the training and the game. I wasn't quite sure I would get to the hotel alive, the roads were hideous. That was the worst traffic I'd ever experienced and it was scary to say the least, especially in a lorry. There were no rules, they just made it up as they went along. It gave you a feeling of being on the crossroads of Europe and Asia.

"Then when we got to the hotel everything had to go through a metal detector, which was a bit frustrating because there was an awful lot. It wasn't just when we went in, it was when we went out again two hours later to train and back in again afterwards. It was a nightmare."

Wanderers were staying in the Ritz-Carlton Hotel, a towering building that loomed over Besiktas' Inonu Stadium.

"The hotel was overlooking the ground, it was a really nice setting," says Marland. "In some places the hotel and the ground were 10km apart and you would have to plan the traffic, but there you could physically walk from the hotel. The team didn't but we did when we were going to the pre-match meeting on the morning of the game."

"I can remember being up quite early that morning, opening the sliding door on the balcony and thinking what a lovely morning it was," Byrne-Fraser added. "As I did that you heard the call to prayer wafting through the window from the mosques. It made you realise that culturally you were somewhere really different."

Apart from the few who had travelled independently, Wanderers supporters arrived on official charter flights at lunchtime on the day of the game. They were transported from the airport in the south west of the city via the maddening streets to the central Taksim Square, from where they were free to roam Istanbul for the afternoon before being transported by bus to the stadium for the match.

Fans had been given a long list of dos and don'ts before leaving for Turkey. First of all they had been warned that anyone arriving in Turkey without a match ticket risked being prevented from obtaining a visa at the airport, and deported straight back to Britain. How exactly that would work we were unsure. It would surely be a bit of a blow to any unsuspecting tourists arriving from England that day. 'Have you got a ticket for Besiktas v Bolton Wanderers? What do you mean you've never heard of Bolton Wanderers? No ticket, no visa, you're going straight home'. Somehow we were dubious about that piece of advice, particularly as many travelling Bolton fans would actually have to collect their match tickets in Istanbul in any case.

Supporters were also told that anyone found to be drunk in public could be arrested and fined, which seemed a little more believable. In addition we were warned of things to avoid because culturally they were considered offensive in Turkey. Don't point with your finger, don't stand with your hands on your hips and don't show the bottoms of your feet. Based on that combination, woe betide John Travolta if he turned up in the centre of Istanbul doing the Saturday Night Fever routine.

Rather wary of getting stabbed though, we tried to take heed of those warnings. That was until approximately five seconds after we got off the coach in Taksim Square. 'Where shall we go?' our group pondered. 'Over there,' I pointed. D'oh. Thankfully the locals didn't seem to be offended, and I survived to tell the tale.

Some fans were content to spend their time in the bars and restaurants near Taksim Square. In 2013 the square was the scene of barricades made out of destroyed cars during violent protests, when the government announced plans to bulldoze the adjacent and popular Taksim Gezi Park and then sent in riot police to brutally deal with dissenters. But that day it was tranquil with some street salesman selling food from stalls and others approaching Wanderers fans, often quite persistently, to enquire whether they would like their shoes shined. Every passer-by was an opportunity to make money.

Many Bolton fans decided to wander further afield and use the short amount of time they had to explore this frenzied city, which offered eye-opening experiences around virtually every corner. Some opted to take their chances with the local taxi drivers, many of whom were somewhat craftier than your average British black cab driver. Fares had a habit of spiralling.

We made the error of taking the world's most bizarre open top bus tour, which left us windswept and frozen in dipping autumn temperatures and featured possibly the least informative tour guide on the planet. It took about three hours longer than scheduled as we eventually got caught up in the early evening rush hour – the worst gridlock we had ever seen.

But the sights were still spectacular. We travelled south over the little Galata Bridge crossing the Golden Horn, an inlet of the Bosphorus jutting west into Istanbul. All around the water were hills, upon which every last inch was packed with house after house. You got a sense of just how vast Istanbul really is.

Meanwhile on the bridge itself, a mind-blowing number of local angling enthusiasts lined up side by side, fishing for their supper in the Bosphorus as boats and passenger ferries manically darted back and forth nearby – taking people across the water to homes in the eastern part of the city. The traffic in the water was just as ludicrously chaotic as it was on land.

We continued a short distance further and passed the Grand Bazaar – one of the largest and oldest covered markets in the world, a mesmerising hive of wheeling and dealing, with 3,000 shops selling everything you could ever want, and up to 400,000 visitors every day.

From there we arrived at the Blue Mosque, a huge and historic place of worship built in the early 17th century. Nearby was the similarly imposing Hagia Sophia, once a Greek Orthodox church and later converted into a mosque before being transformed into a museum when Turkey officially became a secular country following Ataturk's rise to power.

By early evening Wanderers supporters returned to meet in Taksim Square for a bus journey to the stadium. The Inonu was less than 500 metres away, but fans were under strict instruction as night fell in Istanbul that they must arrive at the ground via the official coaches, rather than risk walking there themselves.

That was fine until there was no sign of the coaches, leaving apprehensive supporters standing en masse after dark in the same square where the two Leeds fans had been stabbed five years earlier. If there were any Turkish hooligans around searching for a target, they would not have far to look. Thankfully, there were no such hooligans in the vicinity and fans were eventually transported to the stadium before being ushered into the away section amid tight security.

The Inonu was a few hundreds yards from the grandiose Dolmabahce Palace, once the headquarters of the Ottoman Empire, in the relatively leafy Besiktas district of Istanbul. Originally called the Dolmabahce Stadium when it opened in 1947, it was renamed in 1973 following the death of the second president of Turkey and Besiktas fan, Ismet Inonu.

The 32,000-capacity stadium, decked in the black and white colours of Besiktas, was an old style bowl that had been renovated on occasions over the years but gave an authentic flavour of Turkish football. The away section was still a basic uncovered area behind the goal. Such were the security problems on occasions at football games in the country, high fences had been erected to separate it from the pitch and protect it from the home areas of the ground. Views near the front of the stand were restricted, although there were not enough Wanderers fans present for that to cause a problem.

To the left was the smart main stand filled with dignitaries, while at the other end of the stadium was the largest stand – a three-tiered structure backing into a hill, atop which Wanderers' hotel stood. The views across the Bosphorus to Asia from that stand made the Inonu the only stadium in the world from which you could see two different continents.

Many passionate Besiktas fans situated themselves behind the goal, but the real crazy people were in the two-tiered Kapali tribune alongside the right hand side of the pitch.

The Kapali was the home of the Carsi ultras, whose fanaticism was far beyond anything Wanderers had ever seen before. Bolton supporters did wonder if the Carsi realised they were named after a toilet, but no-one was about to approach them and point out the error of their ways.

Their catchphrase of 'Carsi, her seye karsi!', roughly translated as 'Carsi is against everything!', rather set their stall out. Their logo referred to the symbol of anarchism, and the group were said to be left wing. The Carsi would later disband in 2008 before becoming a mobilising force for anti-government protests.

The group were actually named after the Besiktas Carsi market, where they would meet on the afternoon before a match and walk en masse to the stadium, taking their places in the Kapali tribune up to three hours ahead of the 9.45pm kick-off. A hostile atmosphere would build well before the start of the match, which made for an unusual experience for secretary Marland.

"The crowd were in three hours before the game started and then we turned up," he remembers. "Before the team got changed and went out, three of us walked across the pitch because the tunnel was on the opposite side to the main stand. They obviously recognised we weren't Besiktas people and I think it's the only time I've ever been booed by opposing fans! There were a few thousand people giving us stick and I was wondering what it was all about, but I suppose that's the norm there."

Besiktas are firmly one of Turkish's big three clubs but have often been regarded as third in the pecking order behind Istanbul rivals Fenerbahce and Galatasaray, the latter of whom still played at the infamous Ali Sami Yen Stadium a couple of miles further north. Besiktas had 12 league titles – lagging behind Galatasaray's tally of 15 and Fenerbahce's total of 16.

Formed in 1903 during the late Ottoman period, Besiktas were not just a football club but also played a host of other sports – basketball, volleyball, handball, athletics, boxing, wrestling, chess, bridge, gymnastics, rowing, table tennis and Paralympic sports. Their colours were changed to black and white as a sign of mourning following the loss of Turkish territories during the Balkan Wars of 1912 and 1913.

Becoming known as the Black Eagles, success in the 1950s and 1960s was followed by years of decline but they reached the quarter finals of the European Cup in 1987 before a man from Preston delivered the most successful period in the club's history. Gordon Milne had initially brought in future Bolton striker Les Ferdinand on loan from QPR in 1988 and in the early 1990s he managed the club to three consecutive titles. They topped the table again in 1995 and 2003 after Milne had departed for Gary Lineker's Nagoya Grampus Eight in Japan.

John Toshack also had a spell in charge of the Turkish club but Spaniard Vicente del Bosque had taken the helm by the time of the 2004/05 season. Del Bosque had already won the Champions League twice with Real Madrid and would go on to win the World Cup and the European Championships with Spain, but his time in Istanbul was a blemish on his otherwise incredible coaching career.

Besiktas finished a distant fourth in the table that season behind Fenerbahce, Trabzonspor and Galatasaray, with Del Bosque sacked before the campaign was over. Former player Riza Calimbay had succeeded him and confirmed qualification for the UEFA Cup.

Besiktas eased through a qualifying round against FC Vaduz of Liechtenstein but made hard work of the first round against once great but by then faded Swedish side Malmo, who won the first leg 1-0 in Istanbul. The Turks triumphed 4-1 in Scandinavia to turn the tie around, thanks to a brace from Guinean striker Souleymane Youla and further goals from Ali Gunes and the talented Tumer Metin.

They had been top seeds for the group stage draw by virtue of their regular participation in European competition. Only once in 22 years had they failed to qualify for Europe, but they were not in good shape going into the Bolton game. A nightmare start to the league season had left them seventh in the table, already 13 points behind leaders Galatasaray. A 0-0 draw at home to Kayserispor four days before Wanderers' visit prompted Calimbay's swift resignation as coach.

Youth coach Mehmet Eksi and scout Ulvi Guveneroglu were in temporary charge for the Bolton game and Milne had also been brought back to the club as director of football that week. It was somewhat of an irony, given that only days earlier Wanderers had been taking advice from Milne on what to expect from Besiktas.

The Turks did have genuine experience in their team, particularly in the shape of 30-year-old midfielder Ahmed Hassan, who was well on the way to earning an incredible 184 caps for Egypt, a world record.

Also in the starting line-up were 2002 World Cup winning midfielder Kleberson – a flop with Manchester United – and fellow Brazilian Ailton, a striker who had previously scored 102 goals in seven seasons in the Bundesliga with Werder Bremen and Schalke. Oscar Cordoba had already broken Rene Higuita's record as Colombia's most capped goalkeeper, while Metin, Ibrahim Toraman, Cagdas Atan, Tayfur Havutcu, Koray Avci and Ibrahim Akin were all Turkish internationals.

Creative midfielder Okan Buruk – formerly of Inter Milan – would miss the game through injury, as would Youla. But this still felt like a genuine test on every level for Wanderers. While they had been expected to sweep aside Bulgarian minnows Lokomotiv Plovdiv, now they were facing famous opposition in one of the most intimidating cities in world football.

Wanderers had lost 2-1 at Wigan on their return from Bulgaria and went into the Besiktas match on the back of 5-1 thrashing at Chelsea.

Sam Allardyce had again decided to make changes for the UEFA Cup – seven in total. As in Bulgaria, Jussi Jaaskelainen, Nolan and Kevin Davies were rested to the bench, this time joined by Bruno N'Gotty and Henrik Pedersen. Jay-Jay Okocha and Ivan Campo were joined on the injury list by Gary Speed and Stelios Giannakopoulos.

Khalilou Fadiga started on his return from a loan spell at Phil Brown's Derby, while in came the likes of Ian Walker, Hidetoshi Nakata, Fabrice Fernandes, Jared Borgetti and Joey O'Brien again. If making his first start for the club in Bulgaria was pretty unforgettable for O'Brien, his second start in the cauldron of the Inonu Stadium was something else.

"To this day it's still the best atmosphere I've ever played in," he says fondly. "It was unbelievable. I remember arriving an hour and a half or two hours before the match and even then the place was rocking."

Wanderers would receive an extraordinary choreographed welcome to the pitch for kick-off. As the teams lined up in the tunnel, a lone man strode on to the turf from the frenzied Kapali stand. This man had clearly seen how Lofty the Lion's strong man act impressed the locals at the Reebok and was determined to blow it out of the water by quite some distance.

He spent some seconds arms aloft, fingers waggling. Home fans copied him to form some sort of bizarre mass jazz hands salute, accompanied by a wall of noise. Then the man put his finger to his lips, urging them to fall eerily silent. Wanderers fans wondered what on earth was going on.

Finally, he waved his arms frantically to start a clearly rehearsed chant that finished with the entire crowd of close to 20,000 home fans bouncing up and down amid a cacophony of noise. It was quite a sight, and it was at that moment that the referee led both sides out of the tunnel for kick-off.

It could have been quite intimidating for a player like O'Brien who was more used to playing reserve matches in front of crowds of less than 100 at Leyland's County Ground.

"I wasn't intimidated, I was just delighted to be playing there," says O'Brien. "People were talking about the atmosphere but that's what you wanted as a kid. If you go to those places and you play in a hostile area and you can't feel that vibe and involve yourself in it, I think you're in the wrong game."

Crazed chanting continued from the Carsi on one side of the stadium throughout the match, accompanied by turbo arm waving and finger pointing, with occasional bouncing. Every supporter was stretching his vocal cords to the absolute limit. The stadium was little more than half full, but the volume had to be heard to be believed. Years later they would claim the world record for noise levels inside a football ground, a remarkable 141 decibels. If English stadiums are often praised for their noise and atmosphere, this was a whole new level.

Frequently, the upper and lower tier of the Kapali stand chanted 'KARTAL GOL GOL GOL!' (eagle goal goal goal) back and forth between themselves, becoming ever more manic, as if competing against one another.

The volume levels rose even more after seven minutes of the match, which unusually was being screened live in England on Sky One. Wanderers were finding that the pitch, described as 'a layer of turf put on a lump of slag', was not ideal for passing football. Tal Ben Haim, playing at right back, scuffed a horrible square pass across the pitch on the halfway line, O'Brien had little chance of controlling it, and Metin pounced on the loose ball to play Ailton through on goal.

The 32-year-old Brazilian did not exactly look in peak condition by this stage of his career – indeed he spent most of the night waddling about in a Mario Jardel sort of way, occasionally pausing to gather breath. But he still knew where the net was and needed no second invitation, instinctively poking the ball into the top corner with his left boot. It was a Romario style toe-bung, but a deadly accurate one.

Besiktas supporters erupted in fanatical joy, setting off flares to celebrate. Wanderers had made far from the ideal start to the group stage, and there were fears this could turn into a difficult night.

Most perhaps would have expected Wanderers to lose this game but Besiktas – playing in all white, with the visitors in dark blue – could not capitalise on their fine start. The tide began to turn as Bolton started to settle into the match.

In the 29th minute Borgetti headed the ball out to the right flank where El-Hadji Diouf collected. Diouf delayed briefly before crossing to the far post, where Borgetti had advanced to slam a left-foot shot past Cordoba into the net. The 450 Bolton fans behind that goal could not quite match the roar that had greeted Besiktas' opener, but they celebrated nevertheless.

Wanderers chairman Phil Gartside attempted to do the same in the main stand but was thwarted.

"The president of Besiktas made me sit next to him for the game," Gartside remembers. "I sat there watching the match not being able to say a word because all our lot were sat at the back. I was on my own and they scored to make it 1-0 and all these blokes around me stood up cheering and jumping up and down. Then we equalised and I jumped up, and the president tapped me on the shoulder and said, 'No'. I replied 'Oh right, okay', and I had to sit down!"

Discontent among home fans, already upset with the direction their club had taken at the start of the season, was now starting to materialise. Wanderers were managing to frustrate Besiktas, who were quickly losing their way and struggling to retain possession.

Bolton kept the ball well and a dart down the left flank from Fadiga – immediately in front of the Carsi – brought the most deafeningly ear-splitting whistles that you could possibly imagine. The home fans had been expecting an easier night than this. Their ire was largely aimed at their own team, although coins were thrown at the Wanderers supporters in the away section.

Besiktas lost Metin to injury before half time and then had to replace Toraman at the interval. Later, substitute Gokhan Zan would also be forced off injured.

The second half continued in similarly encouraging fashion for Bolton. In such a difficult setting for an inexperienced 19-year-old, O'Brien was making a real impression in the midfield holding role – putting his foot in when required, and using the ball intelligently. That performance, perhaps more than any other, would be the making of a career that would see him play in the Premier League for both Bolton and West Ham, and earn caps for the Republic of Ireland.

"It was a great stepping stone for me and I suppose that game really showed to myself and the club that I could be a first-team player for the football club, so it was great for my career," O'Brien reflects. "As a young lad I was just hoping to get a few games. At the time the Premier League was the main thing for the football club and the manager was obviously giving lads a chance. I suppose normally you might get a Carling Cup run and you'd get in there, but as a young player my games were coming in the UEFA Cup against some top teams.

"It was great for me. After playing in that game I got into the first team and had the chance to be a regular. It all came from there. I have the game on a DVD and it's a great memory for me. I have watched the game back and I've always kept it. It was just the occasion and the atmosphere, and it was such a famous ground. It was a fantastic night, everything about it."

Besiktas looked all out of ideas, creating precious little. Bolton could even have won it when Diouf forced the ball over the line from a set piece with 20 minutes left, only for the goal to be ruled out for offside.

For Wanderers and their fans, though, there was huge pride at the final whistle as they secured an unexpected point in the most hostile of environments. For decades Bolton could only look in awe at clubs like Besiktas who were respected around Europe. Now they had gone into their back yard and got a result.

"In that game I was thinking that something is being built at Bolton because we had never played in front of so many people, and their fans put us under so much pressure," says Diouf. "The fans in Istanbul were brilliant, it was so crazy. But we played good football and we drew. We were brilliant in that game."

While Wanderers were happy with a point, Besiktas supporters were rather less impressed at the result and were soon making that perfectly clear. Instead of leaving the stadium and heading for home, large numbers stayed and began starting a number of small fires in the stands. After the coach's departure earlier that week, now they were venting their anger at club president Yildirim Demiroren.

"I never saw the president after the game, he just disappeared," says Gartside. "The fans were burning the stadium down, which I thought was different!"

Wanderers fans – kept inside the away section for some time after the match – could only watch in amusement and incredulity at what was unfolding elsewhere in the stadium.

The riot police were soon sent marching across the pitch in comically over-dramatic fashion akin to the Edinburgh Military Tattoo, in an attempt to send the message that they wouldn't stand for any messing around. Wanderers fans, not taking the situation entirely seriously, urged them on with shouts of 'Attack, attack, attack!'

The police lined up in rows next to the Kapali stand, eye-balling the protesting Carsi. Fans stood their ground for some time, remaining in the stands and continuing their protests. The Wanderers squad were told they could not leave the stadium until the situation had been resolved.

"We couldn't go because the fans went crazy and they mashed up the place," remembers Diouf. "After the game Sam Allardyce said, 'No-one is allowed to go out because you never know in Turkey what could happen'. We couldn't go for a long time. We had to stay in the changing room."

Eventually the riot police's presence persuaded the Carsi that it would be for their own benefit if they left before the situation turned nasty. It was a bizarre finish to the night. You don't get that at Carrow Road or Craven Cottage.

Elsewhere that evening, Zenit St Petersburg beat Vitoria Guimaraes 2-1 in Russia to go top of the group thanks to goals from Oleksandr Spivak and Andrey Arshavin.

In the end, Besiktas' president remained until he stepped up to become president of the Turkish Football Federation in 2012. A fortnight after the draw with Wanderers, the club brought in former Fulham boss Jean Tigana as their new manager. They finished third that season to qualify for the UEFA Cup again, despite ending the campaign 27 points behind second-placed Fenerbahce.

In 2008 they returned to the Champions League, beating Liverpool 2-1 in Istanbul but losing 8-0 at Anfield. A year later they won the Turkish league for the 13th time in their history, and in 2011 they beat lesser known city rivals Istanbul BB to win the Turkish Cup. But that result would later be dogged by allegations of match-fixing, and Besiktas were handed a one-year ban from European competition by UEFA.

In 2013 Besiktas played their final game at the old Inonu. The stadium was demolished to make way for a new modern arena on the same site, although the three-tier home end – regarded as a historical monument – was set to be retained and incorporated into the new structure.

With Fenerbahce's ground much renovated at the turn of the millennium and Galatasaray leaving the Ali Sami Yen in 2010 to move into the plush new Turk Telekom Arena, the demolition of the Inonu spelt an end to the last link with the traditional Istanbul football experience. It is hard to imagine that any of the new stadia can create quite the same hostile and raw atmosphere as their crumbling predecessors.

Wanderers had been fortunate enough to savour it before it was too late. It was quite an experience.

Bolton: Ian Walker; Tal Ben Haim, Abdoulaye Faye, Radhi Jaidi, Ricardo Gardner; Hidetoshi Nakata, Joey O'Brien, Fabrice Fernandes (Kevin Nolan 59); El-Hadji Diouf, Jared Borgetti, Khalilou Fadiga. Subs not used: Jussi Jaaskelainen, Jaroslaw Fojut, Bruno N'Gotty, Henrik Pedersen, Kevin Davies, Ricardo Vaz Te.
Goal: Borgetti 29.

Besiktas: Oscar Cordoba; Tayfur Havutcu, Ibrahim Toraman (Gokhan Zan 46, Mustafa Dogan 70), Cagdas Atan, Adem Dursun; Ahmed Hassan, Koray Avci, Kleberson, Ibrahim Akin; Tumer Metin (Ibrahim Uzulmez 36); Ailton. Subs not used: Murat Sahin, Ali Gunes, Veysel Cihan, Ahmet Dursun.
Goal: Ailton 7.

Attendance: 17,027.
Referee: Ruud Bossen (Netherlands).

Group H	P	W	D	L	F	A	Pts
Zenit	1	1	0	0	2	1	3
Besiktas	1	0	1	0	1	1	1
Bolton	1	0	1	0	1	1	1
Sevilla	0	0	0	0	0	0	0
V Guimaraes	1	0	0	1	1	2	0

4

Underwater with the Russian Submarines

Bolton 1 Zenit St Petersburg 0 – November 3, 2005

If other matches in the club's European journey would go down in folklore for dramatic match action or incredible events off the pitch, Wanderers' first home game in the group stage would be remembered for the farcical conditions in which the fixture was played. Bolton were now into their fourth match in the UEFA Cup, but it was showing no signs of becoming mundane.

Wanderers had been lucky to avoid running into Zenit St Petersburg in the first round, but the Russians finally arrived at the Reebok Stadium on a night like no other.

Sadly the quirks of the group stage meant that this would be Bolton's only match against Zenit, and there would be no intriguing return fixture in Saint Petersburg – the historic city founded by Tsar Peter the Great, where the Bolsheviks stormed the Winter Palace to help bring communism to power almost a century ago.

In the chaotic years after the revolution a number of football clubs in the city amalgamated and the team by the name of Bolshevik were renamed as Zenit in 1936. Three years later under political pressure they merged with the Stalinets, the team from the local metal plant.

For many years the club would be referred to across Europe as Zenit Leningrad, with the city taking the name of Leningrad in 1924 following the death of communist leader Vladimir Lenin. It returned to its original name of Saint Petersburg in 1991.

Zenit won their first honours when they lifted the USSR Cup in 1944, helping to raise the spirits of a city who had just suffered a three-year siege by the Nazis. More than one million civilians died, mostly from starvation. In 1967, Zenit should have been relegated but were saved from the drop because the Soviet leadership did not want a Leningrad team relegated during the 50th anniversary of the October Revolution. In those days they counted among their fans the famous composer Dmitri Shostakovich.

Zenit would face Bolton in Group H at the Reebok Stadium. They had qualified for the UEFA Cup a full calendar year earlier by finishing fourth in the Russian league, which at that time ran from March until November.

With only one league title in 1984 to their name, they could not come close to matching the honours lists of the Moscow teams such as Spartak, Dinamo or CSKA at that stage, but they were starting to emerge as a real force in Russian football.

They had briefly registered on the English radar in 2000 when they beat Bradford City in the Intertoto Cup. The name of Andrey Arshavin attracted little attention at the time, but it was while winning 3-0 in the second leg at Valley Parade that Zenit handed a debut to the 19-year-old as a substitute.

By the time Arshavin faced Bolton in 2005, his first return to England since his debut, the Saint Petersburg-born forward had developed into a Russian international. So too had his strike partner Aleksandr Kerzhakov and Aleksandr Anyukov, the attacking right back. Together with emerging 21-year-old Igor Denisov and goalkeeper Vyacheslav Malafeev, in time the quintet would form the core of the Russian national team. Malafeev was on the bench at the Reebok, after slipping to second choice behind Slovak keeper Kamil Contofalsky.

Zenit were under the management of Vlastimil Petrzela, who appeared in the 1982 World Cup for Czechoslovakia. He had bolstered Zenit's squad with the signing of a rugged-looking centre back called Martin Skrtel from little-known Slovak side Trencin, although the defender would only adopt the skinhead look when he signed for Liverpool in 2008.

Instead it was Skrtel's defensive partner Erik Hagen – a Norwegian nicknamed 'Panzer', or 'Tank' – who the local press warned of before kick-off. It promised to be the sort of physical battle that Kevin Davies relished, with Sam Allardyce fielding a relatively strong team for the game.

Davies and Kevin Nolan started, the latter five days after scoring the winner in a 1-0 Premier League win at Charlton. El-Hadji Diouf was saved for the bench, though, while the loss of Nicky Hunt to injury had seen Joey O'Brien asked to improvise at right back in the matches after his midfield starring role at Besiktas. He had helped Wanderers to three consecutive victories in his new position.

"I was a central midfielder when I was coming through in the academy under Chris Sulley," O'Brien said. "When I made my debut against Yeovil and played against Everton, I came on in the centre of midfield. But the following Sunday after Besiktas, we played and I thought I could have been in the team.

"As the team went up I was looking around the centre thinking I might see my name and my name wasn't there. I sort of looked away, and then I just looked back to see who else was there and I saw my name in the right full back position!

"At the time it was completely new to me but that was it really. From there we went down to the training pitch and the manager said, 'You're playing here, let's do a little bit of coaching'.

"I played there for the rest of the season, and I've played there for him at

West Ham, at right full back or left full back."

There was another start in the UEFA Cup, too, for Hidetoshi Nakata – the Japanese midfielder who did not make a huge impact during his solitary season at Bolton on loan from Fiorentina. Surprisingly he opted to retire at the age of 29 that summer after playing in the 2006 World Cup. But of all the famous players Wanderers had during that era, Nakata had probably the most ardent followers from his homeland – with a strong Japanese turn-out at every game.

As it happened, the conditions against Zenit were not exactly suited to Nakata's silky passing style. Bolton had hosted a Russian club before, securing a 3-1 win over the touring CDSA Moscow – later renamed CSKA Moscow – in a friendly at Burnden Park in November 1957. It is unlikely though that CDSA had to face the weather that Zenit had to deal with on their visit. The 500 vocal travelling fans witnessed the heavens open as rain poured down during the first half at the Reebok.

It did not have a great effect in the early stages of the game when quickly it became clear that Zenit, wearing all blue, would be dangerous with Arshavin and Kerzhakov up front – particularly on the counter attack. The pacy Kerzhakov would later be linked with a move to Bolton, and he had an early chance in this game but fired wide.

Composed in possession, Zenit were a constant threat in attack but their defence did appear vulnerable. Davies directed a free header wide from Nolan's left-wing cross, before the forward outpaced his opponents to race clear two minutes later. In increasingly sodden conditions the pitch was starting to make life tricky, but there were still groans from the crowd of 15,905 as Davies lashed his shot high and wide.

A goal came quickly though, in the 24th minute. A deep free kick from Bruno N'Gotty found its way to Stelios Giannakopoulos who controlled the ball but saw his close range shot blocked by Contofalsky. Nolan, always alert to the loose ball in the box, was on hand to stab home the rebound.

"I remember the ball came in and my job was always to get in behind Davo," says Nolan, who had been named captain for the night with regular skipper Jay-Jay Okocha only on the bench. "The ball just came out to me and I managed to react from six yards, one of my famous ones. I put it in the back of the net before anyone could really react, which I was delighted with."

A minute later a knee injury forced off Skrtel, to be replaced by Ukrainian veteran Oleksandr Gorshkov. Still the rain hammered down and by the time the teams came back out for the start of the second half, Italian referee Matteo Trefoloni had a problem – and not just with maintaining his neatly greased-back hairstyle.

The pitch was starting to resemble a lake in some areas, particularly the touchline by the Nat Lofthouse Stand. Passing the ball was becoming almost impossible, as playing conditions reached comical levels never previously seen at the Reebok Stadium.

"How the match wasn't called off I'll never know," O'Brien recalls. "For rain, that was 100 per cent the worst conditions I've played in. I thought it was going to get called off but it never did. It was unbelievable that night.

"There was obviously some sort of reason why they couldn't call it off. I think if it had been a league game it would have been. You weren't able to pass the ball around on the ground. It was just getting held up, it was mad. I remember Stelios Giannakopoulos was playing scoop passes because that was the best way of getting the ball around the pitch."

Indeed, the little Greek appeared to adapt to the conditions better than others as he combated the deepest water on his flank, bravely wading in without first calling for armbands or a snorkel.

"The sooner you adapt to the situation, the better for you," Stelios laughs in recollection of that match.

"I had a quick adaptation in general in England, that was the thing that helped me to go from the Greek way of playing to the English Premier League.

"It was a very difficult situation to play in because although in England you expect the rain, the weather conditions were extremely bad. The pitch was very hard to play on but not only for us, for them as well, because they had some very good technical players.

"But I'd played in worse conditions than that. For Olympiakos I played in a Champions League game at Croatia Zagreb in 1998. We played on ice in minus 17 degrees – extremely bad conditions to play in – and I scored in that game to help us qualify for the last eight. In bad conditions your mind must adapt a little quicker because you don't have time."

Thankfully no footballers drowned in the hazardous conditions at the Reebok, which might not have exactly suited tiki-taka but did provide the sort of entertainment that many still laugh about now. Even throw-ins provided moments of high farce.

"Back then we had a different sized pitch for the Premier League," recalls club secretary Simon Marland, of a period when Allardyce narrowed the dimensions of the playing surface for league matches to hamper the free-flowing style of Arsenal and the like.

"But for European games you had to have a particular sized pitch. They had their rules, and that was it. We had to move the touchlines from the Premier League game for the European game, but it rained that much that you could see two sets of lines for the game against Zenit. I remember Ricardo Gardner taking a throw-in from the wrong line and the referee didn't see it, he just carried on."

Assessing the conditions, the referee no doubt was mindful of the fact that an abandonment would have created major issues, given the fact that Zenit had travelled 1,300 miles to Bolton.

Even restarting the game on Friday afternoon, as has happened with occasional European games since then, would have caused problems – and not just for the Bolton fans who would have been at work. Zenit were scheduled to make the trip to the Ural mountains, another 900 miles further east of Saint Petersburg, for a league game at Amkar Perm on Sunday and would not have relished having just two days to travel and recover.

"You take into account the travelling and what would happen if the game was postponed, and I think once we'd got it underway it would have to be something major to cancel it," Marland said. "It would have been down to UEFA and what arrangements Zenit had made. If they'd organised a plane and it's sitting at Manchester Airport, you've got to take everything like that into account as well.

"But the game wasn't too far from being abandoned as it was. I don't think there were serious discussions but it must have crossed people's minds. We got away with it, though. The weather probably helped us because on that night, if I'm totally honest, Zenit were probably the better team. You can understand why they're a club who are in Europe every year."

Perhaps the most impressive thing about Zenit that night was how they coped with the drenched pitch in the final minutes. These were conditions more suited to Russian submarines than a Russian football team. The pitch suited Bolton's style more than it did Zenit's short passing game.

So did the scoreline. Bolton were in front and did not have to figure out how on earth to actually score a goal in such conditions. But Zenit persisted with their style, and almost made it work.

"You could see that night that Zenit were a top team," O'Brien admits. "That night was the first time I heard of Andrey Arshavin. He was a smashing player."

Arshavin, the most impressive of all in adapting to the conditions, came so close to a dramatic late equaliser in stoppage time. Jussi Jaaskelainen had already saved an effort from Denisov when the small but highly skilled Arshavin somehow managed to dribble the ball at pace towards the area, evading Gary Speed. He exchanged a smart one-two with Kerzhakov before darting into the box, only for Jaaskelainen to make a fine save – deflecting the ball wide with his shoulder. It needed a tremendous stop to deny what would have been a tremendous goal in the circumstances.

After the game, Allardyce hailed Jaaskelainen as 'one of the top two or three goalkeepers in the Premiership', and it was true. The athletic goalkeeping of the 6ft 4in Finn had been the foundation on which all of Bolton's success had been built. Every good team needs a good goalkeeper and Bolton had one in Jaaskelainen.

Victory put Wanderers top of Group H, after Sevilla beat Besiktas 3-0 in Spain in the other game of the evening thanks to a goal from Javier Saviola and two from Frederic Kanoute. Already Wanderers knew that a win in their next match, in Portugal against Vitoria Guimaraes, would confirm their progression to the last 32.

"It was another great night," says Nolan. "At that time I don't think we realised what we were doing for the town. We had 28,000 for games on a Saturday and I don't think we were hitting 20,000 for the European games. I don't think we all appreciated what we had until a few years later, when unfortunately the club started dropping down the league.

"To beat Zenit was massive, the players they had such as Arshavin and a few others who went on to play across Europe in top leagues. Zenit play in the Champions League regularly now, so it was such a massive thing for us."

Just a month later, Zenit's steady progression as a team would be given a real shot in the arm as they were taken over by Russian gas giants Gazprom. They would reach the quarter finals of the UEFA Cup that season but really kicked on under next manager Dick Advocaat, the former Rangers and Netherlands boss.

When Zenit were crowned Russian champions in 2007 for only the second time, it opened the door for more league titles to follow as money was spent on star signings from abroad. Arshavin starred as Zenit won the UEFA Cup in 2008, beating Rangers 2-0 in the final. New Portuguese forward Danny, a Russian record signing at €30m, then scored the winner as they beat Manchester United in the Super Cup.

That summer Arshavin had helped to guide Russia to the semi finals of Euro 2008, shocking the Netherlands, the favourites, in the last eight. Arshavin moved to Arsenal, scoring four times in a 4-4 draw at Liverpool before his star waned.

Without him, Zenit continued to progress under former Roma manager Luciano Spalletti and became Champions League regulars. They spent €80m in one day in September 2012 when they signed Brazilian forward Hulk from Porto and Belgian midfielder Axel Witsel from Benfica.

But in 2005, they were beaten by Bolton Wanderers and the Reebok rain.

Bolton: Jussi Jaaskelainen; Joey O'Brien, Bruno N'Gotty, Tal Ben Haim, Ricardo Gardner; Hidetoshi Nakata (Jay-Jay Okocha 66), Abdoulaye Faye, Gary Speed; Kevin Nolan (El-Hadji Diouf 85), Kevin Davies (Jared Borgetti 74), Stelios Giannakopoulos. Subs not used: Ian Walker, Jaroslaw Fojut, Radhi Jaidi, Ricardo Vaz Te.
Goal: Nolan 24.

Zenit: Kamil Contofalsky; Aleksandr Anyukov, Erik Hagen, Milan Vjestica, Martin Skrtel (Oleksandr Gorshkov 25); Igor Denisov, Oleg Vlasov (Mikhail Kozlov 90), Velice Sumulikoski, Jan Flachbart; Aleksandr Kerzhakov, Andrey Arshavin. Subs not used: Vyacheslav Malafeev, Oleg Kozhanov, Dragan Cadikovski, Robertas Poskus, Viktor Stroev.
Booked: Hagen, Flachbart.

Attendance: 15,905.
Referee: Matteo Trefoloni (Italy).

Group H	P	W	D	L	F	A	Pts
Bolton	2	1	1	0	2	1	4
Sevilla	1	1	0	0	3	0	3
Zenit	2	1	0	1	2	2	3
Besiktas	2	0	1	1	1	4	1
V Guimaraes	1	0	0	1	1	2	0

5

A Goal for the Ages

Vitoria Guimaraes 1 Bolton 1 – November 24, 2005

Perhaps more than any other UEFA Cup match, the trip to Vitoria Guimaraes will forever be linked to one man. On paper at least, a 1-1 draw against an unfancied Portuguese side does not seem one of the more remarkable moments in Bolton's recent history. But for the 4,000 supporters who were there, it was.

Mention Guimaraes to anyone who made that trip, and it will not take long for them to utter the name of Ricardo Vaz Te. It was Vaz Te who scored THAT goal, the fairytale goal that made Vitoria Guimaraes a match to remember.

As a fan there are classic games, and then there are classic moments – split seconds in time that live forever. Each person will have their own personal favourites. For me it's John McGinlay scoring the winner at Hull in 1993, or doing the same against Swindon in the Coca-Cola Cup semi final. Fabian DeFreitas' late equaliser against Reading in the play-off final, Michael Ricketts' winning goal at Old Trafford, Lee Chung-Yong's FA Cup quarter final decider at Birmingham. That perfect footballing moment in time. When it replays in your mind, even years later, you can still remember exactly how it felt.

Vaz Te's goal in Guimaraes stands alongside those moments, arguably more than any other single UEFA Cup goal – maybe even those against Bayern Munich. Often fans visit YouTube to relive the memory. The clip has close to 50,000 hits now. "I was there, I will always love Vaz Te for that moment," one fan comments underneath the video.

When I told people I was writing this book, one of the first questions they asked was, 'Are you going to speak to Vaz Te about Guimaraes?' So when I travelled down to West Ham's training ground, I was particularly keen to hear the Portuguese forward's memories about the night he returned to his homeland and catapulted himself into the hearts of Wanderers fans forever. He did not disappoint, bounding into the room and instantly speaking with real warmth about that goal. Scored with his mother watching on from the stands, it was obvious how special it still remained to him.

"I cherish the moment very much," he admitted. "People still talk to me about it. If I was to walk through town in Bolton they would talk to me about that goal, I'm sure it's going to live forever. If it's a happy memory for people and I'm part of that, I can only be grateful. It's good to be remembered in a good way rather than a bad way."

When the draw for the group stage was made, largely for understandable financial reasons many supporters decided that they would travel to only one of the two away matches. The first away game at Besiktas was at shorter notice and carried with it safety fears, so only around 450 made the journey.

Most instead chose the friendlier climes of northern Portugal. In the end, an incredible 4,000 tickets were sold for a match in a little known town 900 miles away.

Under normal UEFA rules, Bolton would have been entitled to only 1,500 tickets in the 30,000-capacity Estadio Dom Afonso Henriques. But Vitoria, whose attendances averaged at around the 16,000 mark, gave Bolton the entire two-tier away end in their newly renovated stadium.

Work had been carried out on the venue in time for Euro 2004, when Guimaraes played host to two group matches – a 0-0 draw between Italy and Denmark, and a 2-1 win for Italy over Bulgaria. Future Bolton winger Martin Petrov scored Bulgaria's goal.

The stadium had also been the venue of the tragic death of Benfica's Hungarian forward Miklos Feher, who collapsed during a league match in 2004. Sympathy went out not just to Feher's family, but to everyone who had been in the stadium to witness such a shocking event. Soon, though, Bolton fans would come close to seeing something identical – not once but twice.

Later in 2004 Khalilou Fadiga – a player with a history of heart problems from his time at Inter Milan – would collapse during the warm-up of a Carling Cup tie at home to Tottenham. Thankfully, the swift response of players, staff and medics averted a major disaster. Fadiga made a full recovery, returning to the Bolton first-team squad. He would be named on the bench for Wanderers for their UEFA Cup match in Guimaraes.

After the Fadiga incident, Bolton took a defibrillator wherever they went – a piece of equipment that was not always easy to get through airport security during European away trips. But it would prove important when another Wanderers player had an altogether closer brush with death in 2012, again in a cup tie against Tottenham.

Most Bolton fans thought they had lost Fabrice Muamba when he collapsed in an FA Cup quarter final tie at White Hart Lane – lying unresponsive on the field as the attempts of the medical staff to restart his heart went on and on, with no success. It was a harrowing experience far beyond anything most had ever witnessed in a football stadium. The confusion and panic, the despair on his team-mates' faces as they prayed on the pitch. The away fans chanting Muamba's name, knowing that in truth they were helpless.

I thought of Feher that night. Muamba would never play football again but miraculously he survived, revived in hospital after 78 minutes without a heartbeat. Feher was not so lucky. Just as Benfica fans had witnessed the tragedy, so too had the Vitoria Guimaraes supporters that day. It was a sombre part of the stadium's history.

Guimaraes was a small city of just 50,000 inhabitants 35 miles to the north east of Porto, the country's second largest population centre. A few miles over the rolling hills to the north of Guimaraes lay Braga, Vitoria's footballing rivals.

A historical city whose centre had been declared a UNESCO World Heritage Site in 2001, and which would be European Capital of Culture in 2012, one imagines that Guimaraes is normally a tranquil sort of place. By the end of Bolton's visit though, the town must have been wondering what had hit it.

The squad, like a significant number of Bolton fans, stayed in Porto rather than Guimaraes itself. "Guimaraes was the ideal place for us to play, it was a really lovely place," said club secretary Simon Marland. "I'd been fortunate that I'd already been there for the European Championships, so when we drew them I thought it was brilliant. I knew what we were going into and it was perfect.

"The only issue we had from a team point of view was there weren't any reasonable hotels in Guimaraes itself so we stayed in Porto. But it was only about 40 minutes away. The place, the people and the club were good."

Our group of four were among the many fans who flew to Porto on the Wednesday before heading on to Guimaraes on matchday. We almost never made it to Porto at all, after problems en route.

Our flight to Portugal was via Frankfurt, where we had time for a couple of hours in the Christmas markets in the chilly city centre. Unfortunately none of us spoke German, so when we embarked the train back to the airport we did not understand the public address announcement that it had been diverted in another direction. We got the first train back to the centre of Frankfurt, but the same thing happened again – leaving us scrambling for a taxi and only just making the flight.

When Bolton fans arrived in Porto they were greeted by the presence of Rangers fans already in situ. The Scottish side were in the city for a Champions League game against FC Porto on the Wednesday night, 24 hours before Bolton's UEFA Cup match. Securing tickets, we ventured down to the Estadio do Dragao to watch the Gers claim a surprise 1-1 draw against the post-Mourinho era Porto, thanks to a late equaliser from a 19-year-old Ross McCormack. There were reports of an altercation between a small number of Bolton and Rangers fans in Porto city centre that night.

The majority of Bolton supporters arrived in Portugal on Thursday morning via the club's chartered flights. Buses took them from Porto to Guimaraes and by mid-afternoon what was previously a sleepy venue had been transformed.

Peruse the tourism photographs and you'll see that the central Praca da Oliveira in Guimaraes is normally a peaceful square with cobblestones and al fresco dining. That image changed considerably when 4,000 Bolton fans turned up and set up base in the square. Anyone in the local houses hoping for an afternoon nap might have found peace and quiet in short supply.

The bars though, were recording the sort of sales figures that would have bought their owners a small island in the Caribbean. For Bolton supporters, it is hard to imagine that there has ever been a sight quite like that square that afternoon. Hardly a cobblestone was left unoccupied by a Wanderers fan supping beer in the pleasant Portuguese autumn sun. Songs were sung about old heroes, an entire community transposed across Europe and placed among an unsuspecting Iberian populace.

The locals were warm and friendly. House owners allowed fans to hang Bolton flags from seemingly every window in the entire circumference of the square. One elderly Portuguese lady spent the afternoon curiously watching the proceedings in the square from her open first floor window, unaware of the juxtaposition between her stern-looking face and the comedic banner directly beneath her. 'El-Hadji Diouf will spit on you,' it said.

This was a party, a joyous celebration of just how far Bolton Wanderers had come in more ways than one. The chain railings around the square provided a hazard that caught out many a tipsy beer-carrying fan, to the laughter of those around them.

Wanderers chairman Phil Gartside remembers arriving at the square with dignitaries that afternoon and fearing the worst.

"The tradition is that you're invited to lunch with the home club before the game," says Gartside. "In England we did it the night before, we had them for dinner. In Guimaraes they wanted us to go for lunch and we had to go and meet the mayor. We had this lunch, which was very nice, and we had a few glasses of wine.

"Then the mayor decided he'd take us on a tour of the town. We're walking through the streets and you could hear all this noise and I thought, 'Oh God, what are we going to see next?' People were all over the place, drunk as skunks the lot of them! Then the closer we got to the town square I was thinking, 'Jeepers, what are we going to find here?' The mayor was so proud of this town and I was thinking, 'If our lot are wrecking this, it's going to be bad!'.

"But when we got to the square it was like a big party with all these flags hanging out of the houses around the square, mixed in with the washing. It was unreal. It was 4,000 Bolton fans in Portugal, having a great time and not causing any trouble."

Just around the corner in the Toural Square though, a mischievous Bolton tradition had been born as soap powder was surreptitiously introduced to the city fountain. By night-time, the fountain would resemble the largest bubble bath in the world. Fountains in further cities across Europe would later suffer a similar fate. It was a long-running source of amusement for Wanderers fans. No real harm was done.

Later in the afternoon we ventured up the hill to the Palace of the Dukes of Braganca and the statue of Dom Afonso Henriques, who became the first king of Portugal in 1139 and is said to have been born in Guimaraes – although that fact is still disputed. The statue features prominently on Vitoria's crest and it was after him that the club's smart, two-tier all-seater stadium was named.

It does not require a linguistic genius to work out that Vitoria is the Portuguese word for victory and Guimaraes had recorded no shortage of them on the way to qualification for the UEFA Cup. They had finished fifth in the Primeira Liga behind the big three of Benfica, Porto and Sporting, as well as Braga.

The club's nicknames included the image-conjuring moniker of 'Os Conquistadores', or 'The Conquerors', although Portuguese football has long been dominated by the big three and Guimaraes have never won the league title.

Indeed their only major honour at that stage was the Supertaca de Portugal, the equivalent of the Community Shield, which they won in 1988 after losing in the final of the Portuguese Cup. But this was their 13th European campaign, having lost to Southampton in 1969, Aston Villa in 1983 and Celtic in 1998.

Vitoria had been in the Portuguese top flight since 1958, although by the time Bolton arrived for the latest UEFA Cup fixture they had been plunged into a relegation battle after taking only 10 points from their opening 11 games of the 2005/06 league season.

Bolton, in contrast, were fifth in the Premier League and fancied their chances of getting the victory they needed in Portugal to confirm progression to the last 32. The win over Zenit in their previous group match had been followed four days later by a 1-0 home triumph over Tottenham, when Kevin Nolan scored a stunning long-range winner. Nolan was perhaps at the peak of his Bolton powers at around that time, when he was tipped for an England call-up that did not come.

Bolton had been due to play on the Monday night before the Guimaraes trip in what seemed a rather unhelpful piece of fixture scheduling. But the Premier League match at Birmingham City was called off an hour before kick-off because of heavy fog at St Andrew's.

Ahead of the match in Guimaraes, news came in that Zenit had beaten Sevilla 2-1 in the earlier kick-off in the other group game in Saint Petersburg. Aleksandr Kerzhakov scored twice.

It moved Zenit above Bolton to the top of the group, and meant Guimaraes – still without a point – would surely need victory over Sam Allardyce's team to give themselves a chance of being among the three qualifiers.

Vitoria, who played in all white, were managed by the shaven-headed figure of Jaime Pacheco – back at the club for a second spell after a successful period as boss of Boavista, and once a member of the Portugal team that beat England at the 1986 World Cup. The Guimaraes team included former Arsenal youngster Sebastian Svard, Tunisia midfielder Selim Benachour and Poland striker Marek Saganowski, but was largely made up of Portuguese names unfamiliar to Bolton fans.

Bolton left Kevin Davies at home but did include players such as Kevin Nolan, Jussi Jaaskelainen and Jay-Jay Okocha.

The 4,000 travelling fans crammed mostly into the large upper tier of the two-tier away section. With no running track and the stands close to the pitch, the stadium had the feel of an English venue. By the time of kick-off a large number of Bolton fans who had enjoyed the afternoon were rather worse for wear, some stumbling to their seats and one nodding off for a period during the first half.

One of Wanderers' backroom staff would also miss the action despite travelling to Portugal.

"I was ill with food poisoning," says kit man Russell Byrne-Fraser. "I never left the hotel, I spent the entire evening sat by the toilet projectile vomiting."

Perhaps he did not miss the finest opening period of football ever seen. With the away supporters expecting their team to sweep away little-known opposition, Bolton were not playing well and wasting possession on far too many occasions. A less than silky approach to the game was encapsulated at one point when, for reasons known only to himself, Abdoulaye Faye opted not to look around for a square pass but instead launched the ball from his own half and what seemed to be about 50 feet over the crossbar at the far end.

It was not a shot, and it was not a pass. If it was a clearance it was a bizarre one, but Faye's midfield skills were always about power rather than subtlety.

Jaaskelainen saved comfortably from Svard, while Nolan poked an effort just wide at the far end of the ground. But opportunities were few and far between for either side.

The second half continued in the same fashion. Allardyce introduced Gary Speed in midfield for Hidetoshi Nakata on 59 minutes. Five minutes later El-Hadji Diouf was brought on up front for Borgetti.

If it was a big night for Vaz Te back in his home country, the match had significance for Diouf too.

"Before the game it was special because I hadn't seen my dad for many years and he lived in Portugal," Diouf says. "I hadn't seen him for so long and when we played Vitoria Guimaraes I invited him to come to watch the game. My dad never missed the games when I played on TV but for him to watch me live was massive for me. It was the second time I had met him in my life.

"He was very proud, he invited all of his friends, met Sam Allardyce and all the staff, and had a little laugh and joke with them. It was a big game for me because all my family were there. I had never seen my brother and sisters before, and they came to watch the game too."

Diouf's father, Boubacar Diallo, was also a footballer and left Senegal to play in France and then for Portuguese side Barreirense. A complicated relationship in his homeland resulted in the birth of El-Hadji Ousseynou Diouf in 1981. Diallo saw his son after the birth – something Diouf was too young at the time to remember – but returned to the Lisbon area and did not see him again until an emotional reunion many years later. Now they were meeting up for a second time, and Diouf was determined to play well against Guimaraes to impress his father.

His introduction as a substitute did start to change the game. Welcomed like a hero by the Bolton supporters, he finally helped Wanderers to retain more possession. Diouf's skill at coaxing fouls out of the opposition was used to great effect. He won free kick after free kick from French referee Laurent Duhamel, as Bolton attacked the end where their fans were housed.

Nolan came close to scoring when his shot found the side-netting, before Stelios Giannakopoulos forced a save from keeper Paiva.

But what had been a thoroughly enjoyable trip for supporters looked set to be tarnished four minutes from time when Guimaraes took the lead. Saganowski, who would later play for Southampton, was known to be Vitoria's biggest threat and it was he who came up with the goal.

Targino worked half a yard from Tal Ben Haim on the left flank and crossed to the back post, where Saganowski had pulled away from Ricardo Gardner to divert a free header into the net. Jaaskelainen did not dive, so little could he do to prevent the close-range attempt from finding the net.

The Portuguese crowd of around 20,000 exploded with passion, believing an upset was on the cards. Their side had held their own for most of the game, without showing too many signs of genuine quality until then. But this was the lifeline they needed as they attempted to get out of Group H.

The ubiquitous goal music of the Hermes House Band's cover of Gloria Gaynor's I Will Survive, much used across the continent, rung out across the stadium.

Bolton had a problem. Defeat could leave them needing victory over the fancied Sevilla in their final group game to progress.

Allardyce acted instantly. From the bench he summoned the 19-year-old forward Vaz Te, back in his homeland of Portugal for the first time in club football.

Vaz Te had signed for Bolton from Portuguese side Farense at the age of 16. Born in Lisbon, he had moved to live with his father in the west African country of Guinea-Bissau as a child, only to flee because of the increasing perils of a civil war. As the bombs dropped, Vaz Te joined his brother and other family members on a boat to Senegal before returning to his mother in Portugal.

Despite such a turbulent childhood, the boy could play. To all those who saw him at youth and reserve team level at Bolton, where he would score most weeks, it was apparent pretty quickly that he was something special. Pace, power, skill, aerial ability, goalscoring instinct, Vaz Te appeared to have the lot.

He made his debut in an FA Cup tie at Tranmere in 2004, and scored his first goal to give Bolton victory in the same competition at Oldham a year later. By the time the Guimaraes game came around, Vaz Te had still only shown fleeting glimpses of his talent at first-team level but had impressed for Portugal under 20s at the Toulon Tournament.

Some wondered whether the script might be written for him when Bolton were drawn away to Guimaraes, allowing Vaz Te's mother to see him play for Bolton for the first time.

"That game was something extra because it was at home," Vaz Te said. "For me I was just happy to be at home and especially to play in front of my mother. She could never really go to the games. When I was growing up I know she cared but she had to work so hard, two jobs at times just to put food on the table. So for her to actually take time off at that time and come and see me play, it was just massive for me."

Within seconds of Saganowski putting Guimaraes ahead, Allardyce had put Vaz Te on, sacrificing midfielder Okocha for an extra forward. Vaz Te needed only a minute to produce the moment that Bolton fans remember so well.

"Obviously strategically I don't think the manager was going to bring me on at 0-0," Vaz Te said. "I was pretty desperate to get on. I kept warming up even though the manager didn't send me to warm up. I just kept running and showing them that I was ready to be put on.

"It was only when Guimaraes actually scored and he had to throw more men forward that he had a change of heart and put me on. I had no time to think negatively, I just wanted to be out there. Luckily I had the opportunity to score. It came very fast. I was running around everywhere just trying to get a touch of the ball, but I remember the manager telling me to just stay up front, stay up front.

"When I did actually stay up front, Gary Speed played a wonderful ball to Dioufy. We all know Dioufy had an amazing touch of the ball and he laid it off for me quite nicely. I just took it in my stride and hit it second time."

Diouf's instinctive flick with the outside of his boot from Speed's long diagonal ball had been inch perfect. Vaz Te advanced the ball to the edge of the area with his first touch, before hammering an angled shot towards goal with the outside of his right foot. On their feet in anticipation, Wanderers fans knew it was in as soon as it left his boot. The shot rocketed across Paiva and into the top corner.

"WHAT A GOAL!" Channel Five commentator John Helm exclaimed to the audience back home in England.

One of the best strikes of Vaz Te's career? "Yes, I think so," he chuckled. "The feeling was just incredible. I was speechless to be honest."

Allardyce raised both hands aloft in celebration. Behind the goal in the away end, Vaz Te had unleashed a maelstrom of ecstasy.

It was the perfect storm. A dramatic late goal away from home, right in front of the visiting supporters, is always pretty special. When it is a scorcher into the top corner, even better. When it is in front of 4,000 fans in one of the club's first ever European away games, it becomes the stuff of legend. That it was delivered by the boy from Portugal made it a fairytale.

Vaz Te leapt to his feet and celebrated in front of the Bolton fans. He had made his name right there and then. Team-mates leapt on him in amazement and joy at what he had just produced.

"I always remember that game because of Ricardo Vaz Te," said Joey O'Brien, one of those who raced to celebrate with him. "Obviously coming through the academy with Ricardo and with him being Portuguese, to score that night was just a magical moment for him.

"Everyone was so pleased for him, and especially me because I'd been in the youth team with him and played games with him. I'd been on the minibus with him going to training, we were two young lads and I knew how delighted he was to be going back to Portugal... and then scoring!

"It was brilliant, another great night. You hear people at clubs say, 'Oh, those European nights are special'. But those away trips really were special."

Vaz Te's late goal had earned Wanderers a draw. It was not the perfect result, but it felt like a victory given the way events had unfolded. With Bolton not in action on matchday four, qualification would be assured if Guimaraes lost at Sevilla, and Besiktas were beaten at home by Zenit.

Vaz Te said: "It was great for everybody because obviously we needed the point to help us qualify and to be able to score in front of my mother and my brothers was extra special. They were very proud. It's probably among the best goals of my career, together with the one I scored at Wembley to get West Ham promoted in the play-off final."

Both Vaz Te and Diouf, the man who set up the goal, had proud families in the stand that night. "When I made the goal I was so happy," says Diouf. "My dad was so happy as well."

Vaz Te's strike gave the forward real confidence for the months ahead. "I think he left Portugal like he was Ronaldo!" laughs Nolan.

It proved to be the launchpad for more goals for the Portuguese striker that season, six in total, before injuries decimated his Bolton career.

"For that season it was massive for me because it just gave me that boost, that confidence that I needed," he said.

Vaz Te's goal though, did have some unwanted consequences in his homeland, where he later returned to play for Portugal under 21s. His strike played a big part in Vitoria Guimaraes ultimately failing to qualify for the next phase. In turn, the country's ranking points in UEFA competitions suffered.

"They hated me for a while," Vaz Te laughed of the reaction to his goal back in Portugal. "They did not like me for a while at all. They were just upset that I knocked out one of the Portuguese teams who were doing so well. For the ranking as a country it would have helped if they qualified. But I was just doing my job."

Things got worse for Vitoria Guimaraes that season. Pacheco left his post as manager only a month after the Bolton game and the club were relegated out of the top flight for the first time in 48 years.

They bounced straight back though, and finished third in the Primeira Liga in 2007/08 to qualify for the Champions League. Basel denied them a place in the group stage however, before they drew 2-2 at home to Portsmouth in the UEFA Cup.

In 2013 Guimaraes finally won the Portuguese Cup for the first time in their history, beating Benfica in the final.

Three days after their draw in Guimaraes, Wanderers were away to Fulham in the Premier League. The squad returned to Porto rather than flying straight back to England, hoping to prepare in the right way to gain a positive result at Fulham.

"What we used to do back then was instead of travelling back the night after the game, we used to stay over," Marland said. "So you play the game, go back to the hotel and then your body clock doesn't get out of kilter.

"We never travelled back the night of the game because for what it's worth to keep the plane there for an extra day versus getting the players right, if you're landing back at Manchester Airport at 4am or 5am then you can forget the following day. At least by staying where we were we could do warm-downs and get them prepared then for the game on Sunday.

"So after the match we trained the following day at Boavista and then we flew back. With it being Fulham we just flew into London, and stayed in London for the game on the Sunday. There are different schools of thought, some say it wasn't worth it, some say it was. It all depends on what result you get on the Sunday."

As it turned out, Bolton lost 2-1 at Fulham. Vaz Te was an unused substitute this time. But he had already etched his name into Bolton folklore with that goal in Guimaraes.

Bolton: Jussi Jaaskelainen; Joey O'Brien, Tal Ben Haim, Bruno N'Gotty, Ricardo Gardner; Hidetoshi Nakata (Gary Speed 59), Abdoulaye Faye, Jay-Jay Okocha (Ricardo Vaz Te 87); Kevin Nolan, Jared Borgetti (El-Hadji Diouf 64), Stelios Giannakopoulos. Subs not used: Ian Walker, Radhi Jaidi, Nicky Hunt, Khalilou Fadiga.
Booked: Jaaskelainen, O'Brien.
Goal: Vaz Te 88.

Vitoria Guimaraes: Paiva; Mario Sergio, Attila Dragoner, Cleber, Rogerio; Sebastian Svard, Flavio, Selim Benachour, Neca (Paulo Sergio 82); Dario Monteiro (Targino 60), Marek Saganowski. Subs not used: Pedro Freitas, Pedro Geromel, Moreno, Manoel, Zezinho.
Booked: Dragoner, Targino.
Goal: Saganowski 86.

Attendance: 20,000.
Referee: Laurent Duhamel (France).

Group H	P	W	D	L	F	A	Pts
Zenit	3	2	0	1	4	3	6
Bolton	3	1	2	0	3	2	5
Sevilla	2	1	0	1	4	2	3
V Guimaraes	2	0	1	1	2	3	1
Besiktas	2	0	1	1	1	4	1

With five teams in Group H, each matchday left one club without a game. Bolton's turn to sit it out came on matchday four, a week after the draw in Guimaraes.

This time Vitoria Guimaraes would lose 3-1 at Sevilla, confirming their exit from the UEFA Cup and Sevilla's progression to the last 32. Javier Saviola struck twice and Adriano Correia made it 3-0, before Selim Benachour pulled a goal back for the Portuguese side.

Needing only a point to qualify, Zenit went ahead through Oleksandr Gorshkov at Besiktas. The Turks were again struggling to live up to the tag of top seeds, but did just enough to keep their own qualification hopes alive as Ibrahim Akin levelled to secure a 1-1 draw.

With Zenit and Sevilla through, all that was left to decide was whether it would be Wanderers or Besiktas taking the final qualification spot.

Group H	P	W	D	L	F	A	Pts
Zenit	4	2	1	1	5	4	7
Sevilla	3	2	0	1	7	3	6
Bolton	3	1	2	0	3	2	5
Besiktas	3	0	2	1	2	5	2
V Guimaraes	3	0	1	2	3	6	1

6

The Champions Elect

Bolton 1 Sevilla 1 – December 14, 2005

Sevilla may not have been the top seeds in Bolton's group, but their ability was clear by the time they arrived at the Reebok Stadium. Five months later, they would be lifting the UEFA Cup after an emphatic victory in the final in Eindhoven.

Wanderers went into their final group match still needing a result to confirm their place in the last 32, but knowing it would take a real turnaround for Besiktas to take the final qualification spot. Bolton lay three points ahead of the Turks, with a four-goal advantage. Besiktas, whose last group game was at Vitoria Guimaraes, traditionally did not travel well.

A point at home to Sevilla would be enough for Wanderers, but they could not relax because of the talent that the Spaniards possessed. Some of their squad had already made their names at the top clubs, while others were on their way.

Just the strikers at their disposal said much about their quality. Javier Saviola, still only 24, was on loan from Barcelona where had burst on to the scene as a teenager after a £15m move from River Plate in his native Argentina. Also in Sevilla's squad was the former West Ham and Tottenham forward Frederic Kanoute, of renowned ability if sometimes questionable temperament. Both had been in good form and had played up front for Sevilla three days before the Bolton match, in a La Liga fixture at Barcelona. Kanoute had put Sevilla ahead before goals from Samuel Eto'o and Ronaldinho prevented an upset, but it was still an impressive performance.

Sevilla's 'third' striker, who they had the luxury of bringing off the bench at the Nou Camp, was Luis Fabiano. This was the same Luis Fabiano who would go on to lead the Brazilian forward line at the 2010 World Cup. His first move to Europe with Porto, which coincided with the kidnap of his mother back home in Brazil, had not gone well. But Sevilla would be the springboard for the revival of his obvious goalscoring ability, and he would get his chance to impress at the Reebok, as Saviola and Kanoute were rested to the bench.

Already qualified, the pressure was off for Sevilla, so two talented wide men also started the game as substitutes. Some wondered whether 20-year-old Jesus Navas would travel at all, such were his problems with homesickness at the time. He had left training camps on more than one occasion because of the issue. Later he would overcome the problem and help Spain win the 2010 World Cup, before joining Manchester City. Also on the bench for Sevilla was Adriano Correia, who in time would play for Barcelona and Brazil after converting into an attacking left back.

Left at home was Dani Alves, the marauding right back who was one of Sevilla's best players. It was little surprise when he went on to stardom at Barcelona and with the Brazilian national team.

As much as the resting of key players aided Wanderers' cause, at the same time it was a shame to miss out on the chance to see all of Sevilla's stars in action. This was a squad jam-packed with quality, and they spent the day before the game making a tourist visit to Bolton's Victoria Square – possibly the most fearsome visitors to the square since a lion killed its one-armed tamer there in a circus show in 1872.

Under manager Juande Ramos, Sevilla were going places – both individually and collectively. Ramos had taken over as boss after they had qualified for the UEFA Cup by finishing sixth in La Liga. Sergio Ramos and Julio Baptista were both part of that team, but the club raised €50m from their double sale to Real Madrid that summer. Their exits made the success achieved in the following season all the more remarkable. Sevilla were formed in 1905 but had only one league title in 1946 to their name. They were hungry for trophies and for them the UEFA Cup was a realistic possibility.

Wanderers had actually played Sevilla in a little publicised friendly during the September international break in 2004. Allardyce had taken players not on international duty away for a training camp in the south of Spain and squeezed in a match while they were there. El-Hadji Diouf played his first game for Bolton after signing on loan from Liverpool. Sevilla won 2-0 but few players on either side would play again when the clubs met competitively in the UEFA Cup 15 months later. The Spanish side's goalscorers Javier Casquero and Carlos Aranda had departed. Ariza Makukula, who would later have an unsuccessful loan spell with Wanderers, had also played for Sevilla in that friendly but missed the UEFA Cup trip to the Reebok through injury.

Wanderers' final group game was again live on Channel Five and the attendance at the Reebok was only 15,623. Almost 27,000 had been present 11 days earlier when Wanderers beat Arsenal 2-0.

"I think the only thing that disappointed a little bit in the whole European experience was probably some of the home gates," admitted Simon Marland. "It didn't really fire a lot of people up. Some gates were great, and we did deals. For the Atletico Madrid game I think we did well with the gate. But one or two of the other gates were just a wee bit disappointing because you strive to get to where you are to do that and then for whatever reason people don't buy into it. But I think other clubs in Europe have had the same issues."

Allardyce concurred. "I think the fans, our players and myself will probably remember the away games more than the home matches," he said. "The home games were big for us but it wasn't a full house. It was difficult to get a full house on Thursdays. But when we went and played away, the fans would be somewhere in some city or town, all afternoon singing the Bolton songs, singing away. All the Bolton public would say, 'I remember when we went here and we played that game', like Guimaraes when Vaz Te scored in the last minute."

The Sevilla game was actually played on a Wednesday night, with UEFA Cup fixtures split between Wednesday and Thursday that week because there were no Champions League matches.

While Sevilla made eight changes from the side that were narrowly beaten at Barcelona, Allardyce made six alterations from the team that drew 1-1 at home to Aston Villa four days earlier. Rested to the bench were the likes of Jussi Jaaskelainen, Stelios Giannakopoulos and Bruno N'Gotty. Kevin Nolan would also only be named as a substitute, although the 23-year-old was still on a high after being confirmed as Wanderers' permanent captain weeks earlier in place of Jay-Jay Okocha, no longer guaranteed a place in Allardyce's starting line-up at the age of 32.

"Jay-Jay hadn't been playing for a while and Gary Speed had a little bit of a niggle or something, so the gaffer made me captain for a couple of games," remembers Nolan, who netted 11 goals that season. "I think I scored a couple and did really well, and then he just pulled me into the office and said, 'I've spoken to Jay-Jay and I'm going to give you the captaincy.'

"I was so surprised, I thought when he was calling me into his office he was going to rollick me for some reason. I hadn't done anything wrong but that was normally why you got called into his office!

"To get the captaincy was a huge honour and I remember ringing my dad up that day and he was in tears, he was delighted. It was a fantastic season for me personally anyway and the honour of getting the captaincy at that young age was even better."

Among those coming into the side against Sevilla were Khalilou Fadiga, Nicky Hunt, Hidetoshi Nakata and Ian Walker.

The first half was relatively even, with Tunisian defender Radhi Jaidi sending an acrobatic volley just over the bar. But even with so many changes Sevilla, wearing light blue at the Reebok rather than their traditional red and white, looked comfortable on the ball.

"Any Spanish football team are pass, pass, pass and Sevilla were no different," Hunt remembers. "They rested a few people but they still had international players."

Sevilla came so close to taking the lead when Fabiano – eager to oust Saviola or Kanoute from the regular line-up – cut inside before hammering a fierce effort against the post. It was a fortunate escape for Bolton, particularly as Besiktas were leading at Vitoria Guimaraes in the other group game. There,

Marek Saganowski cancelled out Ibrahim Toraman's opener for the Turks, but Souleymane Youla put the visitors 2-1 up after 17 minutes. Another couple of goals for Besiktas against a Guimaraes side possibly dispirited by their early elimination, and defeat for Wanderers would put them out.

At half time Bolton had to make a change as Ricardo Gardner was forced off injured. Hunt switched to an unfamiliar left back position, with Tal Ben Haim moving to right back and N'Gotty introduced from the bench.

N'Gotty had been one of Bolton's first notable Premier League buys, arriving a month into the club's first season following promotion. He brought with him considerable European experience from the likes of AC Milan and Marseille. Allardyce credited N'Gotty as the start of a snowball effect at the club – the man whose presence helped to convince other stars to join Bolton. Youri Djorkaeff followed, then Okocha and Ivan Campo.

N'Gotty was a pacy defender, strong in the air and fearless in the tackle. He was a key part of a defence that produced many resilient rearguard actions during Allardyce's tenure. The Frenchman scored only six goals in 155 appearances for Bolton, but one of them came against Sevilla.

Besiktas had extended their lead to 3-1 at Guimaraes on the hour mark, with Toraman scoring again in Portugal. Meanwhile at the Reebok, Fadiga swung in a corner from the right, which just cleared the head of Ricardo Vaz Te – seconds after the forward's arrival as a substitute. Behind him, the ball fell for the unmarked N'Gotty to control and lash home from six yards past Antonio Notario, the back-up keeper standing in for Sevilla's regular stopper Andres Palop.

Bolton were suddenly on course to leapfrog both Sevilla and Zenit to win the group, which would have been no small feat given the European experience of the four teams they had been drawn with. It would also have given them a potentially easier draw in the last 32. Group winners would play a side who had finished third in another group, and would have the advantage of the second leg at home.

But Sevilla boss Ramos quickly responded to N'Gotty's goal. He introduced Adriano on the wing, and minutes later Saviola was also brought on for ineffective homegrown forward Kepa Blanco. Unfortunately for Bolton, the changes worked. As Sevilla attacked in rapid fashion, Adriano came off the right flank and was played clear on goal. Outpacing the retreating Hunt, the Brazilian fired a clinical finish across Walker and into the far corner. It was a moment of quality from a player on the way up.

"Adriano came on and scored, and you could see they were a very good team," Diouf admits.

"They had to bring on the big men and Adriano was an absolute brute," Hunt says. "I've got his shirt at home."

Adriano almost bagged a second, firing wide. Another Sevilla goal would have left Bolton facing a nervy final few minutes. All it would have taken then was one more goal for Besiktas in Guimaraes and Bolton's UEFA Cup experience would have been over.

As it turned out, Wanderers and Sevilla reined back in the final minutes, content with a draw.

"It seemed like Sevilla were happy to take the draw because then they finished first and we also qualified," says Nolan, who watched the whole game from the bench as an unused substitute. "They just sat off us and let us come at them, but I don't think we really wanted to give anything away either because we wanted to qualify. It was that tension of 'Shall we try and win it to top the group, or shall we just hold back and take the draw?' In the end I think we settled for the draw, which was a fantastic result again against another top club who are in Europe year in year out."

"I think our main focus in the preparation for that game was that a point was enough," Hunt says. "Obviously three points would have been absolutely brilliant but we knew that if we didn't lose we were through and I think we went in with that mindset. We used to have a good record at home."

Indeed, Wanderers have never lost at home in European competition. With the match at the Reebok finishing all square, Besiktas' 3-1 win in Guimaraes was in vain. A point was all Wanderers had needed to book their place in the last 32. Being in Europe after Christmas has often been regarded as a feat for even some of the biggest clubs, but Bolton had ensured that would be the case in their very first European campaign. They remained unbeaten in the UEFA Cup too, having won one and drawn three of their Group H fixtures.

Adriano's equaliser, however, meant that Bolton's progression would be in third place, with Sevilla taking top spot and Zenit finishing second. Wanderers would have to take on a group winner in the next round, and the second leg would be away. In the end, while group winners Sevilla beat Lokomotiv Moscow in the last 32, Bolton ran into Marseille.

After defeating the Russians, Sevilla's progress continued. They overcame Lille in the last 16 before they were drawn to face their group opponents Zenit once more in the quarter finals. They found a fixture in their own stadium rather more comfortable than the group match in Saint Petersburg. Sevilla won 4-1 at home, going through 5-2 on aggregate, and then edged out Schalke in the semi finals.

In the final against Steve McClaren's Middlesbrough in Eindhoven, a Fabiano goal was followed by a brace from Enzo Maresca and a late strike from Kanoute to seal a crushing 4-0 win. Sevilla had claimed the first European trophy in their history and Ramos was starting to gain recognition.

Bolton faced Sevilla again that summer, for a third time in two years, after being invited by La Liga team Recreativo Huelva to play in the pre-season Trofeo Colombino tournament. Sporting Lisbon also arrived in Huelva, a small coastal city 50 miles from Seville, to take part in the four-team competition. Bolton were beaten 3-2 by Recreativo in the semi finals before losing 3-0 in the third-place play-off to Sevilla, for whom Fabiano scored a hat-trick. Sporting won the tournament.

If 2005/06 had been successful for Sevilla, 2006/07 was off the scale. At the start of the season they beat Barcelona 3-0 in Monaco to win the UEFA Super Cup. Later that season they finished third in La Liga – no prize for guessing the top two – to qualify for the Champions League for the first time. They also won the Copa del Rey. On top of that they became only the second club ever to retain the UEFA Cup – after Real Madrid in the 1980s – when they defeated fellow Spaniards Espanyol on penalties in the final at Glasgow's Hampden Park.

Sevilla would win the competition under its new guise of the Europa League for a third time in 2014, beating Benfica in Turin under the tutelage of Unai Emery.

The Juande Ramos era at Sevilla ended in October 2007, when he accepted Tottenham's offer to replace Martin Jol at White Hart Lane. He won the League Cup with Spurs but, largely a cup specialist, he left after only a year with the club bottom of the Premier League.

A couple of months before Ramos' departure from Sevilla, the club had suffered tragedy. Antonio Puerta was a product of the club's youth system and was one of the starters in the 1-1 draw against Bolton 18 months earlier. Capable of playing on the left wing or at left back, he had looked a useful player that night at the Reebok. Later in that UEFA Cup run he had written his name into Sevilla history with the winner in the semi final against Schalke.

After 35 minutes of Sevilla's opening game of the 2007/08 season against Getafe, Puerta collapsed and lost consciousness after suffering a cardiac arrest. He recovered and was able to walk to the dressing room, but collapsed again. Puerta was taken to hospital, but three days later he died at the age of just 22.

The club and the city were left in shock. Sevilla were beaten days later in the UEFA Super Cup against AC Milan, but it barely mattered in comparison. A statue was unveiled to Puerta in 2010 and when Spain lifted the World Cup later that year, former Sevilla team-mates Ramos and Navas wore T-shirts bearing his name.

Even more tragically, Puerta was not the only player who featured in that UEFA Cup game between Bolton and Sevilla to die young. Gary Speed, a substitute for Wanderers that night, was found dead at his home in Cheshire on the morning of November 27, 2011. He had become the manager of Wales after retiring as a player and the day before his death had appeared as a pundit on the BBC's Football Focus programme, showing no signs of distress. The entire world of football was in disbelief when news emerged that Speed had hung himself.

"Gary was a massive influence on my career," says Nolan. "He made it easier for me making that step of becoming a captain. He was someone who

I could always speak to. Even when I went to Newcastle, I spoke to Gary about it and he knew a lot of people who could look after me up there. I spoke to him quite often until he sadly passed away."

"I found out that Gary had died about half an hour before the story broke on the news," recalls Russell Byrne-Fraser, who grew friendly with Speed during his time at Bolton. "One of the lads I used to work with at Bolton, Ally Marland, texted me that Speedo had hung himself. I texted back something like 'Don't be stupid' – almost to say that's not even funny. But the text came back, 'No seriously, so and so has just told me'. As soon as that name was mentioned I knew it was true. I couldn't take it in.

"Like a lot of people I'd seen Gary the day before on Football Focus, and he'd texted me earlier that week with a new phone number. I texted him back saying flippantly, 'Have you got a stalker?' He just texted back, 'Something like that', which he meant ironically, not seriously. That was the last I ever heard from him.

"If you were to pick anybody in that dressing room for that to happen to, he probably would have been the last one – probably the last one that any of us knew inside and outside the game. He was a talented individual with a lovely wife, lovely kids, a great mum and dad, a lovely house, a great circle of friends, you just cannot think of a less likely candidate.

"There was no history of mental illness. Don't get me wrong, he used to get fed up like anybody else. When you're on the backroom staff at a football club if somebody is out of sorts for whatever reason you'll tend to find it won't be one of the lads in the dressing room they'll confide in, it will be a member of staff – a physio, masseur, kit man. I'd done that for Speedo once or twice, but no more than any other player. He just struck you as a very well balanced individual who had the same faults as anybody else, but was a star. I was happy to call him a friend.

"The worst thing is not having an answer. It's not just Gary but anybody in that situation who takes their own life without leaving any sort of communication. It had a profound effect on me. You think, 'If he can do it, find that dark place, with everything he had going for him, I'd better check what's going on with me'.

"It made me examine the subject of mental health more thoroughly than I ever would have done. We assume it was depression, we don't know it was depression, but logically that's the path you go down. I've prompted one or two footballers since to pick up the phone and address their own problems head on and do something about it.

"It's hard to define what Sam's best bit of business was but signing Gary was right up there. It just confirmed everything that Sam had preached, by bringing in this model professional who was very popular with everybody. He was a massive influence and a massive part of that team."

Speed had played a significant part in Wanderers' qualification for Europe and their progress to the last 32. In his final years at the club before his departure in January 2008, he would continue to have a major impact. Just as at his previous clubs Leeds, Everton and Newcastle, he will be forever remembered for what he did for Bolton. Not only was he a fine player, but he was an extraordinary man.

Bolton: Ian Walker; Nicky Hunt, Tal Ben Haim, Radhi Jaidi, Ricardo Gardner (Bruno N'Gotty 45); Hidetoshi Nakata, Abdoulaye Faye (Gary Speed 55), Jay-Jay Okocha; El-Hadji Diouf, Kevin Davies (Ricardo Vaz Te 65), Khalilou Fadiga. Subs not used: Jussi Jaaskelainen, Kevin Nolan, Stelios Giannakopoulos, Jared Borgetti.
Booked: Nakata.
Goal: N'Gotty 65.

Sevilla: Antonio Notario; Jose Angel Crespo, Pablo Ruiz (Aitor Ocio 58), Pablo Alfaro, Ivica Dragutinovic; Jordi Lopez (Adriano Correia 67), David Prieto, Jose Luis Marti, Antonio Puerta; Kepa Blanco (Javier Saviola 73), Luis Fabiano. Subs not used: Andres Palop, Jesus Navas, Diego Capel, Frederic Kanoute.
Booked: Puerta.
Goal: Adriano 74.

Attendance: 15,623.
Referee: Michael Weiner (Germany).

Group H	P	W	D	L	F	A	Pts
Sevilla	4	2	1	1	8	4	7
Zenit	4	2	1	1	5	4	7
Bolton	4	1	3	0	4	3	6
Besiktas	4	1	2	1	5	6	5
V Guimaraes	4	0	1	3	4	9	1

7

Paying the Penalty

Bolton 0 Marseille 0 – February 15, 2006

The UEFA Cup reached the business end after the turn of the year, and with it a tie against one of Europe's biggest names. Only the baffling decisions of a man from Portugal prevented Wanderers from celebrating a famous victory at the Reebok.

With the minnows eliminated, after Christmas the competition was two-legged knock-out football all the way. Wanderers would have to face respected European opposition, knowing that if they came up short the run was over.

When the draw for the last 32 was made two days after Bolton's final group game against Sevilla, Wanderers had only six possible opponents. They would face a group winner but could not be paired with fellow English side Middlesbrough, who had finished top of Group D. That left Romanian duo Steaua Bucharest and Rapid Bucharest, Italian side Palermo or one of the trio from the French league – Marseille, Monaco or Strasbourg. Monaco were the glamour option in terms of location, but Wanderers were quickly followed out of UEFA's little yellow balls by a scrap of paper bearing the words OLYMPIQUE DE MARSEILLE. The draw for the last 16 was carried out at the same time and the winners would face Rosenborg – the Norwegian side who had finished third in their Champions League group – or Zenit St Petersburg, who Bolton had already beaten in Group H.

There was a lot of work ahead though, if Bolton were going to get that far. Marseille was a daunting but exciting draw for Wanderers. This was what everyone wanted when Bolton qualified for the UEFA Cup – the chance to take on one of Europe's big names, head to head over two legs. Marseille were a club famous all over the continent, having won the French league on nine occasions and having become the first winners of the renamed Champions League in 1993.

The club had been quickly embroiled in scandal, when it was revealed that Valenciennes players had been bribed to lose a league match against Marseille – so allowing them to win the title without exertion and prepare for the Champions League final. Marseille were stripped of the league title, relegated to the Second Division and banned from the 1993/94 Champions League, as well as the Super Cup and the Intercontinental Cup.

But they were allowed to retain their Champions League title, achieved with a 1-0 win over AC Milan in Munich thanks to Basile Boli's header. Famous names such as Marcel Desailly, Didier Deschamps, Alen Boksic, Rudi Voller and Abedi Pele had also helped Marseille win that final.

So too had Fabien Barthez at the age of only 22, the youngest goalkeeper to win the European title until his record was beaten by Real Madrid's Iker Casillas in 2000. Thirteen years on from his Champions League triumph and Barthez was back with Marseille, after four up and down seasons with Manchester United.

Barthez won two league titles with United, but also became a figure of fun in some quarters for the occasional gaffe. He had history with Bolton, too, having been United's goalkeeper when Sam Allardyce's side won at Old Trafford in each of their first two seasons after promotion to the Premier League. On the second occasion, Kevin Nolan's winner had squirmed unexpectedly through his grasp.

Barthez would play a major part in this UEFA Cup tie, but he was not the only big name in the Marseille team of 2005/06. Their biggest star, Franck Ribery, had almost cost Marseille their place in Europe before they even reached the first round of the UEFA Cup.

L'OM, as they called themselves, had not won the French league since days of the bribery scandal but made regular appearances in the Champions League and were UEFA Cup finalists in 1999 and in 2004, inspired by Didier Drogba on the latter occasion. Drogba, however, was sold to Chelsea in the summer of 2004 and Marseille only finished fifth in Ligue 1 in the following campaign.

As a result, in the summer of 2005 they went into the much-derided Intertoto Cup – a pre-season European competition that handed UEFA Cup places to the three 'winners'. Marseille's European campaign started way back on July 16 with victory at Young Boys of Berne. They then had to beat Lazio and Deportivo La Coruna just to progress through the Intertoto Cup and reach the first round of the UEFA Cup – the round in which Bolton played Plovdiv.

In the Intertoto Cup 'final' against Deportivo, Marseille looked all but out after losing the first leg 2-0 in Spain. An incredible 50,000 were present for the second leg at the Stade Velodrome when Ribery quickly scored for Marseille. But an away goal for Deportivo left Marseille needing to win 4-1 and in the 12th minute, the hot-headed Ribery was dismissed for violent conduct. The game was still 1-1 with 25 minutes left when Abdoulaye Meite, the centre back who would join Bolton a year later, headed L'OM back in contention. Marseille then dramatically added three more to seal a 5-1 victory on the night.

Even in the UEFA Cup first round, Marseille needed a penalty shoot-out to overcome Belgian minnows Germinal Beerschot, although they then won a group containing Levski Sofia, Heerenveen, CSKA Moscow and Dinamo Bucharest.

Ribery was only 22 years old when the last-32 tie with Bolton came around, and yet to make his senior debut for France. But already he was starting to be talked about as the next big thing. His appearance marked him out and led to his predictable nickname of 'Scarface'. A car accident when he was two led to more than 100 stitches and left him with considerable scars down the right side of his face.

Ribery's early career was turbulent. He played for Lille, Boulogne, Ales, Stade Brestois and Metz before joining Turkish side Galatasaray. After only five months in Istanbul, Ribery controversially joined Marseille after asking FIFA to invalidate his contract, saying he had not been paid all of his wages and that his former agent and a Galatasaray director had threatened him with a baseball bat. Galatasaray went to the Court of Arbitration for Sport seeking €10m in compensation from Marseille but lost the case.

The 2005/06 season was Ribery's first campaign with Marseille and he was shining to such a degree that he would win the French PFA's young player of the year award. Operating on the other flank was the 18-year-old Samir Nasri. Born in Marseille of Algerian heritage, the quickest of glances at YouTube revealed that he had the sort of dazzling skills that made him destined for great things too. Ribery would go on to become arguably the best player in one of Bayern Munich's best ever sides, while Nasri moved to Arsenal before winning the Premier League with Manchester City. It would not be until the second leg against Bolton, though, that they came to the fore.

Under manager Jean Fernandez, who had been part of the coaching staff during the Champions League winning season of 1993, Marseille arrived at the Reebok Stadium for the first leg sitting sixth in the French table.

The Africa Cup of Nations had left them without five players during January. The tournament finished only five days before the first leg, but by then Nigerian duo Taye Taiwo and Wilson Oruma had returned to club duties for L'OM, as well as Senegal's Mamadou Niang and Habib Beye. Ivory Coast defender Meite was also back but only on the bench at the Reebok.

Wanderers similarly had Nigeria's Jay-Jay Okocha, Tunisia's Radhi Jaidi and Senegal's Abdoulaye Faye back from the tournament. Fellow Senegal star El-Hadji Diouf had picked up a hernia problem and would miss both legs of the Marseille tie however, to the disappointment of a player who had started his career in France with Sochaux, Rennes and Lens.

"I had a lot of friends there but I had two operations and I couldn't play against Marseille," Diouf says. "I was very disappointed because I loved to play against Marseille, I always scored against Marseille when I played in France. They wanted to sign me before I went to Liverpool. It's the biggest club in France."

Bolton's squad had been decimated to such an extent during January that Allardyce had surprisingly played reserve team goalkeeper and lifelong

Wanderers fan Sam Ashton up front as a late substitute in an FA Cup third round win at Watford.

Despite that, they were unbeaten in the opening stages of 2006 and sat eighth in the Premier League with games in hand. Astonishingly, they had thrashed Everton 4-0 at Goodison Park in December with the help of a brace from Stelios Giannakopoulos, who later scored the winner in an FA Cup fourth round win at home to Arsenal. Bolton met the Gunners again four days before the first leg with Marseille, this time in the league, when Kevin Nolan's smart lob put Wanderers in front on their last ever visit to Highbury. Gilberto Silva's last-minute equaliser prevented them from going above Arsene Wenger's side in the table.

Bolton were without the injured Henrik Pedersen, Ivan Campo, Gary Speed, Matt Jansen and Khalilou Fadiga for the first leg, while Hidetoshi Nakata was suspended for picking up three yellow cards in the earlier stages of the UEFA Cup. Midfielder Oscar Perez, a surprise January signing from Spanish third division side Cordoba, was named on the bench but did not get on to the field and would never make a first-team appearance for Wanderers.

Allardyce did field more or less his strongest starting line-up however, seeing the chance to claim a real scalp in the last 32. Kevin Davies and Jared Borgetti both started, while Bruno N'Gotty faced the club he left to join Bolton in 2001 – initially on loan and then on a permanent deal.

"I think we didn't expect that we would end up in the last 32 of the UEFA Cup, but there we were, ready to play the great Marseille, a big team who normally play in the Champions League," Allardyce says. "The important thing for me was the players wanted to go as far as they could, because we were still in the top half of the Premier League after Christmas so we'd managed to cope with the burden of all the extra games."

A respectable crowd of 19,288 was present at the Reebok for the first leg. Around 900 flag-waving supporters came from Marseille. The match, again shown live on Channel Five, was a tight affair. Marseille knew a draw would put them in the driving seat for the return to France, and were content not to take too many risks.

"I remember they were a smashing team," said Joey O'Brien, who played at right back that night. "I knew before the game that they were good and had some very good players. They had Nasri and Ribery, and Niang the centre forward. But at the end of the game we had regrets at not going in with a lead."

Bolton's main frustration on the night was with referee Olegario Benquerenca. If his name was flamboyant, so too was the Portuguese official's rather Latin penchant for over-dramatic hand signals. He was clearly an ambitious man determined to assert his authority. Later he would referee top Champions League and European Championship matches, as well as the 2010 World Cup quarter final between Uruguay and Ghana when Luis

Suarez infamously handled on the line.

At the Reebok, Bolton felt they had four justifiable penalty claims as they sought a crucial lead to take to Marseille. But all four were turned down by Benquerenca.

Defender Frederic Dehu appeared to have handled Okocha's cross before half time – a certain penalty in Allardyce's view. "It was an absolute screamer, blatant, definite, 120%-er," Allardyce said after the game. He was never one to sit on the fence.

Barthez looked shaky throughout the match but did save early on from Okocha, before denying substitute Ricardo Vaz Te in the second half.

There had almost been disaster just after the interval though, when the speedy Niang raced clear. Going 1-0 down, to an all-important away goal, would have put Bolton in big trouble and Niang's impressive strike rate at Marseille was such that he seemed likely to score. Thankfully, he overran the ball slightly and Jussi Jaaskelainen raced off his line to intercept as Niang tried to round him.

Jaaskelainen had to save again from Ribery, but Bolton knew that even a 0-0 draw would give them serious work to do in France. They pressed forward in search of a goal but had more penalty shouts denied by the referee. Barthez appeared to fell Davies as he attempted to collect a cross, then Stelios was tripped by Albanian midfielder Lorik Cana.

"We were robbed of a penalty for the foul by Cana in the box," Nolan recalls now, the frustration flooding back.

To make matters worse, Stelios was elbowed by Dehu in the area and still no penalty was given. Marseille, operating with three centre backs, were defending in determined and uncompromising fashion. Occasionally there are matches when you sense you are destined never to score, and this was one of those nights. A fine chance came to the normally clinical Stelios in the closing seconds, but he headed Ricardo Gardner's cross wide of the post from six yards. It summed up Bolton's frustrating evening.

Now any sort of victory at the Stade Velodrome, where Marseille were strong, would put the French side through.

"We felt we needed something to take over there, a little lead maybe, because we knew it was going to be hard there," Davies reflects. "But it was just one of those games. They didn't score an away goal and playing Marseille at home and holding them wasn't bad."

"They were a very good side with a lot of talented individuals at the time, but I thought we definitely deserved to at least win the game in the first leg," says Nolan. "We were very unlucky. They didn't really do much to upset us and we dominated the game throughout. But it's just about having that little bit of luck when you need it and we didn't get it.

"In the end that was what probably harmed us, not going over there to their place with a 1-0 lead and having that either to sit on, or if you get another goal then they've got to score three."

The tie was still in the balance, but it would now require a night of heroics in France if Bolton were to extend their European run.

Bolton: Jussi Jaaskelainen; Joey O'Brien, Bruno N'Gotty, Tal Ben Haim, Ricardo Gardner; Kevin Nolan, Abdoulaye Faye, Jay-Jay Okocha (Gary Speed 60); Kevin Davies, Jared Borgetti (Ricardo Vaz Te 67), Stelios Giannakopoulos. Subs not used: Ian Walker, Nicky Hunt, Radhi Jaidi, Jaroslaw Fojut, Oscar Perez.

Marseille: Fabien Barthez; Demetrius Ferreira, Habib Beye, Frederic Dehu, Bostjan Cesar, Taye Taiwo; Samir Nasri (Christian Gimenez 73), Lorik Cana, Wilson Oruma, Franck Ribery; Mamadou Niang (Alain Cantareil 90). Subs not used: Cedric Carrasso, Abdoulaye Meite, Renato Civelli, Jose Delfim, Thomas Deruda.
Booked: Oruma, Cana, Cesar, Barthez, Ferreira.

Attendance: 19,288.
Referee: Olegario Benquerenca (Portugal).

8

Au Revoir to the Wacky Warehouse

Marseille 2 Bolton 1 – February 23, 2006

Wanderers' first season in Europe would come to a brave end in the south of France, on a trip that became embroiled in controversy long before the first Bolton supporter touched down at the Aeroport de Marseille Provence.

From the moment Bolton were drawn against Marseille in the last 32 in mid-December, the demand for tickets for the away leg was always going to be high. This was the club's first knock-out match against genuine top quality opposition, in a location close enough to tempt thousands of fans to make the trip.

Given that Wanderers were not exactly European regulars and Marseille were the firm favourites to win the tie, who knew whether Bolton would ever play in a match like this again? Flight and hotel availability would quickly diminish in the hours and days after the draw, so many booked online immediately.

But there were two problems. Firstly, tickets. When Bolton travelled to Guimaraes, the Portuguese side had offered them 4,000 tickets – 2,500 more than they were technically required to under UEFA regulations. They were gratefully lapped up by the visiting supporters. Similarly, there were no problems gaining admission against either Plovdiv or Besiktas.

In Marseille, it was different. The French club were required to offer five per cent of the capacity of the Stade Velodrome, so five per cent was what they offered. Not a ticket more. Bolton were handed 2,800 tickets. It was never going to be enough.

It quickly became apparent that Marseille's inflexibility was due to the history of the club and the city. France may not be particularly known for its feisty football fans, but Marseille is a case in isolation.

The city is close to the western end of the Cote d'Azur, otherwise known as the French Riviera, and the swank of the likes of Saint-Tropez, Cannes, Monaco and Nice. But nice is not the word you would always use to describe Marseille. The coastal area of La Corniche in the east of the city has its moments but for the most part Marseille is rough and ready.

The city is France's second largest settlement behind Paris, with a population of around one million, but it has a dark side. Drugs gangs have made it the country's murder capital – a subject matter touched upon in the 1970s film The French Connection. Its geography and sizeable port made it the gateway to France for heroin smuggled in from Turkey.

Immigrants from the north African countries of Morocco, Tunisia and Algeria have also arrived in significant numbers over the years – among them the parents of Zinedine Zidane, who left Algeria for Marseille in the mid-1960s. Zidane grew up as a Marseille fan and, although he started his career along the coast at Cannes, he remains a virtual deity in the city. By the sea, a huge imposing poster of his face covered the entirety of the gable end of a building. It was an advert for Adidas. Next to Zidane's picture were simply the words 'Made in Marseille'.

"Marseille was a rough place, it was a docks really, an industrial place, but you just saw this huge picture of Zidane," remembers Russell Byrne-Fraser. "Not only did it make you realise how big Zidane was but how big football was in Marseille that it could dominate the skyline like that. It did give you a sense of being in the big time."

Marseille was a one-club city. The population mix of African immigrants and French was reflected in the support at home games at the Stade Velodrome, where the atmosphere can take on the sort of added fervour found more readily in the football stadiums of northern Africa.

The Marseille authorities had learned to take no chances. The uncovered away section at the Velodrome, tucked away in the corner of the stadium, was bordered by high fences and netting on either side. There were 2,800 seats, and it could not be extended for segregation and safety reasons. In the scramble to secure tickets some were left disappointed, as the 2,800 tickets sold out long before they went on open sale. Those who had already booked flights but now did not have a ticket were faced with the dilemma of whether to cancel the trip, or travel and try to find some other way into the ground on the night.

Even for those who had tickets, there was a further problem. It was announced that away fans would be shepherded 400 at a time into a warehouse known as 'The Hangar' before the match. There they would be individually searched and held for a lengthy period of time. If you wanted food or drink, forget it. If you'd already had a drink, there were no toilet facilities on offer either. Other items such as bottles and umbrellas would be confiscated, the latter of which was not particularly helpful given that the away section had no roof.

Wanderers fans were advised to arrive as much as two hours before kick-off. Chief Superintendent Dave Lea, the head of Bolton Police, said that although the police stance seemed tough, 'when you see their fans you will know why.'

The news about the warehouse did not go down terrifically well with Bolton fans, particularly when it became obvious that Marseille supporters would not have to go through the same rigmarole. When pictures emerged of the unappealing, dark location in which supporters would be held – taken by Newcastle supporters who had travelled to Marseille two years earlier – Wanderers fans became even less impressed. Many complained it was an unnecessary infringement on human rights for people who simply wanted to watch their team play football, but would instead be treated like animals.

Looking back, club secretary Simon Marland admits Wanderers were not exactly happy when they discovered the police's plans during a preparatory visit to Marseille weeks earlier. But they felt they had little choice but to go along with it.

"They do that for all their home games," Marland says. "When we went to the recce there, we actually went to a game. They played Lens I think, who had maybe 200 fans there. It was exactly the same scenario. They just told us, 'This is what we do with the away fans, we do this, this and this'.

"We said okay. It's not ideal but you're caught between the devil and the deep blue sea because if you start fighting their organisation and it backfires and doesn't work, then it's our fault.

"They were experienced at it, they did it week in week out, so we had to live with it even though we felt it wasn't perfect. We would always like our supporters just to be able to make their own way there, to do their own thing, but you have to think about due care and attention."

Trouble had infamously occurred in Marseille in 1998, ahead of England's opening World Cup game against Tunisia at the Stade Velodrome. Given the large Tunisian population in Marseille and the reputation of England supporters at the time, it was probably an incident waiting to happen. England fans fought pitched battles with Tunisians, local youths and police in the Old Port area, leaving many injured.

The Old Port was normally the most tranquil part of the city, with a plethora of bars surrounding the harbour where boats rocked gently in the mistral breeze. Monte Carlo it wasn't, but it was pleasant enough. Bolton fans largely based themselves in that area, with many of those who arrived a night early taking in the Champions League match between Chelsea and Barcelona on television in the local bars.

Overlooking the harbour was L'OM Cafe, the official city centre bar for Marseille fans. That it should take up one of the city's most prime locations was a symbol of just how big the club was, and what it meant to the people there.

From there was La Canebiere, which sadly for Bolton fans did not mean 'the can of beer', but instead was a boulevard that ran up the hill and away from the harbour. Travelling supporters were advised to avoid that area, particularly at night. But some had already booked hotels there, and took their chances.

Pickpockets were said to be a danger, and streets in some areas were dirty and littered with dog excrement. Marseille's status as the European Capital of Culture for 2013 would have raised eyebrows with many Bolton supporters.

"You went there thinking how fantastic Marseille would be, and when you got there it was a bit of a dump really," admits chairman Phil Gartside.

A large number of fans arrived on the day of the game with the club's official travel, with some of the young supporters passing the time in the afternoon with impromptu games of football in the street.

By Thursday night, the attention turned to the match. I can still remember boarding the metro to the stadium that evening, with a feeling that this may be the biggest Bolton match I ever see. Wanderers had played big domestic games before, of course. But this was the sort of game Bolton fans had dreamed they might one day be involved in, as they watched at home on television year after year as other clubs had their big European nights.

Now it was us playing one of the most famous clubs in Europe, in one of the most famous stadiums. It was the knockout stages, it was them or us. They were the former European champions, and we were little Bolton Wanderers. But we felt we had a chance. For all we knew, we might never get another one.

Those inside the club knew the gravity of the occasion, too. "Marseille was bigger than the Bayern Munich game for me because it was new to us," says Byrne-Fraser. "I can remember watching highlights of European football in black and white with the commentator sounding like he was talking into a baked bean tin, staying up as a kid to watch highlights of Steaua Bucharest or whoever. It just seemed so exotic and glamorous, and out of reach. You thought you were never going to be there and involved in it.

"That game was a massive moment. Everyone has heard of Marseille. That was the first really big game."

Marseille were the undoubted favourites, as French national sports newspaper L'Equipe proved statistically on the day of the game. History showed that clubs who drew the first leg at home 0-0 were usually eliminated, despite myths to the contrary. An away goal would put the pressure on Marseille, but all they needed was any sort of victory at the stadium where their record was so strong.

Outside the Velodrome, there was an edge in the air, and a sense to move quickly to the entrance for away supporters. Some Marseille fans were looking for trouble and a few isolated skirmishes in the area around the ground resulted in minor injuries. Wanderers supporters who had avoided problems walked through a courtyard that housed the official coaches before entering the dreaded warehouse.

Supporters were penned into a small area in the centre of the dark building. "There was a lot of moaning, people saying it was outrageous and that we were being treated like cattle, and we were," says Carl Crook, who had made the trip to Marseille.

Some fans passed the time by kicking a football around. When enough supporters had arrived, the police opened the door at the other side of the building and allowed people into the stadium.

For those supporters who had taken the risk of travelling without tickets, their gamble paid off. Marseille took a late decision to set aside a small part of the home section for an overspill of Bolton supporters. Guarded by police, a pocket of fans watched the game in an area adjacent to the 2,800 supporters in the allocated away section.

The away section itself was not exactly befitting of one of Europe's top clubs. Seats were a small flat piece of plastic bolted on to the terracing, and numbering was a luxury that most were not afforded. With one small exit near the bottom of the stand for the entire section of 2,800, and unscalable fences on either side, things might have got a little panicky had an emergency arisen.

"Even at the end of the game there was a crush as everyone was leaving," remembers Dave Blackburn, then the media relations officer of the Bolton Wanderers Supporters Association. "How there wasn't anyone injured I haven't got a clue."

With high netting extending well above the fencing itself, the views of a significant section of the pitch were as if watching the match through the world's biggest sieve.

"My mate took his young son and he couldn't see because of the fencing," says Crook. "He was crying so they had a word with the stewards and they had to let him into the section next to us with the Marseille fans. For a massive club it was unbelievable how basic the ground was."

The Stade Velodrome was opened shortly before hosting games at the 1938 World Cup. Sixty years later the capacity was extended to close to 60,000 for the 1998 World Cup. Glenn Hoddle's England put news of fan violence to one side to beat Tunisia 2-0 there in the group stage thanks to goals from Alan Shearer and Paul Scholes. Later, Dennis Bergkamp's famous goal gave the Netherlands a quarter final victory over Argentina there, before they were knocked out by Brazil at the same venue in the semis.

A year after Bolton's visit, the stadium would also host matches at the 2007 Rugby World Cup, including England's quarter final win over Australia.

But no English football team had managed as much as a draw there when Bolton arrived, needing to avoid defeat to progress. Southampton lost at the Velodrome in the Cup Winners' Cup in 1976, while Manchester United and Chelsea were both beaten there in the Champions League during the 1999/2000 season. Marseille claimed home wins against Liverpool and Newcastle on the way to the UEFA Cup final in 2004.

The stadium has since been renovated ahead of the 2016 European Championships, with a roof added and capacity increased once more. But in 2006 only the main stand had cover, with the other three curved stands open to the elements.

Despite that lack of natural acoustics, Marseille's supporters knew how to generate a racket. The club have a host of supporters' groups and some situated themselves in the Virage Nord, to the right of the away section, led by a man with megaphone who watched little of the game as he focused his attention on whipping up the home fans. Other supporters groups based themselves at the opposite end of the ground, the Virage Sud, where they unveiled impressively choreographed blue and white coloured cards spelling out 'OM' in giant letters just before kick-off.

Chants would be orchestrated between both ends of the stadium too, as Marseille's most ardent fans spent most of the match bouncing up and down – sometimes even facing away from the game itself.

"It was the first time I'd ever been to a stadium where all the supporters had their back to the pitch, it was strange," laughs Henrik Pedersen, who was on the bench that night.

The Stade Velodrome was just behind Besiktas for sheer volume levels, but this was still an eye-opener for many as to what the atmosphere at matches abroad can be like – even in western Europe. Although the atmosphere at English grounds is regularly praised, for sheer imagination and unrestrained enthusiasm it falls some way short of places like Marseille.

"It was a fantastic atmosphere, a really hostile place," remembers Joey O'Brien. "The fans are really on it all the time there. It was one of those European nights again, like Besiktas, where the place was rocking."

"Marseille were one of the big European teams, growing up you see and hear about teams like that so to get the chance to go and play there, it was just a really intense atmosphere and their fans were absolutely amazing," remembers Kevin Davies.

Despite it feeling a world away from Bolton at times, the music that greeted both teams on to the pitch – Van Halen's 'Jump' – was a throwback to Burnden Park, of all places. Always keen to catch the mood, Jump was often the song of choice when Bolton won at home in the latter years of their Burnden days. A bad result was sometimes accompanied by 'The Way It Is' by Bruce Hornsby. 'That's just the way it is, some things will never change,' went the lyrics, adding a touch of light philosophy to a 2-1 defeat against Exeter or Hartlepool. Supporters trudged back to their cars muttering more industrial assessments.

There had been only eight days between the two legs of the Marseille tie. In between Bolton had drawn 0-0 at home to West Ham in the fifth round of the FA Cup. They made one change to the side that started the home leg, with Gary Speed fit enough to start in midfield after recovering from injury and Jared Borgetti dropping to the bench. Kevin Nolan pushed into a more advanced wide role, supporting lone striker Davies.

Marseille had lost a league game at Metz and also lost Slovenian centre back Bostjan Cesar, a key part of their solid back line in the first leg, to a fractured skull in that match. The introduction of future Bolton defender

Abdoulaye Meite in his place was the only change for L'OM.

Bizarrely both managers were struck by illness ahead of the game. Sam Allardyce had been laid low by a chest infection and travelled to Marseille on the morning of the match. Marseille's Jean Fernandez, however, was forced to miss the game altogether after being taken to hospital for surgery to remove gallstones. Assistant manager Albert Emon took charge for the game, and would eventually take over as boss that summer when Fernandez departed for Auxerre, following differences with sporting director Jose Anigo.

By kick-off time, Bolton and Marseille knew the winners of this tie would face Zenit St Petersburg in the last 16. Zenit had won their second leg against Rosenborg 2-1 earlier that evening, to follow a 2-0 triumph in Norway in the first leg a week earlier. It was an appealing tie, the chance to face a side Bolton had already beaten in the group stage, and travel to Russia.

With the first leg of the last 16 taking place only two weeks later, Bolton had already announced potential ticket and travel arrangements in case they progressed. Russian visas would have to be applied for swiftly after the Marseille tie if fans wanted to travel to Saint Petersburg.

For a while, it really looked like Bolton would be going to Russia. Wanderers started well in the Stade Velodrome, knowing that an away goal would put them ahead on aggregate and leave Marseille needing two.

That away goal did not take long to come. Jay-Jay Okocha had already forced an early save from Fabien Barthez with a long-range strike when the Nigerian gathered the ball on the right flank on 25 minutes. He looked up and sent in a looping cross that appeared to be drifting into the hands of Barthez. That was until Barthez provided the sort of gift that he had given Nolan at Old Trafford four years earlier.

Inexplicably, the goalkeeper dropped the tamest of crosses. Stelios Giannakopoulos, ever a goal poacher, immediately pounced on the loose ball. There was no panic, no need to lash the ball immediately towards goal. Instead the Greek controlled the ball and calmly directed it into the net from six yards through the legs of defender Meite who had retreated to the line.

"It was from close range so it was very easy, basically it was a tap-in," Stelios says in typically modest fashion. "Playing in an atmosphere like that was nothing new to me, because back in Greece week in week out it was that kind of atmosphere. To score was a great feeling because we deserved it. It was a really big pleasure for myself and the team to go ahead in the match."

"When Stelios scored I was jumping up and down, very happy, thinking about the next round," remembers El-Hadji Diouf, watching the game as he recovered from a hernia problem. The jumping up and down may not have helped.

Wanderers fans – peering from a distance at the other end of the ground, many through the netting that obstructed their view – could not believe it.

Little Bolton, at Marseille and winning. Not only that, but now with a massive chance of going through. Barthez shook his head in despair at what he had done.

The home crowd silenced, Marseille were struggling. Shunning their traditional white for an ugly yellow-and-blue-halved shirt specially made for the UEFA Cup, this looked like it could be the last opportunity they would have to wear it. Wanderers looked for a second goal that would surely have clinched their place in the last 16. Barthez had to save a volley from Stelios, before perhaps the pivotal moment in the tie.

"We were cruising and then I remember having a bit of a dribble in the middle of the pitch and sending Abdoulaye Faye clear," Nolan remembers.

Once a player for Istres, just a few miles up the road from Marseille, Faye had charged forward from his holding midfield position. He calmly slotted past Barthez, but the offside flag was up. Television replays showed he had timed his run perfectly. He had not been offside. After the penalty decisions that had gone against Bolton in the first leg, the luck just did not seem to be with them.

"Abdoulaye Faye had a goal disallowed for offside that was a good goal," Allardyce reflects, still ruefully. "It would have put us 2-0 up."

They still would have fancied their chances of going through, had they been able to keep the score at 1-0 until half time. Two goals would have been a big ask for Marseille in the final 45 minutes.

But there are moments in football when you get that sinking feeling as a supporter. That night, it arrived seconds before the interval. A Marseille long ball found only Wanderers defender Bruno N'Gotty, the normally reliable Frenchman. Inexplicably, N'Gotty misdirected his header straight to Samir Nasri. Marseille would have one more unexpected chance to attack before the half-time whistle sounded. Inevitably, they made it count.

Nasri exchanged passes with Mamadou Niang before looking up and curling a cross into the box. At the far post, somehow Franck Ribery had managed to line up against the 5ft 8in Stelios. Ribery is 5ft 7in and, for all of his obvious talents as a footballer, he has barely won a header in his life. But on this occasion, he beat Stelios to the ball and nodded it powerfully past Jussi Jaaskelainen.

"It was a fantastic header into the bottom corner," admits Nolan. "It was just before half time and that got their tails up."

Ominous strains of Led Zeppelin's Kashmir, Marseille's usual goal music, rung out across the ground. It was the sound Bolton did not want to hear that night. The game had just changed. Ribery pointed to his head in celebration, in disbelief that he had just used it to find the net.

"It was brilliant to go in front when Stelios scored," says O'Brien. "We knew we were a good team. I don't think people gave us a chance, but to go ahead we realised we were right in it and we could go through.

"I think we just made a couple of individual mistakes that let them back in. They scored just before half time and it changed the whole dynamics of the game going into the dressing room. Maybe we went in a little bit down in the dumps. I think we would have gone through if we'd been 1-0 up at half time. We would have been going in buzzing, they would have been getting booed by their fans.

"The team talk would have been, 'If we keep it tight for the next 10 or 15 minutes, their supporters are going to turn'. That's what probably would have happened and it would have been very hard for them to play in.

"If we'd gone in 1-0 up, they would have been thinking we need to get a couple of goals, and you have a lot to hang on to. At 1-1, it was a tricky scoreline to defend. They came out then and we were under a little bit of pressure. They had that bit of quality."

The second half was not exactly chance after chance for the hosts, but Marseille started to dominate possession with the belief that they needed just one moment of magic and they were through. Wilson Oruma looked to threaten from long range with his powerful right foot, just as fellow Nigerian Okocha had tried for Wanderers in the first half.

Territory presented the opportunity Marseille had been looking for in the 68th minute, before the point when anxiety might have set in about the clock ticking down.

Two minutes earlier the hosts had brought on midfielder Thomas Deruda, sacrificing right wing back Demetrius Ferreira. Habib Beye, previously operating as one of three centre backs, was pushed wide to right back.

The tactical switch paid dividends almost immediately. Deruda picked up the ball in the centre of the field and sprayed a diagonal ball into the path of the raiding Beye. Crucially, Stelios' lack of inches again proved detrimental. Knowing Beye had escaped him, the Greek's attempt to intercept the pass ended in failure. He could not jump high enough to reach the ball and missed it, taking him out of the game.

Beye – a pacy defender who would later have spells with Newcastle, Aston Villa and Doncaster – would make Wanderers pay for that briefest of lapses. He advanced into the area and fired a low cross into the famous 'corridor of uncertainty' between defenders and goalkeeper.

Bolton's Israeli centre back Tal Ben Haim was left with an impossible dilemma, that he must somehow solve within a split second. Leave the ball and allow Niang to almost certainly tap in at the far post, or attempt to clear the ball while stretching and facing his own goal. He chose the latter, and the result was not entirely surprising. Ben Haim stuck out his left leg but could only turn the ball past Jaaskelainen and into his own net. Time for Led Zeppelin again.

With 22 minutes left, the game was not over. But there was a feeling that fate had intervened, that this was just not meant to be. The own goal was the final inevitability of a path that had turned sharply against Wanderers with Ribery's goal on the stroke of half time.

Allardyce quickly introduced Pedersen on the left wing for the more defensive minded Faye, with the Dane making his comeback from a four-month absence with an Achilles problem. He was back, but not for long.

With three minutes remaining, Pedersen was released into a good attacking position on the left. He charged forward, before being cut down by a scything tackle from Lorik Cana. The ball had gone, the chances of Cana winning it had been zero. The midfielder, later to join Sunderland, knew he had to stop Pedersen in his tracks but it was a cruel challenge that perhaps deserved a red card.

As Pedersen lay writhing in agony, Swiss referee Massimo Busacca issued only a yellow card. It seemed a lenient decision. Busacca had frustrated Bolton with a number of decisions on the evening, although he would go on to referee at two World Cups and take charge of Barcelona's Champions League final victory over Manchester United in Rome in 2009. Pedersen had to be replaced, just 14 minutes into his comeback.

"In the beginning I wasn't supposed to travel to that game because I'd had the operation on my Achilles and I didn't think I would be able to go," Pedersen says. "But just at the last moment I said it was okay, I went and suddenly I was playing. Actually there were two tackles on me after I came on. I think the first one was even worse than the second one, but I didn't hurt myself as much as the second time.

"The second time it was a straight tackle on the Achilles that I'd just had the operation on. I thought everything was all over again, that was the first feeling when I was on the ground. Luckily I found out later it was only bruising."

On for Pedersen came Borgetti, while Ricardo Vaz Te had also been brought on in place of Speed. But despite having three forwards on the field, an increasingly desperate Wanderers could not fashion the opening they needed to make it 2-2 and progress on away goals after 90 minutes.

"The manager put me on too late I guess," Vaz Te jokes now, tongue firmly in cheek. "I was kind of working miracles at that time, I think he probably expected it to be like Guimaraes when I came on but I barely had any chance!"

Jaaskelainen charged forward for a late set piece, but succeeded only in clattering into Barthez and conceding a free kick.

The final whistle marked the end of the adventure. It would be Marseille who would progress 2-1 on aggregate. It would be they who would travel to Russia to face Zenit St Petersburg. As their players raced to celebrate with each other, Wanderers players could only stand and stare in deep disappointment. In the away section, fans did the same.

For Bolton – after eight matches in European competition, eight of the most remarkable matches in the club's history – it was over. It was a sad moment.

"In football sometimes you don't get what you deserve," Stelios reflects. "It was a fantastic performance from the team. We didn't deserve that result."

There was pride, though. This was Bolton's first defeat in the UEFA Cup, coming only narrowly and away from home against one of the most famous clubs on the continent. Wanderers had given Marseille a real scare, and had done themselves justice in their first season in the competition. Even if they never qualified for Europe again, heads could be held high.

"I thought we were pretty unlucky in the end to lose," Allardyce admits. "We lost 2-1 and we scored two goals because Tal Ben Haim scored the own goal after we'd gone 1-0 up. It didn't quite go for us but it was a terrific experience for us, and one that I think most Bolton fans will cherish."

"Over the two legs I thought we deserved to win," Nolan says. "But it just shows with the quality they had, because we didn't finish them off when we were on top – and those little decisions, I think it just went against us. They put us under a bit of pressure and they got their reward for it, whereas in the first leg when we put them under pressure we didn't get a penalty.

"But it was such a great experience, something that I've never forgotten. That first season in Europe was absolutely fantastic."

"We went there and gave it our best shot," says Davies. "It was disappointing because we'd worked hard to get there and ultimately you want to try to win the trophy. But we certainly didn't go there and get humiliated. We were playing against a big club and there was no embarrassment about the way we went out. You could look back and be proud."

"I think it was a great achievement to get that far and nearly go through against a big opponent like Marseille," Pedersen adds.

For O'Brien too, the memories of that game, good and bad, stay with him.

"On a different day we could have nicked it, and we would have still been talking about the fairytale now," said the Irishman. "I saw a picture of me not too long ago, sitting on the turf at the end of the game with my head in my hands. A fan asked me to sign it and straight away when I saw the picture, I knew that was the game it was from.

"But what I do remember is after the game I went over and threw my jersey to the fans because they'd been so good. There was a bit of a drop just in front of the fans and I think one of them nearly went over. I could have been up for a manslaughter charge as well as the disappointment of losing the game!"

Despite Marseille's victory, there were more clashes between fans after the final whistle – both outside the Velodrome and further afield.

"It was a fantastic trip, but it was intimidating after the game," says

Crook. "We got off at a metro station and there were people chucking bottles."

Marseille's run in the UEFA Cup did not go on much longer either. Andrey Arshavin scored the only goal as Zenit won the first leg of their last 16 clash 1-0 at the Velodrome, when Ribery was sent off for the second time in Europe that season, this time for a second bookable offence. Without him, Marseille drew the second leg 1-1 in Russia to go out.

After Wanderers' exit, Middlesbrough were left as England's only representatives in the UEFA Cup. They beat Roma in the last 16, then came from 3-0 down on aggregate to score four times in the final hour and beat Basel at the Riverside. If that was not remarkable enough, they did exactly the same thing against Steaua Bucharest in the semi finals. Boro were beaten 4-0 by Sevilla in the final, but Steve McClaren had done enough by then to be chosen to succeed Sven-Goran Eriksson as England manager that summer. It's probably best not to ask how that turned out.

Bolton's performances in Europe that season had earned them ranking points with UEFA for the first time – 10 in total, two for each of their three wins, and one for each of their four draws. It meant at the end of that season Wanderers were officially ranked as the 78th best team in Europe, ahead of the likes of Sampdoria, Fenerbahce, Fiorentina, Manchester City, Everton, Spartak Moscow, Red Star Belgrade, the list went on. Not bad for a town of 140,000 people.

But would that be it? Was that Wanderers' one and only European campaign? The fear was it might be.

Hunt admits: "You do think, 'Is that it for European football for us?' I'd be lying if I said you didn't think like that. All you're thinking about then is trying to do it again."

Despite the difficulties of juggling both Premier League and UEFA Cup commitments, Allardyce's side had remained in contention to qualify for Europe for a second successive season right up until the final day of the 2005/06 campaign.

In fact it was only after their UEFA Cup exit that their form tailed off. They sat seventh in the table in mid-March, with games in hand that could have moved them above Blackburn, Arsenal and Tottenham.

But a long season started to catch up with them, and they won only one in nine, including a run of five straight defeats. With UEFA Cup places going to only fifth and sixth position that season, and the sides above them now out of reach, only an Intertoto Cup spot was left to fight for at that stage.

The Intertoto would have given Bolton a realistic chance of progressing to the UEFA Cup, but in the end a 1-1 draw at home to Middlesbrough in the penultimate game of the season cost them – even though Boro had rested several players for the UEFA Cup final.

It meant Bolton sat two points behind seventh-placed Newcastle going into the final day of the season. Wanderers beat Birmingham 1-0, but Titus Bramble gave Newcastle victory over Chelsea and the Magpies hung on to the Intertoto Cup place. Denied a place in Europe by Titus Bramble of all people. That hurts.

The last day of the 2005/06 season marked the end of an era, as N'Gotty and Okocha played their final games for Wanderers, even if fans did not know it at the time. It was soon announced that the duo were to be released at the end of their contracts, but they were sure to go down as two of the most important players in a special period of the club's history. Bolton remained in their hearts too.

"I was over in Nigeria after that and I met Jay-Jay at a party and I was chatting away to him and reminding him about the UEFA Cup matches," says Channel Five commentator John Helm. "He still spoke very fondly of Bolton."

Okocha had not made the biggest personal impact on Bolton's UEFA Cup campaign, but he was a big part of the club's journey to that point. His sensational role in keeping the club in the top flight in 2003 and his incredible free kick in the Carling Cup semi final against Aston Villa are memories that will never be forgotten. Jay-Jay, so good they named him twice.

Bolton: Jussi Jaaskelainen; Joey O'Brien, Tal Ben Haim, Bruno N'Gotty, Ricardo Gardner; Jay-Jay Okocha, Abdoulaye Faye (Henrik Pedersen 73, Jared Borgetti 87), Gary Speed (Ricardo Vaz Te 84); Kevin Nolan, Kevin Davies, Stelios Giannakopoulos. Subs not used: Ian Walker, Nicky Hunt, Radhi Jaidi, Hidetoshi Nakata.
Booked: Faye, Nolan.
Goal: Giannakopoulos 25.

Marseille: Fabien Barthez; Demetrius Ferreira (Thomas Deruda 66), Habib Beye, Frederic Dehu, Abdoulaye Meite, Taye Taiwo; Samir Nasri, Lorik Cana (Renato Civelli 90), Wilson Oruma, Franck Ribery (Alain Cantareil 80); Mamadou Niang. Subs not used: Cedric Carrasso, Andre Luis, Fabrice Begeorgi, Christian Gimenez.
Booked: Beye, Cana.
Goals: Ribery 45, Ben Haim 68 og.

Attendance: 38,351.
Referee: Massimo Busacca (Switzerland).

9

Play it Again, Little Sam

Just a season after their debut campaign in the UEFA Cup, Wanderers qualified for Europe for a second time. This time, however, they would end the season without their long-serving manager Sam Allardyce.

After missing out on an Intertoto Cup spot on the last day of the 2005/06 season, Bolton were determined that they would return to Europe at the end of the following campaign.

"The hardest thing in life is to be somewhere you've never been," says El-Hadji Diouf. "But if you've been there once, you know how to go again. After we'd been knocked out by Marseille, Sam said, 'We can do it again and we can do it better.' We knew we could qualify again."

Wanderers started the 2006/07 season as they meant to go on, beating Tottenham 2-0 at the Reebok with the aid of a 40-yard daisy cutter from Ivan Campo.

Weeks later came arguably the most sensational signing of an incredible era. If bringing the likes of Youri Djorkaeff, Jay-Jay Okocha and Fernando Hierro to the Reebok Stadium had been surprising enough, the capture of Nicolas Anelka was frankly remarkable.

True, owner Eddie Davies had shelled out a club record £8m to bring the Frenchman in from Fenerbahce after the Turkish club missed out in qualifying for the Champions League. But this was a world renowned player, not just coming to Bolton to see out his career, but in his prime at 27 years old.

Anelka simply oozed class at Wanderers. His career had lost its way a little and he had craved a return to the Premier League, even if it meant signing for one of the division's less fashionable clubs. But he had lost none of the ability that had previously seen him represent Arsenal, Real Madrid, Paris Saint-Germain, Liverpool and Manchester City.

Looking back, it is hard to believe it really happened. Anelka playing for Bolton Wanderers?

"The first season in Europe helped the club grow in stature and helped me to get better players," Allardyce remembers. "Nicolas Anelka decided to come because we'd been playing in the UEFA Cup and ultimately might even be playing in the Champions League."

Anelka completed what was a formidable forward line. Kevin Davies, such a key part of the Sam Allardyce era, moved to the right side but retained his effectiveness as a focal point for diagonal balls. Diouf operated from the left, twisting and turning, frustrating the life out of both opposition defenders and supporters. They were very different players, but it was the perfect mix.

The trio combined exquisitely in a 2-1 win at Newcastle where Diouf scored twice. A fortnight earlier Wanderers had triumphed 2-0 at home to Liverpool when Allardyce had delighted in irking his bitter rival, Rafa Benitez. A week after the Newcastle game, Bolton won 1-0 at Blackburn as Jussi Jaaskelainen incredibly saved two penalties in the final five minutes.

Those three results put Wanderers third in the Premier League with 20 points from their first nine games, just two less than joint leaders Manchester United and Jose Mourinho's Chelsea. It said much about just how good things were at the club then.

It had not all been plain sailing though. As Wanderers were winning 3-1 in a midweek Carling Cup tie at Walsall in September with Anelka scoring his first goal for the club, the BBC were screening a Panorama programme about alleged wrong-doing in football transfers. Bolton and Allardyce were featured in the programme, and undercover video footage focused on the role of Allardyce's son Craig, an agent.

Allardyce, his son and Bolton Wanderers strenuously denied any wrong-doing, but the aftermath of the documentary was a difficult period for the club.

Wanderers though, responded with a 1-0 Premier League win at Portsmouth thanks to a goal from Kevin Nolan. "Kev scored and came into the dressing room afterwards saying, 'That was for you, gaffer'," Nicky Hunt remembers.

Then came the consecutive wins over Liverpool, Newcastle and Blackburn. It was the perfect show of solidarity, the perfect demonstration of how to respond to adversity. As much as it was a very unwelcome distraction, Panorama might just have set Bolton on the road to European qualification for a second time.

Anelka actually failed to score in his first 10 league appearances for Wanderers, but broke his duck in spectacular fashion with two superb goals in a 3-1 victory over his old club Arsenal at the Reebok.

Five straight league wins in December earned Allardyce the Premier League manager of the month award, for the fourth time since the club's promotion five years earlier.

A West Ham side including Carlos Tevez, then ailing at the start of his time in England, were thrashed 4-0 at the Reebok to signal the sacking of Alan Pardew. Gary Speed's penalty was enough for victory at Aston Villa, before Anelka struck twice in a 2-0 triumph at another of his old clubs, Manchester City.

Further wins at home to Newcastle and Portsmouth meant Wanderers were third at the turn of the year. Bearing in mind Bolton have never finished higher than third in the top flight in their entire history, this was incredible stuff.

Manchester United and Chelsea had disappeared into the distance by then, but Wanderers had posted 39 points from only 21 games – only one short of Allardyce's traditional 40-point target for safety after 38 games. Liverpool sat two points behind in fourth, with Arsenal and Portsmouth close behind them. The rest were some way back.

"We were on absolute fire, it was weird really, I don't know why," recalls Hunt. "The players we had obviously helped but we just had a mentality where if you got off to a good start you very rarely let slip what you had.

"I think if you look at the leagues, and look back season by season, teams that start very well don't drop to 17th or 18th, they maintain there or thereabouts in sixth or seventh.

"It's confidence. If you can get to Christmas in the top six, that's going to spur you on because people are all going to be looking up at you thinking about how many points they are behind you, or looking down worried that the teams below them are going to win. If you're already up there you don't really have that worry. You've just got to maintain your confidence and your standards."

Abdoulaye Meite, signed from Marseille after featuring against Wanderers in their first UEFA Cup campaign, had impressed at centre back. Quinton Fortune, the former Manchester United player, had the distinction of never conceding a goal while on the field for Bolton – even though injuries meant he would never add to his six league appearances in the first half of that season.

After picking up 39 points from their opening 21 matches though, Wanderers would collect only 17 points from their final 17 fixtures.

With Bolton in such a strong position in January, Allardyce had wanted to strengthen the squad with key signings in the transfer window to go for a top four finish and earn qualification for the Champions League. The Wanderers hierarchy though, having already spent £8m on Anelka that season, decided they could not spend more. In the end, the club's only January additions were little-known Slovakian defender Lubomir Michalik, and David Thompson on a short-term deal. For years since then, Allardyce has cited the events of that January window as the catalyst for his exit from the club.

"To get the club into Europe twice in three years was a major achievement for a club like Bolton, but the second time we should have gone to the Champions League and we were all set up to go there," Allardyce says. "It was a great shame we didn't really get the resources in January to clinch a Champions League place."

Allardyce had already flirted with departing a year earlier, when the news broke that Sven-Goran Eriksson was set to leave the England manager's job after the 2006 World Cup. The FA were immediately on the look-out for a new manager and the Bolton boss was one of the prime candidates. The man himself made no secret of the fact that he wanted the job, and Wanderers said they would not stand in his way.

Allardyce was interviewed, along with Alan Curbishley, Martin O'Neill and Steve McClaren. The latter eventually got the nod to Allardyce's bitter disappointment. It was clear by that stage that he was starting to dream of a move beyond Bolton, and perhaps the stress of the Panorama programme also took its toll.

As time went on, what had been a stable environment at Wanderers was starting to become increasingly uncertain. Hunt remembers how the questions about Allardyce's future, particularly during the search for the next England manager, affected everyone at the club.

"There was that much uncertainty, lots of stuff was coming out in the press and Sky Sports were at our training ground every other day for weeks wanting players to do interviews," he said. "It was difficult because they didn't let you go, they'd stand in front of your car and ask if you had a couple of minutes. You'd say, 'Not really'. Then security had to come, it was just a bit unsettling. Sam had been the manager so long that the lads were wondering what he was doing, and what was going on."

Allardyce, already tempted by the chance to move elsewhere, saw the lack of a January transfer budget to push for the Champions League in that 2006/07 season as the final straw. As Wanderers struggled for results and performances in the second half of that season and they slid well behind Liverpool and Arsenal to see their Champions League hopes disappear, Allardyce's eight-year tenure at the club came to a shock end with the campaign not yet over.

Fittingly, his final game was a 2-2 draw at Chelsea in late April as Wanderers yet again tweaked the noses of the Premier League's big boys, with an equaliser from Davies effectively ending Mourinho's hopes of a third consecutive title.

News had leaked out in the newspapers on the morning of the game that Allardyce had decided he would leave Wanderers at the end of the season. Once those reports became public, that departure was brought forward. Allardyce decided it would be best to resign after the match, rather than struggling through the final two fixtures of the season when everyone knew he was going.

Allardyce took a few strides towards the away section at Stamford Bridge to applaud the Bolton fans at the final whistle before disappearing down the tunnel. That would be the last time he would appear as Wanderers manager. Within a month he was unveiled as the new boss of Newcastle.

"We'd trained on the Friday before travelling down to Chelsea and he seemed distracted," says Russell Byrne-Fraser. "All the staff used to assemble in the coaches' office in the morning and I picked up on a vibe that he wasn't really there. The staff regularly went out together to a restaurant on a Friday night and Sam used to take a lot of pleasure in us all going out as a staff group. But he didn't go out with us that night. In the previous few weeks he had skipped a few as well, saying he was out with the chairman. I suppose they must have been having discussions about the future, unbeknown to us.

"We had a quiet moment in the dressing room before the game and I asked him outright. He said, 'This is my last game.' There had been interest from Newcastle a few months earlier and he had rebuffed it. The time wasn't right. He decided not to speak to them, expecting that we would get a genuine shot at finishing in the Champions League. But he wanted two or three players in the January transfer window and didn't get them. I think it took the wind out of his sails.

"When he said he was leaving he told me that it wasn't his intention to go to Newcastle, and I do believe him. He just said he felt he was at a dead end and needed a break.

"My biggest regret was that we didn't have another crack at Europe with Sam. If we'd have known as much as we did in the second season, but with Sam in charge, it would have been entirely different. We would have won the thing, or near enough.

"The timing of him leaving was so weird for everybody. I don't think Sam was entirely happy with the timing either. It was really surreal. A 2-2 draw at Chelsea ordinarily would have been cause for celebration but it wasn't, we were just numb. Everyone was so disappointed."

A day after the Chelsea game, Wanderers released a statement confirming that Allardyce had resigned with immediate effect.

"I remember getting the call I think from one of the radio stations that the news had broken," Davies says. "I was at a friend's party and it was a bit of a shock, the timing of it. It was tough because we were doing so well.

"But Sam obviously felt that he wanted the backing because that year we were pushing for the Champions League, which in itself was quite frightening. I think he felt he didn't get the support to try to get us into the Champions League, which would have been even more of achievement.

"Everyone was disappointed. We loved working under Sam but as players you've just got to carry on as normal, do your job to the best of your ability. We were trying to finish the season strongly and get the job done. We just managed to do that."

Indeed Wanderers scraped into the UEFA Cup by the skin of their teeth after the shock of Allardyce's exit. The result at Stamford Bridge had left them fifth in the table. With Chelsea winning the League Cup and then facing Manchester United in the FA Cup final, even seventh would be good enough to qualify for the UEFA Cup – with eighth place earning a spot in the Intertoto Cup.

Chairman Phil Gartside moved swiftly to appoint a new manager.

Within hours of Allardyce's departure, he had dropped a significant hint in a television interview when he suggested that 'maybe good things come in small packages'.

A day later, Sammy Lee was promoted from assistant manager to first-team boss. Some supporters had concerns about the appointment of someone who had never been a manager before, but Gartside and many others within the club saw it as a natural succession and a way of keeping continuity after years of success.

Lee was a vastly experienced coach who had worked not only with Bolton and Liverpool, but also under Eriksson with England. After a brief spell with Wanderers at the end of his playing career in the early 1990s, he had returned to the club as assistant manager in September 2005 following Phil Brown's exit to Derby.

The 5ft 2in former European Cup-winning midfielder had become known as 'Little Sam' to Allardyce's 'Big Sam'. Many within football felt that at the age of 48, Lee now deserved his chance to become a manager in his own right. He quickly appointed veteran midfielder Speed as a player-coach, to join Ricky Sbragia and Jimmy Phillips in the first-team backroom staff.

However, Lee's first game in charge was little short of a nightmare. Wanderers faced relegation-threatened West Ham at Upton Park and found themselves 3-0 down within half an hour. Tevez, now in sensational form after finding his feet in English football, scored twice. Bolton looked shell-shocked at the events of the previous week. It was a defeat that saw Wanderers slip below Everton and Tottenham to seventh, now clinging on to the final UEFA Cup spot with just one match left, at home to Aston Villa.

But European qualification, for the Intertoto Cup at the very least, was confirmed three days before the Villa game when Blackburn could only draw at Tottenham in their game in hand.

Reading and Portsmouth could still overtake Wanderers in the league, but bafflingly both clubs had announced that they would not enter the Intertoto Cup – blissfully unaware of quite how exciting any sort of European competition could be. Blackburn now could not catch Wanderers, so the Intertoto Cup spot was Bolton's if they needed it.

The Intertoto Cup provided a very achievable route to the UEFA Cup, but would mean an early start to the new season. Wanderers were determined to qualify for the UEFA Cup by right, and finish in the Premier League's top seven – ahead of Reading and Portsmouth.

The Villa game was a nervy affair, watched by Allardyce after the departed boss was invited to the directors' box for the final time. Wanderers were twice pegged back after taking the lead through Speed and then Davies. With the match at 2-2 in injury time, and results elsewhere going Bolton's way, Lee instructed his team to keep the ball in the corner and settle for a draw. It proved to be enough to confirm seventh place.

Blackburn, who finished 10th, took the Intertoto Cup spot. But for the second time in three seasons, Wanderers had punched above their weight and qualified for the UEFA Cup. This time they had scraped over the line, but they had done it. The post-match lap of honour for the final home game of the campaign was a moment for players and fans to celebrate.

"I remember parading on the pitch at the end," Hunt says. "It was a fantastic moment."

Allardyce had left two matches before the end of the campaign, but has always regarded qualification that season as his achievement. From now on though, Wanderers had to find a way of succeeding without him.

10

There May be Trouble Ahead

Rabotnicki 1 Bolton 1 – September 20, 2007

By the time Wanderers began their second season in the UEFA Cup, dark clouds were already starting to hang over the club.

Bolton's early adjustments to the post-Allardyce era had not gone well. Appointed as the new manager of Newcastle, a number of Wanderers' backroom staff had quickly followed him to St James' Park.

There was a certain inevitability when the Premier League fixtures were announced a month later. First game of the season – Newcastle at home. It was probably the last opening day fixture Wanderers would have wanted.

After taking charge for the final two games of the previous season, new boss Sammy Lee had started to put his own stamp on the club that summer. In came former England international Gavin McCann from Aston Villa, Heidar Helguson from Fulham and Daniel Braaten from Rosenborg, while Christian Wilhelmsson, Danny Guthrie and Mikel Alonso arrived on loan from Nantes, Liverpool and Real Sociedad respectively. Jlloyd Samuel and Gerald Cid were also additions to the squad, on Bosman free transfers already in the pipeline during Allardyce's time in charge.

Wanderers' preparations for the 2007/08 season had started well. They travelled to South Korea in July to take part in the prestigious Peace Cup, which brought together clubs from seven countries. Wanderers drew against local side Seongnam Ilhwa Chunma before beating the Mexicans Guadalajara and Spanish side Racing Santander, to ensure they won the group and reached the final.

There they faced Lyon, who had fended off competition from Reading, River Plate and Japanese club Shimizu S-Pulse in Group B. Wanderers were beaten 1-0 by the French giants in Seoul but, just as when they won the Asia Trophy in Thailand two years earlier, they were going into a European campaign having again raised their profile on the world stage.

Allardyce's return to the Reebok with Newcastle on the opening day loomed large though. It was an immediate gauge of Big Sam v Little Sam and what impact Allardyce's departure would have on Bolton.

In the end, that pressure told on Wanderers. Newcastle arrived fired up for Allardyce's first game in charge, and raced into a 3-0 lead inside half an hour – just as West Ham had done against Lee's Bolton months earlier. The game finished 3-1, but Cid's debut in defence had ended in disaster and Wanderers also lost Ricardo Vaz Te to a serious knee injury – just as the Portuguese forward had started to look like becoming a regular starter during an impressive pre-season.

Bolton followed that Newcastle loss with defeats at Fulham and Portsmouth to sit bottom of the table from the off, in stark contrast to the lightning start they had made in Allardyce's last season in charge.

Lee quickly brought in Andy O'Brien from Portsmouth in an attempt to bolster the defence, while Abdoulaye Faye left to join Allardyce at Newcastle.

Henrik Pedersen was allowed to depart for Hull after six years with the club where he gained cult status for possibly the world's weirdest goal celebration. 'The Peacock' was dreamed up during a summer holiday in the bars of Ayia Napa and involved flapping his arms about ludicrously in imitation of the colourful bird.

"It was just a small funny thing that got a lot of attention," laughed Pedersen, who opened a pub in his native Denmark following his retirement from football. "The celebration even went on to the FIFA video game the year after. When I scored on the FIFA game, I did that celebration!

"I had six great years at Bolton. It was a fantastic experience."

Wanderers got their first win of the 2007/08 campaign with a home victory over Reading but by the time the UEFA Cup came around they had lost to Everton and Birmingham, leaving them rooted to the foot of the table with only three points from their first six matches.

An attempt to switch from Allardyce's traditional 4-3-3 to a 4-4-2 formation with a much greater emphasis on short passing had proved wholly unsuccessful. A once resilient defence looked all at sea.

Anelka, with four goals in those six games, was left having to single-handedly salvage the situation. It was too great an ask. For Nicky Hunt, the transition from Allardyce to Lee was awkward.

"It was a weird one for us because we'd known Sammy and he was a fantastic coach, probably the best coach I'd worked for, but when he was appointed he was unproven as a manager," Hunt said. "We knew as players as long as we kept the core of the squad we'd be fine.

"But it was difficult because Sammy started coming under pressure. We played Newcastle at home in the first game and got beat 3-1 and he was getting a bit of stick. The players were feeling it because we were thinking we've had Sam Allardyce for God knows how many years and he's always been a big man, a big strong character. We didn't know how to react.

"I think in any job, not necessarily just football, if you've had a boss for seven or eight years and he just suddenly says he's leaving and someone else comes in, you've got to work them out. What do they want? What's their focus? It's hard to work them out. We should never really have let that affect us, but it does as a whole workforce."

"Under Sammy there was big change," Kevin Davies admits. "I remember speaking to Big Sam quite a lot and he said he didn't really need to do anything, everything's in place, just put your photos on the desk and carry on. But I got on really well with Sammy and I still do now."

One of the early changes Lee made was to surprisingly drop El-Hadji Diouf to the bench for the opening game against Newcastle.

"The first game he put me on the bench and no-one knew why," Diouf says. "I was the best player for so long for Bolton. It was the first time ever I was on the bench and I didn't understand. Afterwards I understood I was not his man, but I still knew he was going to need me.

"When Sam Allardyce left he took three or four players with him, and some players wanted to leave. We didn't want to play for the next manager because he was not nice to us.

"Sam used to represent Bolton Wanderers. Everybody thinks he was born here, it's his town, I've known Sam for a long time and he never told me he was born in Birmingham or near there. He was the main man in Bolton.

"He used to control everything and the manager who came next had to control things, but controlling things is not about fighting with the players. He used to be the coach and he used to look after the players well but after he became number one we didn't understand him.

"He started arguing with the players on the training ground and in the dressing room. I remember one day he had a big argument with Kevin Nolan at training. It never happened with Sam Allardyce, you have to respect the players if you want respect back."

"I was amazed how it went," Russell Byrne-Fraser recalls of the way Lee's reign unfolded. "Sammy talked about what he wanted to do and I agreed in principle, but what was needed was evolution not revolution. Unfortunately he tried to instil a revolution. He wanted to play it out from the back.

"Sammy had big shoes to fill, both literally and metaphorically speaking. While I admired him greatly as a coach, management is a different animal. It's a skill that takes time to learn. I think he just tried to do too much too soon and lost a lot of people with his pace of change. It degenerated very quickly.

"If somebody had told me that Sam was going to leave and Sammy was going to get the job, I would have thought that was natural, it was obvious that's what should happen. As much as it was calamitous from day one to the day he left, and everyone including Sammy got very frustrated, I don't think anyone bore him any malice. Everyone wanted him to succeed.

"But if you want someone to do something, the best way is to encourage and cajole them, which Sammy did in buckets as a coach. It sort of didn't work that way though, it was more a management style of 'This is what we're going to do and this is how we're going to do it.' Generally a team can't change tactics in the space of a couple of weeks. It was just too much too quickly."

The disastrous start to the season had largely overshadowed the fact that

Wanderers were about to embark on their second European adventure. Just like in 2005, they entered the UEFA Cup at the first round stage.

The draw took place on August 31, again in Monaco. Wanderers were once more seeded for the draw.

As in 2005, a pre-draw gave them five potential opponents. On this occasion, they were Groningen of the Netherlands, German club Nuremberg, Midtjylland of Denmark, Austrian side Red Bull Salzburg and Rabotnicki from Macedonia.

Rabotnicki were the lowest ranked of the five and appeared the easiest option – even though Groningen had just sold Luis Suarez to Ajax. What the other four did offer, though, was a reasonably convenient away trip rather than a trek most of the way across Europe to a little visited city in the former Yugoslavia.

Wanderers' European days being what they were, Rabotnicki was the name that was pulled out of the hat. Just as they had started their UEFA Cup campaign in 2005 in the random location of Burgas in Bulgaria, this time they would be heading to Skopje. Unlike two years previously, on this occasion they were drawn to play the first leg away from home.

Not much was known about Rabotnicki – save for the fact that they played their home games at the national stadium, the Philip II Arena, where England had triumphed in European Championship qualifying in 2003 and 2006.

Rabotnicki's Skopje rivals Vardar had long been the most powerful team in Macedonian football. It was they who had regularly played in Yugoslavia's top league. It was also they who produced striker Darko Pancev, arguably the greatest ever Macedonian player, winning the European Cup and the European Golden Boot with Red Star Belgrade in 1991.

Rabotnicki, in contrast, spent only two seasons in Yugoslavia's top league in the socialist era. Most of their time was spent either in the second tier or in the Macedonian Republic League, which they won a record 10 times.

Macedonia declared its independence from Yugoslavia in 1991 after a referendum. Slovenia and Croatia had already attempted to do the same earlier that year as Yugoslavia crumbled 11 years after the death of long-serving ruler Josip Broz Tito. Their secession was met with resistance but Macedonia, the southernmost of the six Yugoslav republics, was able to leave peacefully as 500 US soldiers were deployed to protect the border under the UN banner.

Since then the country has however been embroiled in a long-running argument with Greece over its name. Objections were made to the nation being called simply 'Macedonia', because large parts of ancient Macedonia were actually in Greece and also Bulgaria.

As a compromise, when Macedonia joined the UN in 1993 they had to do so under the name of FYROM, or Former Yugoslav Republic of Macedonia. To this day controversy remains, and even the name of Rabotnicki's stadium gives reason to irritate Greece, who point out that King Philip II of Macedon was in fact a Greek. A similar argument rages about the heritage of Alexander the Great, despite statues being erected of the ancient Macedonian king in Skopje.

Macedonia has remained a relatively stable, if poor, country since 1991 – although around 360,000 Albanian refugees arrived from neighbouring Kosovo during the Kosovo War in 1999. Insurgency from Albanians in the country in 2001 was resolved with the aid of NATO.

On the football pitch, Vardar had the better of the early years of the new Macedonian League but Rabotnicki emerged as a force after being bought by metal company Kometal in 2001.

FK Rabotnicki became Rabotnicki Kometal following the investment and won the league in 2005 and 2006. They finished second to Pobeda in 2007 however, meaning they went into the UEFA Cup in the first qualifying round. From there they defeated Slovenian side Gorica and Bosnian club Zrinjski Mostar to earn their place in the first round.

Managed by Dragoljub Bekvalac, a Serbian whose daughter Natasa was a famous pop star in the Balkans, they had no players known to the average Bolton supporter. But they would soon show they were no mugs.

Wanderers took around 800 supporters to Skopje – a respectable number given the less than glamorous location, although much fewer than they might have taken to a venue closer to home.

The club's official charter flight departed Manchester Airport early on Thursday morning – just as news of Jose Mourinho's shock exit from Chelsea was breaking.

Some fans used the week to travel independently – a few going via neighbouring Bulgaria, bringing back memories of the trip to Burgas two years earlier.

Skopje's Alexander the Great Airport was not exactly one of Europe's busiest hubs. Very few planes came and went each day, and the place was virtually deserted when fans and players arrived – apart from the presence of some rather threatening military helicopters.

"I just remember landing there with all these abandoned MIGs down the side of the runway," says Byrne-Fraser.

The coach to the city centre took fans past horses and carts, the like of which they had not seen since Bulgaria. A mangy stray dog, looking ill with huge areas of bare skin all across its back, lay in the car park as the bus pulled in to the drop-off point. A tourist resort this was not.

Skopje is surrounded by hills, lying in the valley of the Vardar River, which flows south to the sea, just west of Thessaloniki in Greece.

Many European capitals are set against the backdrop of a wide, dawdling river, offering wonderful vistas and summer boat opportunities. There was not a bit of this in Skopje. The river was a narrow stretch of water, a raging torrent thundering along in a fashion that made you wonder whether white water rafters might zoom past at any moment en route to the Zambezi.

On the other side of the river to the city centre stood the Turkish old town, complete with narrow winding streets, an expansive bazaar and with minaret after minaret dominating the area. The crumbling Kale Fortress looked across the river at the stadium. Half a dozen multi-lingual information boards had been erected, apparently in over optimistic readiness for an influx of tourists during the 2004 Olympics in Athens – 300 miles away. By now they were covered in graffiti.

Skopje was ruled by the Ottomans for 500 years until they were expelled in 1912, quickly replaced by the Serbians. Nazi Germany occupied the city during World War II, when Skopje's Jewish population was deported to the gas chambers of Treblinka in Poland.

An earthquake killed 1,000 in 1963, destroying 80 per cent of the city and leaving more than 200,000 people homeless. The population stands at about 500,000 today and work is still being done to rebuild Skopje.

Since Bolton's visit a major project has been launched to build monuments to give the city a more classical feel, although that has been fiercely criticised for both its vast expense and the tackiness of designs some feel are more akin to Las Vegas.

In 2007 Skopje was a simpler affair. A straightforward stone bridge across the river connected the bazaars with the wide city square where many Bolton fans set up camp for the day underneath the huge Skopsko beer sign.

Seven supporters had been released from the cells on the day of the game after a confrontation with taxi drivers outside a night club the evening before. Reports suggested that the Wanderers fans had not become violent and their arrest was a misunderstanding.

One of those held claimed a Macedonian man had tried to goad them by singing 'Glory, Glory Man United', before another attacked them. Insisting the Bolton supporters were innocent, he described his arrest as the most frightening three-and-a-half hours of his entire life.

As Wanderers fans passed the time on the main square on matchday, the area became increasingly filled with beggars – many of them young children looking for enough money to buy food. It was a stark reminder of the poverty felt by some in the country.

"I'd never been to Macedonia before and it was a proper third world country," remembers Dave Blackburn, the supporters club spokesman at the time. "There were a lot of gypsies and beggars, young and old. It was an eye opener."

We walked through the pleasant enough streets of the city, passing the statue of Mother Teresa, born Anjeze Gonxhe Bojaxhiu in Skopje in 1910.

For lunch, a local barman – an expat former West Midlands policeman – pointed us in the direction of a quiet restaurant. Once inside it became clear it was themed in honour of Tito – the former Communist leader, not the member of the Jackson 5 – complete with imposing picture on the wall. The bust of Lenin and the poster of Che Guevara added to the impression that the restaurant owner might possibly be a bit of a lefty. Just a hunch.

The attempts at English translation on the menu were equally baffling. Among the fish offerings was a dish entitled 'crap', without any visible sign of irony. At a price of 950 Macedonian denar, we didn't risk finding out what that was.

As we wandered towards the stadium, a few hundred yards from the main square we stumbled across a large-scale student protest outside the main government building. As it turned out, Macedonia weren't threatening to appoint Gary Megson or Steve Kean as their new national team manager, the protest was a call for more funds for education.

We continued on for an afternoon look at the Philip II Arena, situated in the middle of a pleasant park with training facilities for the local sports teams.

When we arrived at the main stand, the door was open and the place seemed deserted. Out of curiosity, we went through the door to see what was inside. Still no-one was there, so we ventured a little further until we inadvertently found ourselves beside the decrepit-looking dressing rooms. We bumped into a little old cleaning lady, who seemed to be saying we could go inside the dressing rooms if we liked. From there we kept walking and ended up in the tunnel, then on the pitch itself. All this in the national stadium, only a few hours before kick-off. Somehow, you couldn't see it happening at Wembley.

Stadium staff were pitchside as cheerleaders practised their half-time routine, but no-one batted an eyelid as we took our seats in the dugout and generally mooched around for a few minutes before heading back to the city centre.

Wanderers had arrived a day before the game, training at the stadium on the Wednesday evening. A suitable hotel, the Aleksandar Palace Hotel, had been found in Skopje for the squad when club secretary Simon Marland and other officials made a fact-finding visit to the Macedonian capital weeks earlier.

"In Skopje the hotel was good but it was the only one of that level," Marland said. "Some of the others were like Holiday Inns which, don't get me wrong, were fine but obviously you wanted something that had enough bedrooms and things like that.

"From the team point of view there weren't any problems, but when we got taken round to see some the corporate people were going to use, there were hotels that were crossed off straight away. It wasn't necessarily the hotel, but you looked around the area you were in and decided that you wouldn't really want to walk out there at night.

"Safety comes into it. The last thing we wanted was for people travelling with us or under our banner being put in a place where they couldn't step out of the hotel."

Macedonia was a whole new experience for Wanderers defender Nicky Hunt, who admits the squad did not enjoy their surroundings too much.

"The players had never visited there before and didn't know how to take it," he said. "The only time we went out of the hotel was to get straight on the coach, train, then straight back on the coach and back to the hotel. We never saw any of the place, although obviously you could see out of your window and it wasn't great.

"But we only went the day before, it wasn't like it was three or four days. We tried to keep it down to a minimum, which was probably a blessing in disguise. If we'd stayed there for another two or three days it would have sent the lads loopy just in a hotel like that."

"We were followed everywhere for our own safety by a guy with a machine gun," says Byrne-Fraser. "It may have been to do with the threat of kidnap or something because although the place was settling down, I think everyone was still a bit on edge.

"You had your own private guard all day. I'd say, 'No, you're all right', but they'd say, 'No, it's okay, I'll wait here'. You'd even go to the loo and they'd stand there outside the loo!

"There were half a dozen at least floating around the hotel at any given time. The players would meet for lunch and then go off to their rooms, sleep and get up later. While they were on their own I was still working, so the guys with the machine guns had nothing to do and they just tended to follow the staff. It was the most bizarre scenario."

The Philip II Arena has been expanded to a 33,000-capacity stadium since Bolton's visit, and modernised to an extent that now it would not look out of place in any western European country. In 2007 the capacity was 18,000 and the stadium was more basic.

"FIFA's rules about stadiums are so rigid and yet you went to Rabotnicki and the place was falling down," remembers chairman Phil Gartside.

With its aesthetically pleasing curving roof, the main stand was a smart and imposing structure, albeit bizarrely placed behind a rather incongruous pitchside hedgerow. The rest of the stadium would later be built to the same design, but back then the other three stands were standard Eastern European fare, 20 rows of open seating, separated from the playing surface by fencing and a running track.

Fine weather meant the lack of a roof was no real problem on the night, with Wanderers fans situated along the length of the open side of the pitch.

Rather paranoid policing meant supporters were relieved of every last coin in their possession outside the stadium, just in case anyone felt tempted to lob one in the direction of the pitch during the match.

"Before the game a lot of police suddenly appeared from nowhere and we were all searched," recalls supporter Blackburn. "It was a real European ground. The loo was just a hole in the floor."

An attendance of 16,000 was officially recorded for the game, with Bolton being the most high profile visitors to Macedonia for a club match for some time. Rabotnicki usually played league games in front of an almost deserted stadium, but this time locals virtually filled the main stand, waving balloons and cheering enthusiastically. A small group of ultras, the 'Romanticari', positioned themselves in the top corner of the stand.

There were giant footballs pitchside next to huge inflatable footballers, as well as cheerleaders and a rather impressive firework display at half time. If the students protesting outside the government buildings wondered where all the money for education had gone, it was probably being spent on the matchday entertainment for this game.

Unlike in Wanderers' first season in Europe, when every match was shown live on television, this game could not be watched back home in England. In 2005/06, Bolton had been joined in the UEFA Cup by Middlesbrough and Everton, with the latter going out in the first round. In 2007/08 Tottenham, Everton and Blackburn were all competing in the competition and there were not enough television channels to go around.

Negotiating live TV rights was down to the home club and no deal was agreed between Rabotnicki and any UK broadcaster.

Wanderers' match started at 8pm local time, by which time Blackburn had already lost 2-0 at Greek side Larissa. Lee opted to field the strongest side available to him. That was in contrast to the teams fielded by Sam Allardyce in the early matches of the UEFA Cup in 2005, and perhaps was an indication that Lee knew he needed a result to try to kick-start Bolton's season and avoid embarrassment in Macedonia.

So against the little fancied Rabotnicki, Wanderers started with their best forward line of Nicolas Anelka, El-Hadji Diouf and Kevin Davies – the latter starting after surprisingly being an unused substitute in a defeat at Birmingham days earlier. Perhaps the hope was that the strike trio would quickly impose their quality on their opponents and allow Bolton to take control of the tie. But that was far from what happened.

The match in Skopje was one of the biggest illustrations of just how badly confidence had been affected by Wanderers' disastrous start to the season. In truth they could so easily have lost.

"The stadium was awful, the pitch was awful," remembers Hunt. "You should never let surroundings affect you but they do, you're only human at the end of the day. Rabotnicki gave us a hard game. They had a winger who was good, and they had a number 10 who played just behind the striker who was very good technically, very good on the ball. Every free kick, every corner, he took. He was a good player."

The 'number 10' was Rabotnicki's captain, a balding left footer by the name of Nderim Nedzipi. His skill in possession caused Bolton untold amount of trouble that night in Skopje. His confidence reached such levels that he even took the chance to showboat on occasions to entertain the crowd.

Some might have wondered just what a player with such natural talent was doing playing for the red of Rabotnicki. Nedzipi had in fact been picked up by Hertha Berlin as a teenager but made only fleeting appearances before moving on to Wolfsburg and then leaving Germany to return to Macedonia. His form for Rabotnicki would later earn him a move to Belgian club Lierse.

The winger that Hunt refers to was the pocket-sized Serbian Nemanja Milisavljevic, who would score Rabotnicki's goal.

Also threatening was young forward Ivan Trickovski, who gave the increasingly hapless Gerald Cid nightmares with his pace – something that Wanderers fans realised by now the Frenchman did not possess. After the Bolton game Trickovski would later earn moves to Red Star Belgrade, APOEL Nicosia and Belgian side Bruges. He helped Cypriots APOEL to the quarter finals of the Champions League.

Wanderers were disjointed and wasteful in possession in Skopje, with Gary Speed and Nolan having off nights in midfield. Speed was growing increasingly frustrated with the way Rabotnicki players were going to ground easily. He protested at one point to Hungarian referee Zsolt Szabo by a doing a mock dive to the turf – reminiscent of Francis Lee's famously comical complaint about George Best in a Manchester derby in 1971.

Anelka did have a chance to put Bolton in front before half time when he went round Rabotnicki keeper Filip Madzovski, but as he swivelled he screwed his shot into the side netting.

The fireworks at the interval were followed by fireworks on the pitch, as Wanderers' poor performance resulted in them falling behind. The home crowd had been encouraged by Rabotnicki's display, making an increasingly hostile atmosphere for the visitors, and both players and fans celebrated as if they had won the World Cup when their side struck in the 53rd minute.

Jussi Jaaskelainen had already had to save from Trickovski at the start of the second half before the forward turned provider. His header was embarrassingly misjudged by Cid, who was caught under the ball – allowing the bright Milisavljevic to race through and volley left footed into the bottom corner.

Wanderers were now facing real embarrassment, losing in Macedonia after an already horrendous first few weeks of the season. Not only that, but defeat in Skopje would leave them with major work to do in the second leg at the Reebok. On the evidence of this display, you would not have been entirely confident of them salvaging the situation.

The travelling fans were becoming increasingly frustrated. Things could and should have been even worse as Trickovski darted clear and looked set to make it 2-0, only to fire over the bar. It was a let-off.

Cid was hauled off and replaced by Andy O'Brien. After being a regular in Wanderers' Premier League side until that point, he would find himself axed after his nadir in Skopje. Although the Frenchman did appear in a number of UEFA Cup games later in the season, he made only one more league appearance for the club. He will not go down as one of Bolton's all-time great defenders.

Lee also brought on Braaten for McCann, before introducing Joey O'Brien at right back for Hunt with 75 minutes gone. It was the Irishman's first appearance for 15 months, after a knee injury had completely wiped out the 2006/07 season for him. Just as he had made his name with the Wanderers first team in the club's first season in the UEFA Cup, now fate would decide he would return at the very start of their second run in the competition.

"My whole career as a first team player at Bolton was basically associated with the European runs," said O'Brien, who would go on to play in a number of UEFA Cup games in 2007/08.

"The first year we played in Europe was my first year as a player, then I was out for the next year with my knee. That was the start of my knee problems. But then the following year I was fit and back playing in Europe.

"I remember my first game coming back was Rabotnicki. I only came on for about 15 minutes at right back. I'd been out for the best part of 18 months. I was just delighted to be back after being out with a potentially career-ending knee injury.

"Obviously things weren't going great under Sammy Lee so there was massive pressure to go to Macedonia and get a result. It was a massive relief to get an equaliser."

That equaliser came with only six minutes left, in rather fortuitous and unlikely fashion.

Just as time appeared to be running out, Wanderers won a free kick on the edge of the box. Anelka stepped up to deafening whistles from the home crowd, who were well aware of the Frenchman's reputation in the game and his status as Bolton's main danger man.

Anelka curled an effort over the wall but straight at Madzovski. The keeper should have claimed the ball relatively easily, but spilled it a couple of yards in front of him. On hand, perhaps surprisingly, was Abdoulaye Meite. The centre back had gone forward hoping for a cross into the box, but displayed a striker's instinct to pounce in no time and stab the loose ball over the line.

It was a moment of great relief as much as anything. No-one could claim that a 1-1 draw in Macedonia was the world's greatest result, but it meant that Blackburn would instead take the headlines for their surprise defeat in Greece.

An away goal also put Wanderers back in firm control of the tie, needing only a 0-0 draw at the Reebok to go through. No matter how badly they had been playing, surely they were capable of that.

After the final whistle, Wanderers opted to depart without using the less than luxurious shower facilities at the stadium, instead quickly returning to their hotel. The club were forced to deny it was a snub to Rabotnicki, explaining that the dressing rooms were not big enough to house the players' usual post-match ice baths and that the home club had been informed in advance of Wanderers' plans.

After taking their ice baths at the hotel, the squad headed to the airport for a midnight flight. Under Lee, Wanderers had decided to return to England that night to begin preparations for their home game against Tottenham three days later.

Supporters waited at the airport for their own chartered flight back to England, some already disgruntled at the performance and further irritated by the news that they could not board the plane until the Wanderers squad had departed.

"We weren't allowed on our flight until the players had gone, and there were some fans who wanted to confront the players and manager over such an inept performance," recalls Blackburn. "But they were sneaked in through a back door. The last we saw of them was them flying off in the distance."

After the couple of days they had just had, most were glad to be out of Macedonia, hopeful they would never return.

Bolton: Jussi Jaaskelainen; Nicky Hunt (Joey O'Brien 76), Abdoulaye Meite, Gerald Cid (Andy O'Brien 63), Ricardo Gardner; Kevin Nolan, Gavin McCann (Daniel Braaten 63), Gary Speed; Kevin Davies, Nicolas Anelka, El-Hadji Diouf. Subs not used: Ali Al Habsi, Mikel Alonso, Andranik Teymourian, Danny Guthrie.
Booked: McCann, Speed, Hunt, Diouf.
Goal: Meite 84.

Rabotnicki: Filip Madzovski; Lukmon Adekunle, Vasko Bozanovski, Miroslav Vajs, Lazar Stanisic; Nemanja Milisavljevic (Krste Velkoski 72), Nikola Gligorov, Ertan Demiri, Minas Osmani (Ivan Pejcic 65); Nderim Nedzipi; Ivan Trickovski (Ismet Selim 89). Subs not used: Tome Pacovski, Emir Sabani, Saso Gjoreski, Mensur Idrizi.
Booked: Milisavljevic, Nedzipi, Osmani, Vajs.
Goal: Milisavljevic 53.

Attendance: 16,000.
Referee: Zsolt Szabo (Hungary).

11

In the Nic of Time

Bolton 1 Rabotnicki 0 – October 4, 2008

Wanderers had climbed off the bottom of the Premier League table by the time Rabotnicki arrived at the Reebok for the second leg, but Sammy Lee's position as manager was becoming increasingly precarious.

Three days after the first leg in Skopje, Wanderers had drawn 1-1 at home to Tottenham. Their goalscorer had been Ivan Campo, brought back in from the cold for his first appearance of the season.

Campo was a cult hero at Wanderers. He had come a long way from his disastrous initial days at the club, when he struggled badly after arriving on loan from Real Madrid in 2002, shorn of confidence after being virtually hounded out of the Bernabeu by frustrated fans and the press.

Watching him play in central defence for Wanderers, you could understand their frustration. Clearly a classy player who had played in Real's Champions League final victory over Valencia in 2000, Campo was also lackadaisical at times and had the tendency to needlessly lose possession trying to do too much in defensive areas. He was badly exposed for pace too, and he knew it. On one occasion, the Spaniard was so outpaced by Harry Kewell during a 3-0 home loss to Leeds that he simply resorted to the most spectacular of rugby tackles.

Campo produced such comedy moments on a regular basis during his Bolton career, whether it be theatrically diving on the ball to award his own free kicks when he was fouled, or his split-second rage – where the Spaniard would leap to his feet looking ready to punch someone before quickly thinking better of it.

From his overdramatic arm waving at referees to his frizzy mop of hair, which he insisted on regularly flying back to Madrid to get cut, some around the country wrote off Campo as a clown.

But to Bolton fans he became much more than that. It soon became clear he could play, and play really well.

That transformation came when Sam Allardyce moved him into a position in front of the back four. He was such a success that many Wanderers fans still refer to that position as 'the Campo role'.

Wanderers were spoiled by many fine passers of the ball in that era, but Campo was up there with the best of them.

He had a big heart, too. It was clear it meant a lot to him when Wanderers fans began to love him, and Campo wigs started to do a roaring trade in the club shop. The open letter he wrote to supporters when he left Bolton illustrated just how sincere his affection for the club was.

Campo's popularity meant it was always going to be controversial when he found himself out of the first-team picture under Lee at the start of the 2007/08 season. Not even on the bench, he took to watching home games pitchside a few yards from the dugout, disconsolate that he could not be out there himself. Briefly it appeared that his time at Wanderers was over as he held talks with Qatar Sports Club, where Jay-Jay Okocha had moved after leaving Bolton a year earlier.

It was around that point that Lee had to submit Wanderers' 25-man squad for the UEFA Cup, on September 1 after the transfer window shut. This was a novelty for Bolton in the days before clubs had to officially name a squad of the same size for the Premier League season. Campo was left out – along with Blerim Dzemaili, the Swiss midfielder who never made an impact at Bolton after a serious knee injury but went on to star in Italy for Torino and Napoli.

With Campo looking unlikely to play for Wanderers again anyway, his omission from the UEFA Cup squad went unnoticed to the outside world by the time of the first leg against Rabotnicki in Macedonia. But it had hurt the player and many of his team-mates, such was the affection in which he was held.

When Campo made an immediate impact on his return to the side against Tottenham, Lee had a problem. UEFA regulations meant he could not select Campo for any European game before the January transfer window, and fans would want to know why.

The manager, to his credit, did not shy away from trying to explain the situation when the press started to ask questions. At the time, he explained, leaving Campo out of the squad had made the most sense. But with hindsight it proved to be a mistake, particularly given the fact that one of those selected ahead of the Spaniard was Zoltan Harsanyi, a young Slovakian forward who ultimately never made an appearance in the UEFA Cup. The situation did not help Lee's standing with supporters who were already deeply concerned about results on the pitch.

Lee also had Stelios Giannakopoulos back after a hernia operation, and the Greek scored the winner in a League Cup tie at Fulham, before Wanderers drew unconvincingly at Derby – by now bottom and on the way to the lowest points total in Premier League history.

Then came the second leg of Wanderers' UEFA Cup tie with Rabotnicki. The visitors were bringing few fans, as low wages in Macedonia made airline tickets virtually impossible to afford. Bolton supporters though, decided to help out some of those who had gone out of their way to welcome them to Skopje.

Fans from both countries had conversed online before the first leg, mostly via the Wanderers Ways supporters' message board. When it became clear that two of their new Macedonian friends could not afford the £350 per head travel and ticket package to make a first ever visit to England, the Bolton supporters decided to have a whip-round.

They had already raised close to £1,000 for a Macedonian children's charity by selling specially made Wanderers T-shirts while in Skopje, a donation that made the newspapers in the Balkan country. They also managed to raise the £700 needed to fly their two Macedonian friends to England for the second leg. The money was sent to Wanderers, who contacted Rabotnicki to request that the pair be given seats on the club's charter flight to Manchester.

Sadly, for reasons known only to themselves, Rabotnicki prevaricated before belatedly informing the duo that their flight was full. Wanderers supporters had made a gesture that did much to dispel the myth that the average football fan is merely a tribal boor. But it came to nothing. Their Macedonian friends never did make it to the game.

Only 12 supporters travelled with Rabotnicki to the match, although their number at the Reebok was swelled a little by UK-based Macedonians.

Ticket prices were cut to £5 for the game, attracting a respectable attendance of close to 19,000.

Rabotnicki arrived at the Reebok unbeaten in 13 games but made a change in goal, with Filip Madzovski axed after the mistake that gifted Abdoulaye Meite's equaliser in Skopje. Tome Pacovski, later a regular in the national team, took his place.

Lee made seven changes from the team that faced Derby, hopeful that his side would still have enough to progress. Any victory, or even a 0-0 draw, would be enough for Wanderers to reach the group stage of the UEFA Cup. Anelka and El-Hadji Diouf were rested to the bench, while Kevin Nolan and Gary Speed did not feature.

The match was shown live on Setanta, but Wanderers made hard work of breaking down Rabotnicki. Among those who had come into the side were the Norwegian Daniel Braaten and Swedish winger Christian Wilhelmsson. Both arrived that summer with big reputations, but were disappointments in their brief spells at the Reebok. Wilhelmsson was prone to running head down straight into defenders – a surprising trait for an experienced player with many caps for his country. Braaten had looked good on YouTube, particularly in a clip where he baffled opponents with a 'seal dribble', darting forward with the ball balanced on his head. Sadly, this talent proved particularly useless in the Premier League.

Danny Guthrie twice went close with efforts that were saved by Pacovski, before Kevin Davies had a header cleared off the line. Wanderers brought on Stelios at half time and the Greek came close to opening the scoring when he rounded Pacovski but saw his shot blocked on the line.

Knowing that one goal for Rabotnicki would put Wanderers out, Lee called Anelka off the bench with 25 minutes left. The Frenchman needed just two minutes to ease Bolton's nerves. Ironically, given that he was introduced in place of target man Davies, Anelka's goal came with his head. Never known for his aerial ability, he looped a header over Pacovski and into the net after meeting a cross from Stelios.

It would be Anelka's only UEFA Cup goal for the club. Injured for the trip to Bayern Munich and then rested when they travelled to Red Star Belgrade, the first leg in Skopje was his only away game in Europe for Wanderers. That seemed a pity. When the club had a world class star like Anelka at their disposal, it seemed a shame not to show him off around the continent.

Anelka may only have been at Bolton for 18 months but when they compile the list of the club's best ever players, on ability alone at least, he surely has to be included. Nicknamed Le Sulk from his days at Arsenal, he had a reputation as a man who team-mates supposedly found it difficult to get on with. During his time at Bolton however, there were no such problems.

"He was quiet, he kept himself to himself," is Nicky Hunt's assessment. "At times he was bubbly but he was just one of those who came in for training, had their lunch and then went home. Some players are like that. I think he's very religious too so that always comes into it.

"But it was absolutely brilliant just to be in the changing room with him. He's probably in the top two or three players I've played with. He was unbelievable technically, he was naturally quick and his finishing was second to none. Because he had that burst of pace he ran past defenders and it was easy for him when he got in one-on-one positions just to slot it home."

Kit man Russell Byrne-Fraser became particularly close with Anelka – so much so that the striker invited him on an all-expenses paid trip to the Champions League final in Moscow after signing for Chelsea midway through that season.

"Nicolas is one of my best friends in the game," Byrne-Fraser says. "He moved on from Bolton and although I didn't see him as regularly we still kept in touch. At the end of that season Chelsea got to the Champions League final against Man United in Moscow, and he asked me if I would like to go. I joked back, 'Yes sure, let me just check my wallet!'. Suffice to say I didn't need a penny, so I ended up going to Moscow for three days.

"He invited me to China when he was playing over there too, and he invited everybody at the club to his wedding in Marrakech and told us he was paying. The wedding was unbelievable, think of four of the best parties you've ever been to and that was it for four days on the trot. There were all sorts of people there – actors, celebrities, Charles Aznavour – and about a dozen people from Bolton Wanderers.

"I'd met Nico before he signed for Bolton because Reebok filmed a

Jared Borgetti scores an injury time winner to give Bolton a 2-1 victory at home to Lokomotiv Plovdiv in their first match in the UEFA Cup
© Martin Rickett/ PA Images

Wanderers players emerge for kick-off in their first UEFA Cup away game in Burgas' Naftex Stadium, as Lokomotiv Plovdiv fans hold up pictures of their murdered president Georgi Iliev

Every last inch of land is built upon in the hills of the vast city of Istanbul

The locals fish in the Bosphorus as hundreds of ferries dart backwards and forwards at rush hour in Istanbul

Wanderers fans, sombreros and all, watch their side draw 1-1 in the cauldron of Besiktas' Inonu Stadium

Wanderers striker Jared Borgetti and Zenit St Petersburg's Aleksandr Anyukov slide through a pool of water in farcical second half conditions during Wanderers' 1-0 victory at the Reebok Stadium
© Jon Super/AP

A stern-looking Portuguese lady peers out over the fan-packed square in Guimaraes

Bolton fans flood the central square in Guimaraes on a memorable day in Portugal

The fountain in Guimaraes after receiving the washing powder treatment from Wanderers fans

Wanderers prepare for action against Vitoria Guimaraes at the Estadio Dom Afonso Henriques

Ricardo Vaz Te celebrates with Stelios Giannakopoulos after netting a stunning late equaliser against Vitoria Guimaraes on his return to Portugal

Restricted views for Wanderers supporters at the Stade Velodrome in Marseille

Stelios Giannakopoulos slides the ball through the legs of defender Abdoulaye Meite to put Wanderers ahead in Marseille after an error from Fabien Barthez, but they would lose 2-1 to go out of the UEFA Cup

A statue pays homage to Mother Teresa in the Macedonian capital of Skopje, where she was born

Despite Macedonia's lack of comparative wealth, no expense was spared for the half time entertainment at Rabotnicki

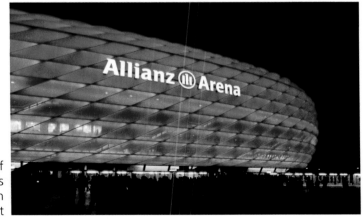

The exterior of Bayern Munich's Allianz Arena on match night

A Wanderers fan's eye view from the top tier at Bayern Munich

Kevin Davies celebrates scoring Wanderers' late equaliser to secure a famous 2-2 draw at Bayern Munich, to the frustration of Brazilian World Cup winner Lucio
© PA Images

There were some unusual spellings for the Wanderers team on the scoreboard at Red Star Belgrade

Wanderers take on Red Star Belgrade as the home side's ultras, the Delije, unveil a banner saying 'Kosovo is Serbia', protesting against imminent independence for Kosovo

El-Hadji Diouf scores to give Wanderers a 1-0 win over Atletico Madrid in the first leg of their last 32 tie in 2008
© Martin Rickett/
PA Images

A mariachi band greet Wanderers fans in the centre of Madrid

Travelling fans and riot police watch on as Wanderers secure a crucial 0-0 draw against Atletico Madrid at the Vicente Calderon, to reach the last 16

The Cristo Rei in Lisbon, inspired by the Christ the Redeemer monument in Rio de Janeiro

Wanderers fans applaud their heroes in an emotional farewell to the UEFA Cup after defeat at Sporting Lisbon

commercial at the Reebok Stadium with the director of Gladiator, Ridley Scott. Nico was at Man City at the time and we got chatting, but nothing too much. Then a few weeks later I was in Manchester city centre, and I passed a jewellers and Nico was in there. He waved and came out of the shop, and we had five minutes talking. I remember thinking, 'What a nice thing, he barely knows me but he's recognised me and he's come out of the shop to talk.'

"I'd be amazed if you can find anyone who's ever worked with Nicolas on a day to day basis who would have a bad word to say about him, probably with the exception of Raymond Domenech (the France manager at the 2010 World Cup). Other than that I think people will say he's never been a problem.

"Mike Forde used to do all sorts of psychometric profiling with players when they came to Bolton, so none of it was chance. If you didn't tick all the boxes, you weren't recruited. There were very few people who ever rocked the boat."

Anelka's goal would prove to be enough to defeat Rabotnicki. The Macedonians still needed only one goal to take the game into extra time, and they did push forward late on. With playmaker Nderim Nedzipi looking to make the same impact he did in Skopje, their one chance came late on when substitute forward Ivan Pejcic fired a shot wide from inside the area.

It was not exactly impressive, but Wanderers had secured a 2-1 aggregate victory to eliminate the Macedonians. Lee had secured Bolton's place in the group stage.

"I was pleased for Sammy that we did do that," Hunt said. "It's on his CV that he got Bolton through in the UEFA Cup.

"Going into that game we knew what we had to do, we had to fight them at what they did, they were physical, they were dirty, so we just had to match them. I think we did that night."

Sadly for Lee, he was no longer in charge when the group stage started three weeks later. Three days after the Rabotnicki win, Wanderers lost 1-0 at home to Chelsea thanks to a Salomon Kalou goal.

It left the club in 19th position, with only five points from their opening nine league games.

Nolan and Speed had both been dropped for the Chelsea game, with Lee insisting Speed's omission would not affect the midfielder's role as player-coach. The duo held talks that week, however, and Speed swiftly stepped down from his role as first-team coach to concentrate on his playing duties.

Lee said he had relieved Speed of the coaching role, but the midfielder insisted he had resigned from the position. It suggested all was not well within the Wanderers camp.

Reports leaked into the newspapers that several senior players were unhappy with Lee's methods. The manager was furious, demanding to know exactly who inside the Wanderers camp had given the press such information.

In the end, a worsening situation inside the club came to a head towards the end of the international break – a full week and a half after Wanderers' last game against Chelsea. It was announced that Lee and his right-hand man, general manager Frank McParland, were leaving the club by mutual consent. After only 171 days in charge – and just 14 competitive matches – Lee was gone.

"None of the players revolted against Sammy Lee or anything like that, or refused to play for him, but something wasn't right and I think everyone knew something wasn't right," says Hunt.

"I just think the chairman thought that results weren't going where they were supposed to be going so he had to do something, he had to change it, and he made the decision. That's what owners or chairmen do if they want to stay in the league and move forward. Sometimes they think it's in their best interests to appoint a new manager."

Davies admitted he was sad at the way things had turned out. After a spell back coaching at Liverpool, Lee would actually return to Wanderers in 2012 to take a coaching position with the club's Academy. Later in the year he briefly stepped up to first-team duties to assist caretaker boss Jimmy Phillips for three matches, following Owen Coyle's exit as manager.

"Coaching is a massive strength of his," Davies says. "I loved training under him in those three games when he stepped back in. He was superb.

"He's won it all himself but it didn't quite work out as manager. Sometimes when you get off to a bad start it's hard to recover."

"Sammy was probably on a hiding to nothing at the time, let's be honest," said Joey O'Brien. "With the success Bolton had, so much of it – a cup final, promotion, being a top six or seven team in the Premier League and qualifying for Europe twice, it would have been a really hard thing to do to repeat that, so maybe it was just a bad time.

"He was a fantastic coach, he put the sessions on with great enthusiasm, but I think he found it hard to change from being a coach to a manager. In football, especially in the Premier League, as soon as a few results start going badly for you pressure comes and people start asking questions. When it starts going wrong, the person who pays the price more often than not is the manager."

Rabotnicki would go on to win the Macedonian league that season and played in Europe for another four consecutive campaigns, losing 4-0 on aggregate to Liverpool in qualifying for the Europa League in 2010. David Ngog, a future Bolton striker, scored three of the goals.

But despite the turmoil at the Reebok, Wanderers were the ones with the group stage to look forward to in 2007.

Bolton: Jussi Jaaskelainen; Joey O'Brien, Andy O'Brien, Lubomir Michalik, Gerald Cid; Mikel Alonso (Stelios Giannakopoulos 46), Gavin McCann, Danny Guthrie; Daniel Braaten (El-Hadji Diouf 75), Kevin Davies (Nicolas Anelka 66),

Christian Wilhelmsson. Subs not used: Ali Al Habsi, Abdoulaye Meite, Ricardo Gardner, Andranik Teymourian.
Goal: Anelka 68.

Rabotnicki: Tome Pacovski; Lukmon Adekunle (Vasko Bozinovski 75), Zeljko Kovacevic, Miroslav Vajs, Lazar Stanisic; Nemanja Milisavljevic, Nikola Gligorov, Ertan Demiri, Minas Osmani (Krste Velkoski 46); Nderim Nedzipi; Ivan Trickovski (Ivan Pejcic 63). Subs not used: Filip Madzovski, Dimitrija Lazarevski, Mensur Idrizi, Bojan Mihajlovic.
Booked: Vajs, Stanisic, Gligorov, Kovacevic, Bozinovski.

Attendance: 18,932.
Referee: Tommy Skjerven (Norway).

12

Protests and Portuguese

Bolton 1 Braga 1 – October 25, 2007

When Wanderers' first game of the group stage arrived, there could hardly have been more distractions. The actual 90 minutes of football seemed like a mere sideshow, given everything else that was happening at the time.

Wanderers had found out their group stage opponents a fortnight earlier. The 40 teams in the draw were divided into five pots, and Bolton's greater UEFA ranking this time around meant that they were in pot two. In 2005/06, they had been in pot three. That in theory meant a potentially easier route to the last 32 this time.

The top seeds, in pot one, were Villarreal, Bayern Munich, AZ Alkmaar, Panathinaikos, Basel, Bordeaux, Bayer Leverkusen and Anderlecht.

Pot three consisted of Spartak Moscow, Braga, Galatasaray, Atletico Madrid, Getafe, Fiorentina, Rennes and Everton – although Wanderers could not be drawn against another English side.

In pot four were Hapoel Tel Aviv, Red Star Belgrade, FC Copenhagen, Toulouse, Dinamo Zagreb, Panionios, Nuremberg and Czech minnows Mlada Boleslav.

Pot five was made up of Aris Thessaloniki, FC Zurich, Larissa, Aalborg, Brann Bergen, Elfsborg, Helsingborgs and Aberdeen.

In the end, Wanderers were drawn into Group F, against one of the top two sides in each pot, at least as far as the UEFA rankings went.

From pot five came little known Greek side Aris, before the potentially tricky opponents of Red Star Belgrade emerged from pot four.

Wanderers seemed to have had a lucky escape in pot three. Braga were ranked highly by UEFA, but did not seem to pose the same threat as the likes of Atletico Madrid, Fiorentina or Galatasaray.

From the top seeds though, they drew the cream of the crop. One name stood out in the UEFA Cup that season, and it was Bayern Munich. The 2007/08 season had been the first time they had missed out on qualification for the Champions League for a decade.

They were heavy favourites to win the UEFA Cup, and this could be Wanderers' one and only chance to play the German giants in a competitive match. It was the game Bolton hoped for when the draw was made, and they got it.

"The draw was happening while we were training," recalls Kevin Davies.

"We got wind of it during the training session that we'd drawn Bayern. I think there was a mixture of excitement and maybe of being a bit daunted! Then it was waiting to find out whether we were playing them home or away. But we managed to draw them away in that fantastic stadium."

In the hour or two after the groups were drawn, it was decided by UEFA that Wanderers would host Braga and Aris, with their away games coming against Bayern and Red Star. It was an appealing draw.

Braga would be Wanderers' first game of the group and many were content to face the Portuguese side at home, given that they had already travelled to Guimaraes – only 10 miles down the road – in the UEFA Cup two years previously.

A trip to Belgrade was not without its problems, and was likely to present a much tougher test than facing Red Star at the Reebok, but it was the sort of unforgettable away day that nothing but the UEFA Cup could provide for Wanderers.

As for Bayern, for the supporters who could travel it was a match that just had to take place at the spectacular Allianz Arena.

The club, however, had been hoping to face Bayern at home.

"I was disappointed not to play Munich at home," says Wanderers secretary Simon Marland.

"All through the years, we've not played many of the very top teams at home, although I remember at Burnden once we played Ajax in pre-season, and we played Inter Milan at the Reebok a few years ago.

"It was great to go to Munich, but we'd have sold out at home and we'd have earned a lot more money. It would have been great, Bayern Munich at home.

"In terms of TV, we never really got the big one. Financially that would have been at home to a German team. That's where the big money was. We played in Munich but we didn't see any big money for that, we saw some but nothing compared to what we would have got with a home game against a German team. The TV rights in Germany at that particular time in European competition were quite high. You could have been looking at a few hundred thousand pounds.

"That was the other side of the coin, by getting into European competition you think you're in the riches but it wasn't as lucrative as you thought when you first went in it. Obviously the prize money for winning games and getting through to the knockout stages helped out when you take into consideration the cost of going abroad, hiring a plane and hotels for a few nights. We made money but it's not like you see in the Champions League, where you earn £5m, £6m, £7m or whatever just for being in it. Certainly in the UEFA Cup it was nothing like that.

"But you look back and it wasn't just about the money side of things. It was putting the club on the map of European football."

The club were clearly on the map by now. That was evident from the quotes that were emerging from Munich within hours of the draw. Given the direction both clubs took in the ensuing years, it serves as a reminder of just what level Wanderers had reached at that point.

Uli Hoeness – West German 1974 World Cup winner and Bayern's general manager, who would later receive a jail sentence for tax evasion – said: "It's not an easy group. We'll have to watch ourselves. Bolton Wanderers and Red Star Belgrade are big name clubs."

Karl-Heinz Rummenigge, Bayern chairman and another national legend, said: "It'll be anything but a stroll, especially against Bolton Wanderers and Red Star Belgrade."

Sammy Lee had still been Wanderers manager when the draw for the group stage was made, but his departure a week later meant that the build-up to the Braga game was overshadowed by the club's search for a new manager.

Archie Knox, who had joined Wanderers a month earlier as a coaching co-ordinator, was put in caretaker charge. Knox had vast experience in the game having worked as assistant to Sir Alex Ferguson at Manchester United and Aberdeen, and number two to Walter Smith with Rangers, Everton and Scotland. The Scot took charge of Wanderers for their Premier League trip to Arsenal, but was unable to prevent a 2-0 defeat.

Wanderers quickly made a request for permission to speak to Birmingham boss Steve Bruce – a request that was refused.

An approach for Real Sociedad manager Chris Coleman was also met with resistance from the Spanish side, who made it clear they would want significant compensation.

Wanderers also asked for permission to speak to Leicester manager Gary Megson. That was initially denied, too. Megson had been appointed as Foxes boss only a month earlier by chairman Milan Mandaric who was keen for him to stay. Megson had still not signed his three-year contract at Leicester, but Mandaric insisted he had a legally binding agreement and wanted £1m in compensation if his manager was to leave.

After that, Wanderers held talks with Graeme Souness but the former Blackburn and Newcastle boss opted to withdraw from the running and it emerged that Megson was Wanderers' first choice – despite Leicester's initial reluctance to play ball. It also became clear that Megson was an unpopular option with Bolton fans. In a poll, only 12 of 699 voters said they wanted Megson.

A hard taskmaster with a reputation for pragmatic, often defensive football, Megson's only Premier League managerial experience was at the wrong end of the league. After being unable to save Norwich from relegation in the final weeks of the season in his first job in management, he had returned to the top flight with West Bromwich Albion in 2002. The Baggies lasted only a season in the Premier League and, although they bounced straight back, Megson was sacked two months into their next top flight campaign following a breakdown in the relationship with chairman Jeremy Peace.

His last win as West Brom boss was a 2-1 victory over Wanderers at the Hawthorns, possibly catching the eye of Phil Gartside – together with a play-off semi final tussle between the two clubs in 2001.

But Bolton fans looked at his results in his next job at Nottingham Forest who were relegated to League One under his guidance. There was also a feeling that Wanderers had earned the right to be setting their sights higher, for managers with greater experience at the top level. Supporters saw a club competing in the UEFA Cup and, despite a difficult opening few weeks of the season, felt Wanderers could still attract better.

Enthusiasm for Megson waned even further when it became clear that some Leicester fans were actively voicing hopes that their manager would join Bolton. A second approach for Megson was rejected but by now reports were suggesting that £300,000 in compensation would be enough to seal a deal. With Megson keen to move to the Reebok, a third approach proved successful.

Megson was announced as boss on the day of the Braga game. The timing did much to detract from the match, but Wanderers wanted their new man appointed as soon as possible with the main focus on turning around the club's Premier League fortunes.

Knox remained in caretaker charge that night, but Megson decided to watch the game from the dugout after introducing himself to the players in the dressing room before kick-off.

"I hadn't really started up to that point, I walked into the dressing room that night when they were preparing for the game, shook hands with the ones I knew and introduced myself to the ones I didn't know," Megson recalls. "I sat there and Archie picked the team, did the team talk and did everything else on that day against Braga. In effect I took over on the Friday.

"I walked out about quarter of an hour early and just sat in the dugout so the photographers could get all the pictures before the game actually started, rather than doing it when the game had begun and therefore not concentrating and focusing on the right thing.

"I walked out and the atmosphere was poor. I don't kid myself, I wasn't wanted as manager. That just gave me an indication of what life was going to be like for me at Bolton.

"I was told there was going to be a demonstration before the game, but I walked out of the main entrance and there were about six kids stood outside. I just had a natter with them and that was it."

A small group of supporters had been protesting outside the Reebok Stadium's main entrance in the hour before kick-off with posters carrying slogans such as 'Gartside Out' and 'Sack The Board'. When Megson was spotted in the main reception area, he was greeted by jeers from the protesters. Megson wandered straight outside, asking: "Who's doing the moaning out here?" It was an opening gambit that could have gone wrong, but instead he quickly found himself signing autographs and shaking hands with fans. It appeared to be a step in the right direction, a sign that bridges could possibly be built.

Inside the stadium, though, there was no warm welcome for Megson from supporters. Chants against the new manager and Gartside continued during the match. With a disappointing 10,848 fans in attendance, despite ticket prices being cut to £10, the situation produced a surreal and distracting atmosphere – given that this remained an important UEFA Cup fixture. Admittedly Braga at home was far from the most glamorous of Wanderers' European matches, but a result was needed here to set up bigger fixtures further down the line.

Braga brought possibly fewer travelling supporters to the Reebok than any of Wanderers' other UEFA Cup visitors, perhaps less than 50.

They had qualified for the UEFA Cup by finishing fourth in the Primeira Liga – despite finishing a full 17 points behind the country's traditional big three. This was their fourth consecutive season in Europe, after becoming a regular name in the upper echelons of the Portuguese league. In 2006/07 they had progressed to the last 16 of the UEFA Cup, matching their best ever run in Europe, before exiting 6-4 on aggregate to Tottenham.

That two-legged tie had seen Spurs visit the rather bizarre Estadio Municipal. The 30,000 stadium, nicknamed 'The Quarry', had hosted two games at Euro 2004 and was distinctive for the fact that it was carved out of the local rocks. Huge imposing stands stood on either side of the pitch, but behind each goal there was nothing but a massive cliff face at one end, and trees at the other.

An urban population of 94,000 put it around 50,000 short of Bolton, but still made it the third largest city in Portugal behind Lisbon and Porto.

The club was officially called Sporting Clube de Braga, named after Sporting Lisbon, although they were commonly referred to around Europe simply as Braga. Their red shirts with white sleeves were a homage to Arsenal, having switched colours from green and white in 1946 in admiration of the Gunners. To this day they remain nicknamed the Arsenalistas.

The year of 1966 may be better known for England winning the World Cup, but for Braga fans it was also the year they won their first major trophy, the Portuguese Cup. By 2007 it remained the only major trophy of their long history.

They arrived at the Reebok managed by Jorge Costa, the former Portugal centre back who had lifted the UEFA Cup and then the Champions League trophy as captain of Jose Mourinho's Porto. Costa also had a loan spell in the Premier League with Charlton during the 2001/02 campaign. Braga was his first job in management after stepping up from assistant.

Costa had been at the Emirates to watch Wanderers' match at Arsenal but Braga's own preparations for the Reebok fixture were not exactly ideal either. The club were only seventh in the table after the opening games of the season and uncertainty surrounded the future of president Antonio Salvador. Braga's most famous player, Joao Pinto, did not travel to England because of 'a disciplinary issue' – something Costa was not keen to expand upon.

Pinto was 36 by this stage and not the player he once was, but it was still a pity that one of Portugal's greatest players of recent years would not be appearing at the Reebok. He had scored in Portugal's 3-2 comeback victory over England at Euro 2000, helping his country reach the semi finals. The striker was not exactly a calm head though, hitting a referee during the 2002 World Cup and a fireman during a match in Portugal. Disciplinary issues were not especially unusual with Pinto.

The Braga side that was fielded at the Reebok mainly consisted of little known Portuguese and Brazilian players, although right back Joao Pereira would establish himself in the Portugal national team after earning moves to Sporting Lisbon and Valencia. Their most potent threat was Austrian forward Roland Linz, who had scored twice in the 5-2 aggregate victory over Swedish side Hammarby in the first round.

Wanderers made four changes, with Kevin Nolan, El-Hadji Diouf and Joey O'Brien rested to the bench, while Ivan Campo was again ineligible. Nicolas Anelka returned from injury with Nicky Hunt another to come into the side.

But the right back admits that everything else going on around the club meant that the match itself does not hold particularly vivid memories.

"When there's a manager there and he's not picking the team, it is hard to focus on the game," Hunt said. "Archie Knox was in charge and it was a bit strange.

"I think it was a bit of a surprise to us that Gary Megson had got the job. But we can't say that we didn't want him to be the manager, because we don't have a say on who is the manager.

"We just thought, 'Great, we've got a new manager in place and let's hope we can kick on from here'. We didn't want to be 17th or 16th in the Premier League, we wanted to be up there in the top 10, which was where we had been in the previous seasons. You don't want to ever let that slip away.

"To be honest I don't remember a lot about the Braga game. There was that much going on at the football club that everything was in everyone's head. But luckily we didn't get beat."

The match was live on Setanta but was not a thriller. Braga, kicking towards the away fans in the first half, were disciplined and composed yet unspectacular. An early free kick from left back Cesar Peixoto was tipped over by Jussi Jaaskelainen.

The visitors' Peruvian centre back Alberto Rodriguez was doing much to keep Wanderers at bay, although his hesitation in possession did present Anelka with a first half opportunity that the Frenchman uncharacteristically squandered. The Wanderers forward tried to chip Paulo Santos from 30 yards but succeeded only in finding the goalkeeper's arms.

Neat Braga interplay led to Jorginho forcing a save from Jaaskelainen early in the second period, but the game was becoming frustrating – for the Wanderers fans and for Megson who was in the dugout but keen not to interfere.

"It was strange, I sat there and I'd see things and ordinarily I'd shout something out or I'd say what I thought," Megson said. "But it was important that I didn't undermine Archie Knox."

The game finally sprang to life in the 66th minute. Knox had brought on Diouf five minutes earlier, and it was the substitute who broke the deadlock. Anelka played the ball wide to Kevin Davies who chipped a cross to the far post for Diouf to head home unmarked from close range.

Braga looked for a leveller and Jaaskelainen did just enough to palm away Peixoto's wickedly swerving 20-yard strike, before Andy O'Brien appeared to escape conceding a penalty for what seemed to be a foul on substitute Ze Manel. Slovenian referee Darko Ceferin, back at the Reebok after officiating Wanderers' opening UEFA Cup game against Plovdiv two years earlier, waved play on. Bolton had a chance to seal victory at the other end, only for Davies to slice a shot against the woodwork.

For the final 15 minutes the visitors introduced Brazilian forward Jailson, on loan from Benfica after previous spells at Vitoria Guimaraes, Russian side Rubin Kazan and Corinthians in his homeland. With just three minutes to go, as Wanderers looked set to hang on for victory, Pereira crossed from the right and Jailson rose unmarked in the penalty area to loop a header over Jaaskelainen and into the top corner. For more or less the first time all night, the small group of Braga fans at the other end had reason to make themselves heard.

This was a game that Wanderers would have regarded as 'must win' if they wanted to put themselves in a strong position to qualify from the group.

Wanderers had made a solid start to the group two years earlier with four points from their first two games against Besiktas and Zenit. They accumulated six points in total, and still only went through on goal difference.

The hope had been that this time around, those six points could have been recorded without too many problems at home to Braga and Aris. Without a win against Braga, now even if Wanderers won against Aris they may still need at least two points from extremely tricky games at Bayern Munich and Red Star. It was becoming apparent that this group would not be easy to get out of.

In the other game of the evening in Wanderers' group, Bayern travelled to

Red Star and took early command of the group by winning 3-2 despite twice trailing. Ognjen Koroman and Nenad Milijas had scored Red Star's goals in front of a vociferous crowd in Belgrade, but Miroslav Klose twice equalised and 17-year-old Toni Kroos won it for Bayern deep into stoppage time.

The day following the Braga game, Megson officially started work as Wanderers boss after being unveiled at a press conference. His first match in charge was a 1-1 draw at home to Aston Villa on the Sunday.

Just as Megson's reign was beginning, Costa's time as Braga boss was coming to an end. Only five days after the Bolton game, a disappointing 1-1 draw with Naval in the Primeira Liga left Braga 13 points behind leaders Porto and Costa was sacked.

Bolton: Jussi Jaaskelainen; Nicky Hunt, Andrew O'Brien, Abdoulaye Meite, Gerald Cid; Danny Guthrie (El-Hadji Diouf 61), Gavin McCann, Gary Speed; Kevin Davies, Nicolas Anelka, Ricardo Gardner (Andranik Teymourian 82). Subs not used: Ali Al Habsi, Joey O'Brien, Kevin Nolan, Mikel Alonso, Daniel Braaten.
Booked: Cid.
Goal: Diouf 66.

Braga: Paulo Santos; Joao Pereira, Alberto Rodriguez, Paulo Jorge, Cesar Peixoto; Vandinho, Andres Madrid (Jailson 76), Castanheira (Stelvio Cruz 68); Jorginho, Roland Linz, Wender (Ze Manel 67). Subs not used: Dani Mallo, Joao Tomas, Carlos Fernandes, Anilton.
Booked: Castanheira.
Goal: Jailson 87.

Attendance: 10,848.
Referee: Darko Ceferin (Slovenia).

Group F	P	W	D	L	F	A	Pts
B Munich	1	1	0	0	3	2	3
Bolton	1	0	1	0	1	1	1
Braga	1	0	1	0	1	1	1
Aris	0	0	0	0	0	0	0
Red Star	1	0	0	1	2	3	0

13

One Night in Munich

Bayern Munich 2 Bolton 2 – November 8, 2007

Sometimes you wait five years, sometimes 10, sometimes longer. Every so often, a match comes along that unites a generation, a match so unforgettable that it ranks above all others. And you were there.

For many Wanderers supporters, Bolton 4 Reading 3 was one of those games. The play-off final at Wembley in 1995, the prize a place in the top flight for the first time in 15 years – only seven years after promotion from Division Four. The sense that this was Bolton's year, followed by the despair as Reading went 2-0 up inside 12 minutes. Then Keith Branagan's penalty save and the comeback of all comebacks, at least as far as Bolton fans are concerned. Coyle, DeFreitas, Paatelainen, DeFreitas, pandemonium, paradise, promotion.

You can watch a team for years and years, and never see a game quite like that. The same is true of Bayern Munich away.

The 12 years in between the two matches produced many great games. Two promotions, one via the play-offs once more, two victories at Old Trafford, the Carling Cup semi final, Plovdiv. That's just a selection.

But Bayern had something extra, that crucial ingredient. The fact that everyone who was there knew it might never happen again.

If ever a night illustrated just how far Bolton Wanderers had come, it was that night in Munich. It might only have been a draw, but it felt better than a hundred victories.

Just playing Bayern Munich, one of the biggest clubs in the world, in the Allianz Arena, one of the most spectacular stadiums in the world, was enough for most. To actually get a result was unthinkable. But it happened.

Only five seasons later, and with a number of that squad still remaining, Bayern battered Barcelona 7-0 over two legs on the way to victory in the Champions League final against Borussia Dortmund. Wanderers, meanwhile, lost at Peterborough in the Championship – although by now with a team that was pretty much unrecognisable from their UEFA Cup years.

The team wasn't exactly recognisable that night in Munich either, it must be said. To do what they did with their first team would have been impressive. To do it with a line-up that was not far from a reserve team was mind-blowing.

If the events on the day of the Braga game had virtually nothing to do with the actual football, the night of the Bayern match was everything to do with the football. Somehow, amid the chaos and discontent of the first three months of the season, an oasis of football bliss appeared that night. The arguments had all been forgotten. It was a night when you could be proud to be a Wanderers fan. There have been very few moments when Wanderers fans have ever been prouder.

At night the spectacular oasis that was the Allianz Arena could be seen for miles around, shimmering bright red, drawing in thousands of fans like moths to a flame. There are few more impressive sights than the exterior of the €340m stadium, lit up on match night. Built in time to host the opening game of the 2006 World Cup, its unusual external design saw the stadium ringed with thousands of luminous plastic panels. The stadium has been compared to a giant tyre or a 'Schlauchboot' (an inflatable boat), which may not sound like it would create the most glamorous of vistas, but the lighting effect after dark was the designers' touch of genius.

When Bayern were at home, the stadium glowed red. When it was city rivals 1860 Munich, who shared the area, it was blue. When it was the German national team, it was white. Police had insisted that only one colour be used for each match, because of concerns that changing colours might distract motorists and cause accidents on the nearby autobahn.

Wanderers' own stadium can be a spectacular sight after dark, its curving stands and space age floodlights piercing out of the night sky as you drive from the M61. There are perhaps few more aesthetically pleasing stadiums in English football, at least from the outside. But the Allianz was something else. It was a fitting stage for what would be a game for the ages, for Bolton fans at least.

As soon as the draw for the group stage was made, a full month earlier, many supporters rushed to book their flights to Munich. Thousands had followed Wanderers to Plovdiv, Guimaraes and Marseille in their first UEFA Cup campaign, and were ready to go on tour once more.

Bayern themselves sold more than 50,000 tickets for the game within a day of the draw, and gave Wanderers 4,000 seats in the 70,000-capacity arena. Travel companies in Bolton reported 'incredible demand', as the club's first official charter flight sold out almost instantly. More planes were lined up to meet the clamour. A total of 1,500 supporters eventually travelled via official and unofficial charter flights, with 2,500 more making their way to Munich independently.

The annual and world famous Oktoberfest had finished in Munich a few weeks beforehand. But that was not going to stop Wanderers fans from enjoying themselves in the city's many beer halls, where some locals still donned traditional lederhosen – completely unconcerned by the fact that it went out of fashion long ago.

"We flew from Edinburgh, we stayed there on Wednesday night and flew to Munich on Thursday morning," remembers Carl Crook. "The first pub we went in when we got to Munich, it was people wearing Bavarian gear, women serving big steins. They were very anti-us, so we only had one drink and moved on. But we found this little bar and got talking to these Germans who really made us feel welcome. We had a German phrase book and I was using that. They were all laughing so I must have cocked it up! The people were superb with us in Germany, and everywhere you went you just saw Bolton lads."

By the day of the game many had gathered in the bars around the picturesque main square, the Marienplatz, which was dominated by the imposing town hall, the Rathaus. In the centre of the square stood the Mariensaule column, erected in 1638 to celebrate the end of Swedish occupation in the city. In the Rathaus was the Glockenspiel, a popular tourist attraction that chimes at 11am and re-enacts 16th century stories with miniature figurines. On this occasion the figurines would have been well advised to cover their eyes, as a small group of Wanderers fans decided to greet the bells by climbing the Rathaus steps and baring their backsides.

The capital of Bavaria in the south east of the country and with a population of 1.5 million, Munich is Germany's third biggest city behind Berlin and Hamburg. With spacious boulevards outside the inner city, it is very pleasant – even in the damp and chilly conditions of November, as snow prepared to fall from the skies and blanket the region for winter.

Like much of Germany, though, Munich has a darker history too. Shortly after the end of World War I, a Bavarian Soviet Republic was proclaimed following the murder of the first republican premier of Bavaria. A republican government was quickly restored but the city became a hotbed of extremist politics.

It was in Munich where the Austrian-born Adolf Hitler based himself and his support grew as leader of the Nazi Party. On the night of November 8, 1923 – 84 years previously to the day – they staged the Beer Hall Putsch, an attempt to seize control of the country from the unpopular and failing Weimar Republic.

Around 2,000 men marched to the centre of Munich as the Nazis attempted to ambush the Burgerbraukeller beer hall, where Weimar Republic leader Gustav von Kahr was making a speech. But the putsch failed and Hitler was arrested. He served nine months at the nearby Landsberg Prison, where he dictated his manifesto, Mein Kampf.

In 1933 the Nazis did take power in Germany and they created their first concentration camp in the north west of Munich, at Dachau. The camp remains open to visitors, not as a tourist attraction but as a warning to the current generation that the unspeakable atrocities that occurred there must never be allowed to happen again. The chilling sign on the entrance gate remains: 'Arbeit macht frei' – 'work makes you free'. Also remaining were the watchtowers, the gas chambers and some of the huts where unimaginably large numbers of prisoners were packed into the smallest of spaces.

It is impossible not to be moved by the experience, even if you arrive on a day when the place is swarming with school outings and exuberant children who appear to have little comprehension of just what appalling moments in human history the place still represents. Around 30,000 died there – many of them political prisoners, many of them Jews – before the camp was liberated in 1945.

British Prime Minister Neville Chamberlain's visit to Munich in 1938 had led only to an ill-fated appeasement plan that failed to stop the war. A total of 71 allied air raids would leave the city heavily damaged as Germany were eventually defeated.

Munich was soon occupied by the US and rebuilt, and by 1972 they had won the right to host the Olympics. But even that normally joyous occasion was overshadowed as 11 members of the Israeli team were taken hostage by Palestinian terrorist group Black September in the Olympic village. All died, nine in a failed rescue attempt at the Furstenfeldbruck airbase.

A memorial to the 11 is situated near the old Olympic swimming pool – where Mark Spitz won seven gold medals – and the Olympiastadion, which still stands today but is now rarely used. The rather basic bowl of a stadium also hosted the 1974 World Cup final, when West Germany defeated the Netherlands, as well as being the stage for Marco van Basten's famous volley as the Dutch won the 1988 European Championships. In 2001 it was the scene of England's 5-1 win over Germany in World Cup qualifying.

The Allianz Arena opened in 2005 and hosted six matches at the World Cup. Channel Five commentator John Helm already knew his way around the venue.

"I'd been there for the World Cup just a year before," he said. "I did the opening match of the tournament, Germany against Costa Rica, when Philipp Lahm scored the first goal of that World Cup. I had some happy memories of the place. It was great to see an English club playing in a World Cup stadium. If someone had said to a Bolton fan a few years before that you'd be playing in a World Cup stadium in Munich they wouldn't have believed you."

Wanderers history had been made at the Allianz Arena before. When Radhi Jaidi scored for Tunisia against Saudi Arabia at the stadium in 2006, he became the first Bolton player to score in a World Cup since Nat Lofthouse in 1954. Jaidi, though, left for Birmingham months later.

From the moment the World Cup finished, the stadium became more famous as the home of Bayern, renowned as one of the biggest clubs in the world. They have long been the powerhouses of German football with a record 20 Bundesliga titles to their name by 2007. Add to that 13 German Cups, six German League Cups, one UEFA Cup Winners' Cup, one UEFA Cup and four European Cups, and they weren't doing too badly.

They had won their only UEFA Cup in 1996, two years after Norwich City had memorably knocked them out of the same competition – winning 2-1 at

143

the Olympiastadion with the aid of a Jeremy Goss volley, before drawing the second leg 1-1 at Carrow Road. One of Norwich's unused substitutes that night in Munich? A midfielder by the name of Gary Megson.

That Bayern side had names like Lothar Matthaus and Christian Ziege and over the years their line-ups have been pretty much a who's who of German football. Franz Beckenbauer, Gerd Muller, Sepp Maier, Paul Breitner, Uli Hoeness, Karl-Heinz Rummenigge, Andreas Brehme, Klaus Augenthaler, Jurgen Klinsmann, Oliver Kahn, Steffen Effenberg, Michael Ballack.

The club were the face of one of the most imperious football countries in the world, with players that exuded discipline, talent, confidence. They were Bayern, and no matter who the opposition were, they expected to win. Always.

Bayern had been affected by World War II as their Jewish president and coach left the country. They were taunted as 'the Jew's club'. It was not until the 1960s that they really began to establish themselves as any kind of force, aided by the majestic defending of Beckenbauer, the goalkeeping of Maier and the predatory goalscoring skills of Muller. Together the trio became known as 'The Axis'.

From there, Bayern never looked back. They beat Rangers to win the UEFA Cup Winners' Cup in 1967 and won their first European Cup against Atletico Madrid in 1974. A year later they defeated Leeds 2-0 in Paris to retain the trophy, and the year after that they won it again with victory over Saint-Etienne at Hampden Park. They remain the last club to win the European Cup three years in a row.

But by the mid-1990s Bayern had earned the nickname FC Hollywood. Their players were attracting as much attention in the gossip pages of the newspapers as they were doing on the sports pages. Beckenbauer, West Germany's former World Cup-winning captain and boss, twice stepped in as manager to steady the ship. He helped them beat Zinedine Zidane's Bordeaux to win the UEFA Cup in 1996.

Bayern installed Ottmar Hitzfeld as manager in 1998, a year after he had led Borussia Dortmund to the Champions League title with victory over Juventus in Munich. In 1999, Hitzfeld's Bayern team lost to two late Manchester United goals in the final in Barcelona. It was a moment that left deep scars in the club's psyche. Bayern were not supposed to lose big matches, and certainly not like that.

Hitzfeld made sure they responded. They won four consecutive Bundesliga titles and in 2001 they did secure that elusive fourth European Cup, beating Valencia on penalties in Milan thanks to three saved spot kicks from Kahn.

Eventually a downturn in form saw Bayern finish second in the league in 2004 and Hitzfeld departed to take a break from the game, replaced by Felix Magath. Future Fulham boss Magath twice did the domestic double but key men Bixente Lizarazu and Jens Jeremies then retired, while Ballack left for

Chelsea on a Bosman free transfer. Dutch midfielder Mark van Bommel and German international striker Lukas Podolski came in, but midway through the 2006/07 season Bayern were struggling to keep pace in the league.

A leviathan of a club whose every move dominates the newspaper headlines in Germany, this was never going to be accepted. Bayern have rarely been far away from internal political struggles either, given that the club were overloaded with legends in key off-field positions – Beckenbauer as president, Rummenigge as chairman and Hoeness as general manager. If Beckenbauer has sometimes tried to be diplomatic, the other two were less shy over the years in voicing opinions to the media, whether positive or not. When things are not going well, being manager of Bayern Munich can be one of the most difficult jobs in world football.

On this occasion, Magath was sacked and Bayern called for Hitzfeld, less than three years after his first spell had come to an end. It was too late to rescue a Champions League spot and Bayern finished fourth – their lowest league position for 12 years. They would play in the UEFA Cup for the first time since they had won it in 1996. While they were not exactly thrilled to be in Europe's secondary club competition, once they were there they were determined to win it. Most around the continent expected them to do just that.

Their response to a disastrous season was to spend big that summer. Arriving from Werder Bremen was Miroslav Klose, a predatory striker already well on his way to becoming the leading scorer in the history of the World Cup finals. Joining him up front was Luca Toni, a world champion with Italy in 2006. Another to sign was Wanderers' old UEFA Cup nemesis Franck Ribery, by then a star of the France national team, from Marseille for a club record €25m.

This then was a relatively new Bayern team, still finding their way but possessing the obvious potential that would later turn them into one of Europe's great sides once more.

They cruised through the first round of the UEFA Cup against Portuguese minnows Belenenses. By the time Wanderers arrived for the second game of the group stage, they were top of the Bundesliga after an unbeaten start to the league season. Bayern had, however, missed 38 chances in a 0-0 draw at home to Eintracht Frankfurt in their previous match. They also had a game at Stuttgart only two days after they faced Bolton, which would have some bearing on the UEFA Cup clash.

Hitzfeld opted to make five changes against Wanderers, resting Lahm and future Manchester City centre back Martin Demichelis. Toni, Ze Roberto and Hamit Altintop all dropped to the bench, although in came the emerging Bastian Schweinsteiger. Podolski was also given a chance to shine up front, after the forward had struggled to convert his strike record with the national team to regular goalscoring form in his first season at Bayern.

Meanwhile, Bolton were still second bottom of the Premier League and made six changes from the side that had drawn at West Ham four days earlier. Megson decided to rest Jussi Jaaskelainen and El-Hadji Diouf, while Ivan Campo was again ineligible and injuries picked up by Nicky Hunt and Abdoulaye Meite ruled them out.

With Nicolas Anelka already injured, the squad that Bolton took to Munich was starting to look depleted. That situation was exacerbated a night before the match when Gary Speed picked up an injury in training.

"There were people playing who hadn't played before and there were people playing who didn't play after that," said Megson, in charge for a European match for the first time in his managerial career. "Gary Speed was going to play and he injured his ankle in the training session at the Allianz Arena, so we had to change it again. We were playing Kevin Nolan because he hadn't been playing much before I arrived, so he needed game time. Danny Guthrie played in midfield too and Mikel Alonso was the one who came in for Gary Speed."

It is incredible to think that Wanderers got a result against Bayern with the team they fielded. Alonso – the younger brother of former Liverpool and Real Madrid ace Xabi Alonso, who joined Bayern in August 2014 – had shown potential after arriving under Sammy Lee but had quickly faded out of the Premier League side. Others to start were misfits Daniel Braaten and Gerald Cid, the latter at left back, as well as Lubomir Michalik. The 6ft 3in Slovakian centre back had been signed from FC Senec as a star of the future but lacked pace and his outing at the Allianz Arena was one of only 17 appearances for Wanderers. Later he moved into the lower leagues with Carlisle, Leeds and Portsmouth before joining Kairat Almaty in Kazakhstan.

If the starting line-up was much changed, with Ricardo Gardner moving forward from his usual left back position to the wing, the bench must not have exactly instilled fear into Bayern either. Stelios Giannakopoulos and Ian Walker had experience but after that it was the injured Speed, the Iranian Andranik Teymourian and three players who never made a league start for Wanderers.

Looking back at the squad that night, Channel Five commentator Helm says: "There are one or two names I need to be refreshed on, Harsanyi, who on earth was Harsanyi? Then there's Sinclair and Sissons! I just find it absolutely gobsmacking that they went to Munich with a substitutes' bench that contained Harsanyi, Sinclair and Sissons and got a 2-2 draw!"

Zoltan Harsanyi's arrival at Wanderers had possibly been partially to accompany fellow Slovakian Michalik in England. The striker never played a first team game and eventually returned to his homeland before moving on to Hungary. James Sinclair and Robert Sissons were youth team graduates. Sinclair went on to play for Gateshead before spells in Israel, Puerto Rico, Poland and Sweden. Midfielder Sissons left professional football at the end of his Wanderers contract in 2009, becoming captain of the University of

Manchester football team before qualifying as a solicitor.

In contrast, Bayern's bench contained 17-year-old midfielder in Toni Kroos, who in time would star with both his club and with the German national team before moving to Real Madrid.

Bayern's 18-man squad had 15 internationals, and 625 caps between them. Even without Lahm, it contained four players who would lift the World Cup with Germany in 2014 – Klose, Schweinsteiger, Kroos and Podolski. Toni and the Brazilian defender Lucio had already won the trophy.

There was simply no comparison between the two squads that night at the Allianz Arena, and even Megson knew it.

"I remember when the players went out and there was only me and Archie Knox still in the dressing room," he recalls of a pre-match conversation with his assistant manager. "I looked at our team compared to their team and said to Archie that we've really got to make sure that we don't get a good hiding from this lot so that it doesn't impact on us in the league."

Megson also had a problem at right back. With both Hunt and Joey O'Brien injured, the manager had tried to bring Polish reserve defender Jaroslaw Fojut into his squad – only to find out that like Campo he was ineligible because he had not been registered for the UEFA Cup in September.

In the end, he had little choice but to select a right back who had never played in the position before – and never played there again. That man was central midfielder Gavin McCann who was not exactly an enthusiastic right back, but professional enough to do a job for the team. He had sensed his fate when Megson approached him the day before the game.

"We had no right back and I remember Megson pulled me to one side the night before," McCann says. "He said, 'Have you got a minute?' I knew straight away what he was going to ask me. I said, 'You want me to play full back, don't you?' He did, but I told him no problem."

One of the biggest gambles had appeared to be in goal. In place of Jaaskelainen, Megson had selected the Oman international Ali Al Habsi for only his second appearance for the club. He had signed from Norwegian club Lyn 18 months earlier, but was completely unproven at this level. How he responded to the opportunity was one of the stories of the night.

"We had confidence in him because we'd seen him in training a little bit and he was a good lad," Megson says. "He handled it really well."

"Signing for Bolton was massive for me, I was the first player from the Middle East to sign in the Premier League," Al Habsi reflects. "I was delighted not just for myself but for my family and my country. It was one of the best moments of my life.

"I remember my first game was against Fulham in the Carling Cup, and then two days before the Bayern Munich game Fred Barber and Gary Megson told me I was going to play. I was shocked as I didn't expect that I would play in a game like that. I was going to be facing one of the biggest teams in the world. I was so happy.

"The good thing was that they told me two days before so you could relax, think about the game and prepare yourself. I was waiting for my chance at that time and you are not going to get a better opportunity than to play against Bayern Munich. I just went there and really enjoyed myself."

Thrown into such a match, nerves would have been perfectly understandable. But Al Habsi did not feel that way.

"I always like to play big games," says the keeper, who would later play in the Wigan side that won the FA Cup final at Wembley in 2013. "When you play big games you have to enjoy it because you are playing against big players, a big team, with a big crowd in a big stadium. Millions of people tune in to watch you. You have to enjoy that and you have to perform."

Determined to savour every last second of this once in a lifetime experience, Wanderers fans had started to arrive at the Allianz Arena well before kick-off. It was located in a wide expanse of land in the north of the city beside the Frottmaning metro station.

Unlike some previous away matches, there was no hint of menace in the air, just 66,000 football enthusiasts gathering to cheer on their heroes. This, perhaps more than any other European away day, had the sort of civilised ambience that Wanderers fans had become accustomed to in the Premier League.

Inside the stadium, Bolton supporters were determined to make their voices heard. The 4,000 travelling fans were housed in the top corner of the stadium – most in the third tier, some a little further below in the second tier. At the top, the pitch seemed a mile away, with players starting to resemble ants in the distance. But the view of the stadium as a whole was spectacular.

"They call Manchester United's ground the Theatre of Dreams, but it was nothing like that Allianz Arena," said Crook. "It was a fantastic stadium. We were high up but the atmosphere was brilliant."

Asked what crossed his mind as he walked into the arena, Al Habsi says: "I felt like I was going into the World Cup. Many teams had played in that stadium in the World Cup. The atmosphere was great, it was something you dreamed about, especially when you were young."

Like Al Habsi, it would be the arena where Kevin Davies would have arguably his greatest night as a Bolton player.

"We had the opportunity to go down and train there the day before, and it was such a good stadium, although you felt quite tight and tense at the same time," he says. "Munich was a great city, my family travelled over, my missus went with some of the other wives and girlfriends.

"Everyone wanted to play, you didn't want to be left behind for that one, that's for sure. We went there just to enjoy it, I don't think we were really expecting to get anything as there were a few changes in the team. But what an arena. Driving in and seeing it lit up and then actually getting inside ... the atmosphere, the feeling around the place, it was just amazing."

Underneath the stands, Bayern did not miss the opportunity to make some money. To buy food or drink, fans first had to purchase an ArenaCard for the price of €10 that they could top up as and when required but could only use within the stadium. For a one-off match, that did not seem a particularly appealing deal. In any case, many Bolton fans had already discovered that the world famous German bratwurst – on sale from stalls around the city – was something of an acquired taste.

The match was a sell-out with Bayern's most vocal, flag-waving fans situated in the lower tier at the far end of the stadium. As Bayern's pre-match hymn 'Stern des Sudens' ('Star of the South') played around the arena, they were surely expecting a comfortable victory.

But Bayern, playing in their European kit of all black, got a shock right from kick-off. The ball was played to German international left back Marcell Jansen, who quickly discovered that Davies was no respecter of reputations – on the football field at least. Within six seconds of the game starting, Davies had charged over to Jansen, steamed into him, and won the ball with the perfect sliding tackle. From there he started an attack that won Wanderers a corner.

If there was any trepidation among the Wanderers team about the task that lay ahead of them, within an instant it had gone. Bayern may have been one of the best teams in the world, but they could be rattled by an in-your-face, wholehearted English display. With one tackle, Davies had just proved it.

"The first thing that happened was Davo won a tackle straight away and instead of them going forward, we did," Megson said. "We used to instil it into the players all the time that it was vital to start games on the front foot. Davo certainly did that for us that day. We scored early on because of the start we got.

"In those European games it used to make me laugh because they couldn't handle some of the things that we were doing. The only way teams were trying to handle it was by waving imaginary cards from the sidelines, trying to get people sent off and booked. We were playing against some exceptional players but in some respects of the game they just couldn't handle it. It was quite amusing."

"We had a plan to get off to a good start and I was often the one who tried to set the tempo," Davies said. "You don't know them that well and we did that quite a lot, we pressed teams high up and got into team's faces, people like Arsenal and Liverpool. We had to do that because they had better players so you've got to give them less time on the ball.

"I think we caught Bayern a little bit by surprise because they probably didn't know an awful lot about us. They would have done their homework but with our team being a little bit weakened, we probably caught them a bit by surprise. We started the game really well, forced a few corners and then Ricardo scored."

Less than eight minutes had passed when one of the most remarkable moments of Wanderers' recent history happened. They took the lead against Bayern Munich at the Allianz Arena.

Nolan sent in a long throw from the left and Lucio won the first header, but could only clear as far as Guthrie on the edge of the box. The midfielder poked the ball back into the danger area where Braaten, with his back to goal, laid the ball off for Gardner to get in an angled shot with his weaker right foot from 15 yards.

The Jamaican had been at Bolton for almost 10 years, arriving from Harbour View shortly after the 1998 World Cup. He had not scored for five years but this, along with his solo goal to seal a 3-0 victory over Preston in the 2001 play-off final, was his finest moment in a Wanderers shirt.

He rarely used his right foot at all, but his shot flicked off the boot of Jansen, deflected down into the turf and then up past Kahn into the top corner, going in off the post. It felt like slow motion.

In a split second, the away section behind that goal was transformed into a sea of delirium and disbelief. Most thought Wanderers would turn up, give their best and lose – probably comfortably. Few even contemplated that this could happen.

"And Bolton have scored!" Helm exclaimed to Channel Five viewers, in a tone that suggested he did not expect to be saying those words that night.

Gardner raced away to celebrate, the shock and joy written all over his face. In contrast, Kahn could not hide his disgust. This was not part of the Bayern plan.

"We were all thinking that we couldn't believe we were winning," Davies admits.

Wanderers were not having things all their own way though. Even in those early stages, Ribery was starting to cause serious problems at the other end. Wanderers knew all about him already from their meeting with Marseille in 2006, but Ribery was two years older now. Before he was good, now he was seriously good. It was quite a test for the makeshift right back McCann.

"I was lucky because before the fans had even sat down Ribery had beaten me twice," he laughs. "Because it was in the first couple of minutes I don't think the fans saw it. Then for some reason he went over to the other side and I was happy with that because he was red hot. It was everything he did, his touch, his ability, he knew where everyone was and he had that awareness. He was great."

Ribery was no less effective on the other flank, dribbling at the Wanderers defence to his heart's content, twisting, turning, befuddling. It was impossible to predict his next move. Bolton fans knew they were watching a truly great player.

"Ribery was sensational that night, absolutely sensational," says Helm.

Despite that, Bayern could have been 2-0 down. Just as Ribery was terrorising Wanderers, Davies was giving Lucio nightmares at the other end. A World Cup winner in 2002 and previously a Champions League finalist with Bayer Leverkusen, Lucio was one of the best known defenders on the planet. He would later win the tournament with Jose Mourinho's Inter Milan in 2010. But he simply could not cope with Davies' marauding presence up front for Bolton – harassing, chasing, determined to make the most of this opportunity on the big stage.

Davies' performance was already deserving of a goal and he came so close to getting it just before the half hour mark. McCann carried the ball out of defence and played a slide-rule ball that released the striker. Davies side-stepped Daniel van Buyten and found himself bearing down on goal. He took aim with his right foot but dragged the ball inches wide of the post, just as Wanderers fans thought a two-goal lead was theirs.

Within two minutes, Bolton were made to pay. Podolski worked his way in from the left flank and passed to Ribery, who darted into the box and found Schweinsteiger. In an instant the midfielder laid the ball off for Podolski to brilliantly steer home an angled effort with the outside of his left boot. It was a wonderfully crafted goal. Just too good.

Unbelievably, it was Podolski's first goal of a difficult start to the season, as he struggled to cope with the pressure of playing for Bayern. Wanderers had run into the Podolski everyone knew existed, the one who had been such a threat for Germany at the 2006 World Cup.

Cue the Zillertaler Hochzeitmarsch, Bayern's curiously parochial goal music which seemed to have come straight from the album Now That's What I Call Accordion Music 1972. Sadly this was not accompanied by Beckenbauer leaping from the stands in full lederhosen, but by the world's loudest PA announcer.

"TOOOOOOOOOOR FUR DEN FC BAYERN MUNCHEN (Goal for FC Bayern Munich)," he bellowed. "DURCH DEN SPIELER MIT DER NUMMER ELF (scored by number 11), LUKAS..."

"PODOLSKI!" replied the crowd.

"LUKAS..."

"PODOLSKI!"

"LLLLLUKAS..."

"PODOLSKI!"

"NEUER SPIELSTAND (new score), FC BAYERN..."

"EINS!"

"BOLTON WANDERERS..."

"NUL!"

No matter what the actual scoreline, the tradition was that the Bayern fans would always shout 'NUL!' for the opposition. Such was Bayern's strength at the Allianz Arena, most times it probably was nil. But this time it wasn't.

The home side were starting to push forward for a second goal though, and Wanderers needed Al Habsi to be on top form to keep them at bay. Everything they threw at him, he saved. Podolski's backheel played in Schweinsteiger, but the midfielder was denied by the keeper before lashing the rebound into the side-netting with Al Habsi still on the floor.

Wanderers held out to half time at 1-1, at which point Megson made a tactical change.

"Gavin McCann's a good lad and he said he'd give it a go at right back, but it became obvious that it wasn't going to work," Megson said. "One minute he was marking Podolski and then when they'd decide to swap, over would trot Ribery, so we had to change everything. We put Bibi Gardner, a left-footed winger, to right back and put Gavin more or less into the place where he plays in midfield."

Bayern's momentum continued at the start of the second half. After Wanderers' bright start, when they could have been 2-0 up, the tide had well and truly turned.

Three minutes after the interval, Bayern were ahead. Schweinsteiger played Ribery into the right-hand channel and the Frenchman darted past Alonso before pulling the ball back for the unmarked Podolski to sidefoot home from six yards. It was another brilliantly worked goal.

"TOOOOOOOOOOR FUR DEN FC BAYERN MUNCHEN."

Bayern fans were in full voice by now, and the game looked to be over for Wanderers. They'd had their fun, but the hosts had flexed their muscles and seemingly done the job. If any side looked like scoring the next goal, it was Bayern. Wanderers brought on Stelios for Alonso, before Hitzfeld withdrew Podolski. That might have been a relief, had he not replaced him with Toni, the club's regular striker in the Bundesliga.

Bayern continued to attack. But then came the save.

It was a save that has gone down in Wanderers folklore, a save that earned Al Habsi instant hero status with Bolton fans. The keeper had already made a number of stops when Ribery cut in from the right on the hour mark, wriggling away from Cid before playing one-twos with Schweinsteiger and then Klose. The Frenchman shot left footed and looked to have found the bottom corner to make it 3-1. That was until Al Habsi stuck out his left hand and somehow, almost impossibly, lifted the ball over the crossbar.

It was a save that earned comparisons with England goalkeeper Gordon Banks' stop from Pele at the 1970 World Cup.

Wanderers fans knew little about Al Habsi before that night. Ever since, he has been associated with that save, a key moment in one of the club's greatest nights. Aside from Branagan's penalty save against Reading in 1995, few other saves have been quite so memorable in Bolton's recent history. Al Habsi played only 18 games during his Bolton career, but he is remembered just as fondly as some who played 180.

"Bayern battered us at times but Habsi was brilliant," McCann says. "I remember the save from Ribery and the fact that he got cramp. He's the first keeper I've ever known to get cramp. I was made up for him because it was a massive game for him. We all knew how good he was from training but that set him up for his career."

"Ever since that day I had a great reception from the fans," Al Habsi says, smiling with the memory. "Even after I left the club I didn't move out of Bolton, and every single day when I go shopping or walking in the street I have all the respect from the Bolton fans. Every time I walk in the street fans remind me of the Ribery save.

"It was one of my best saves of my career and the next day they compared it to the World Cup save of the England goalkeeper. It is good to make a great save but when it's against a top player it makes it even better. Ribery has been one of the best players in the world, winning the Champion League, winning many things.

"It was good because it was 2-1 and that save kept us in the game. I was so happy on that day because I was on top form. Even now sometimes I watch some of the saves on YouTube to remind me of that game.

"All the Middle East people watched that game and they remind me of it too. I had a big reaction from everyone back home. You play against Bayern Munich, my second game for Bolton and my first game in Europe and then the result, it was special. That game helped me a lot."

Denied the goal his majestic performance deserved, that moment proved to be Ribery's last act in the game. Kroos had already been readying himself on the touchline to come on, and to everyone's surprise it was Ribery that Hitzfeld brought off. Perhaps believing Bayern had already done enough to win, the manager was starting to think about the Bundesliga game against Stuttgart two days later.

Now without both Ribery and Podolski, Bayern's momentum slowed. Having look close to being dead and buried, Wanderers suddenly got a second wind. Megson took off Braaten and replaced him with Andranik.

With eight minutes left, an equaliser came. Wanderers won a throw on the right and Andranik took it quickly, catching Bayern napping. He found Nolan who had broken from midfield beyond marker Van Bommel. From there the captain lifted the bouncing ball over Lucio and advanced into the box. Such has always been Nolan's goalscoring instinct, most expected him to shoot. Instead he flicked the ball past Christian Lell into the path of Davies, who needed no second invitation to fire a shot past Kahn and into the net.

One of the most famous German goalkeepers of the modern era – by now 38 years old but still an intimidating, snarling presence between the sticks – had been beaten for a second time on the night. Davies dashed away, arm raised aloft to the sky.

"I knocked it over Lucio's head and just laid Davo on. He got all the plaudits, ran away and didn't even come and celebrate with me," Nolan laughs.

Davies' team-mates eventually caught up with him, burying him at the bottom of a ruck. The goal came at the far end of the stadium to the Wanderers fans, but despite the distance Davies was well aware of the ecstasy his goal had created in the away section.

"To score and see the pocket of Bolton fans up there was an amazing feeling," he says. "Bayern had got back into the game with the quality they had and Ribery played well. But they took him off when they thought the game was over.

"For the goal, it came to Kevin Nolan and I thought he might get his shot off, but he played me in and I just managed to get a decent volley on it and it went through Oliver Kahn's legs.

"That was my first goal in Europe, and a nice place to do it. The celebrations were brilliant. All the lads just piled on. After that we hung on. I thought we deserved the point. It was a big achievement."

Davies' goal has been celebrated ever since. He was already on the way to becoming a Wanderers legend but that goal cemented it, providing an iconic moment to symbolise everything he had given the club in what would eventually be just short of 10 years of service.

The picture of his celebration is one of the most famous of recent times, used on commemorative T-shirts and other merchandise. "Who put the ball in the Munich net? Super Kevin Davies," was a chant heard for years afterwards.

"The goal comes up quite a bit when I speak to people, and I know there are a few pictures on T-shirts, and songs about putting the ball in the Munich net," says Davies, who regards that night as the highlight of his 10 years playing for the club.

"Bayern Munich went on to become one of the best teams in Europe, dominating cup finals, and unfortunately Bolton went a little bit the other way, which was a little bit of a contrast.

"But that result is something that is in the club's history now. I haven't particularly reflected on past games too much while I've still been playing. I've got all the cuttings and shirts but you haven't got time to reflect.

"We've got the DVDs and when I retire I'll sit down and assess what we achieved. But I've watched the game back and I've seen the goal a few times. I show the kids occasionally on YouTube.

"I enjoy seeing people's videos from their phones, I like looking at some of them from a fans' point of view. Sometimes as a player it's so different being down there and you look back and see what's it like for the fans. It's nice to look at some of the videos, with people just in disbelief that we went ahead. Then to get a late equaliser was probably beyond their wildest dreams."

Bayern looked for a winner in the closing stages but by then their play had become rushed and imprecise. They resorted to sending the ball long, looking for the head of Toni, but to no avail.

The final whistle was greeted by celebrations greater than many victories. Wanderers had secured a draw in the Allianz Arena, in the sort of action-packed match that those who were there will remember forever.

"They had a fantastic side and were really going for it and wanted to give us a good hiding," says Nolan. "But they couldn't. We stuck in there. It was well deserved."

Those who missed out still rue the fact that they could not be part of it.

"I'd done my hamstring and I was absolutely gutted to miss the game, but I was so pleased watching it," says defender Hunt. "I was just absolutely made up for the boys."

Joey O'Brien had to watch it at home, too.

"Out of all the European nights that was probably my only regret," he says about his absence. "I had a niggle so I missed that match. I was pretty sick about it. But I watched it at home and it was great for Ricardo Gardner and Kevin Davies to score – players who had been there and done 10 years at the club. There was a massive buzz around the place when the squad came back from Germany."

Perhaps the most surprising absentee of the night was Wanderers chairman Phil Gartside.

"I don't think many people know this, but I didn't go to the Bayern Munich game," he said. "I was away on business in India and I was actually walking in the hills there when the game was on. I've never ever admitted that to anybody because it seems a bit strange to have done that for a game as big as that. But it was just unavoidable, I couldn't get out of it.

"I listened to the game on the radio, one of those internet radio things. I got Jack Dearden commentating in Germany, with me stuck in southern India. A big part of me was gutted, to go there and get a draw in a stadium as fantastic as that and I'll probably never get a chance to do it again. But there was no way I could get back."

Having been an unpopular appointment as manager, for a period at least the result at Bayern started to turn opinions towards Megson. He earned the nickname of 'the Ginger Mourinho', a tag that was largely in jest but did show some small signs of affection towards the man who had guided them to a draw in the Allianz Arena with a vastly depleted team.

"It was a brilliant result and it was a great effort by everybody concerned," Megson says. "It makes me smile now but I'm still not popular in Bolton. I look at some of the huge teams in Britain who go across to Bayern Munich and can't get a result yet we did with the reserve team and it was a fantastic trip, the supporters seemed to enjoy it.

"Bolton did it brilliantly, they brought the staff to games and because we did well, especially away from home, there were some good nights afterwards. The players couldn't enjoy it but as staff we could.

"In Munich everyone looked after us really well. For the training session on the day before the game, police outriders took us to the ground and they brought us back. On the day of the game they were with us again and they took us wherever we wanted to go. They took us to the game, but then after we got a really good result they just left us and going back we had no police escort. They just disappeared! I think if we'd been beaten 4-0 we'd have had a police escort but because we got a good result they weren't having it. They just left us to our own devices and it took ages for us to get back."

There was also a surprise when Wanderers got home. Players found that playing at the Allianz Arena had, quite literally, come at a cost.

"When we got back we found out we had to pay some taxes for playing in Germany, so a few of the lads weren't happy about that," Davies laughed. "It wasn't too much but they were saying, 'Bloody hell, we didn't know anything about that, you didn't tell us about that or we would have stayed at home'."

"It's something to do with the German tax rules, if you play over there and get paid then you're liable to German tax," explained Marland, the club secretary. "Obviously they weren't getting paid over there, they were getting paid here, but I suppose it's like the tennis players when they come over here and they're subject to British tax rules."

The draw in Munich had also given Wanderers an unexpected bonus in their hopes of qualifying from Group F. On the same night, Aris defeated Red Star Belgrade 3-0 in Greece thanks to two goals from Sakis Papazoglou and one from Koke. Bayern still controlled the group, but Wanderers knew victory at home to Aris in their next game would put them in a good position to qualify as well.

Things got better for Megson and Bolton two weeks later as Wanderers beat Manchester United 1-0 thanks to a goal from the returning Anelka. It was Wanderers' first home win over United since 1978.

"Bayern Munich and United, what a few weeks," remembers lifelong fan Crook. "Years ago if you'd have said we'd been playing Bayern Munich and we'd get a draw, you'd have said, 'Get out.' It was unbelievable."

Bayern lost 3-1 at Stuttgart two days after the Wanderers match – meaning Hitzfeld's decision to substitute Podolski and Ribery against Bolton to save their legs had been in vain. The substitutions had earned criticism from Bayern chairman Rummenigge in the press.

"I'm really annoyed," Rummenigge said after the Wanderers game. "It would have been very easy to win and advance. The spectators have a right to see the best team play. Football is not mathematics. You can't calculate everything."

In the end Bayern would go on to reclaim the Bundesliga title that season by a convincing 10 points. The expectation that they would win the UEFA Cup did not come to fruition, though. After progressing through the group, they overcame Aberdeen in the last 32 after a 5-1 second leg victory at the

Allianz Arena. They then beat Anderlecht 5-0 in Brussels in the first leg of their last 16 tie, before coming from two goals down with five minutes of extra time remaining to defeat Michael Laudrup's Spanish minnows, Getafe, in the quarter finals.

Their luck ran out in the semi finals when they came up against Zenit St Petersburg, who drew 1-1 at the Allianz before incredibly triumphing 4-0 in the second leg in Russia. Bayern's hopes of another European trophy were over in humiliating fashion. Hitzfeld, already due to step down as Bayern boss at the end of the season, saw his glorious career in European competition come to a sad end.

In Bolton, Hitzfeld will always be remembered most for that Ribery substitution. But Wanderers had to seize the opportunity presented to them, and seize it they did. Many of the players who played that night had unremarkable careers with the club. But for one night at least, they were heroes. Every last one of them.

Bolton: Al Al Habsi; Gavin McCann, Andy O'Brien, Lubomir Michalik, Gerald Cid; Kevin Nolan, Mikel Alonso (Stelios Giannakopoulos 56), Danny Guthrie; Ricardo Gardner, Kevin Davies, Daniel Braaten (Andranik Teymourian 77). Subs not used: Ian Walker, Gary Speed, Robert Sissons, James Sinclair, Zoltan Harsanyi.
Booked: Davies, Braaten, Cid, Andy O'Brien.
Goals: Gardner 8, Davies 82.

Bayern Munich: Oliver Kahn, Christian Lell, Lucio, Daniel van Buyten, Marcell Jansen; Bastian Schweinsteiger (Hamit Altintop 73), Mark van Bommel, Andreas Ottl, Franck Ribery (Toni Kroos 60); Miroslav Klose, Lukas Podolski (Luca Toni 57). Subs not used: Michael Rensing, Ze Roberto, Jose Ernesto Sosa, Jan Schlaudraff.
Goals: Podolski 30, 49.

Attendance: 66,000.
Referee: Jaroslav Jara (Czech Republic).

Group F	P	W	D	L	F	A	Pts
B Munich	2	1	1	0	5	4	4
Aris	1	1	0	0	3	0	3
Bolton	2	0	2	0	3	3	2
Braga	1	0	1	0	1	1	1
Red Star	2	0	0	2	2	6	0

14

Aris in the Autumn Time

Bolton 1 Aris 1 – November 29, 2007

In the months to come, Wanderers' European journey would take them to victory over Atletico Madrid, and controversy against Sporting Lisbon. None of it would have happened but for the events of the final minute of stoppage time against Aris.

Wanderers had cut it fine in Europe before – scoring twice late on to beat Lokomotiv Plovdiv, and equalising in the 88th minute at Vitoria Guimaraes. But never before had they cut it quite this fine.

After the glory of the draw in Bayern Munich, and a Premier League victory over Manchester United, Wanderers almost came crashing down to earth with a painful thud against Aris. It seemed a world away from that night at the Allianz Arena – almost hard to believe that this was the same competition, the same group, the same aim that Wanderers had been fighting for in Munich just three weeks earlier. After taking 4,000 supporters to Germany, all of a sudden very few people were interested in the UEFA Cup again.

A crowd of only 10,848 had seen Wanderers draw at home to Braga in their opening group game. Aris brought 1,500 supporters to the Reebok, and yet the attendance dropped further to 10,229 – Wanderers' lowest European gate. How could a competition that had provided one of the greatest moments in the club's history three weeks previously now be so irrelevant?

Even for league games home gates had been falling alarmingly, such had been Wanderers' poor start to the season. Having played in front of 66,000 in their last UEFA Cup match, Bolton now ran out to a stadium that was little more than a third full.

Despite the Bayern result, Bolton had only two points from their first two group games and knew they needed to beat Aris to give themselves a realistic chance of progressing to the last 32. They could not afford to squander another home game after failing to beat Braga at the Reebok. Had they played like they did in Munich, there would have been no problem against Aris. But they did not play like they did in Munich.

The bottom seeds, Aris had been predicted to be the whipping boys of Group F but Wanderers soon discovered that, like Braga, they were not without ability.

Aris hailed from Greece's second city, Thessaloniki, 200 miles north of Athens. With an urban population of close to one million, it is a pleasant sun-drenched city in summer, overlooking the Thermaic Gulf and filled with monuments from its days as an important settlement in the Byzantine Empire.

Aris were one of three Greek top flight teams from Thessaloniki, together with rivals PAOK and Iraklis. PAOK had enjoyed more recent success and were maybe better known in England after knocking Arsenal out of the UEFA Cup in 1998. But Aris had more league titles to their name – three to PAOK's two, even if the last had been in 1946.

The club was named after Ares, the god of war, who is depicted on the club's badge. The name was chosen because the club was founded shortly after the two Balkan Wars, when Greece fought the Ottoman Empire before doing battle with Bulgaria.

Their home ground, the Kleanthis Vikelides Stadium, is bedecked in bright yellow and black, the club's colours, and named after Aris' most famous player, who helped them to two league titles. The last came only two years after the city had been liberated from the Nazis.

Aris lost to Chelsea in the UEFA Cup Winners' Cup in 1970 and Bobby Robson's Ipswich in the UEFA Cup 10 years later, although they did famously defeat Benfica in 1979.

Financial troubles saw them slide to the brink of bankruptcy though, and they were relegated in 1997. They bounced straight back and briefly played in the UEFA Cup in 1999, 2003 and 2005 before they went down again in 2006. From there, their revival was swift. After immediate promotion back to the Greek Superleague they finished in fourth place in their first season back in the top flight, qualifying for the 2007/08 UEFA Cup.

They were major underdogs against Real Zaragoza in the first round, but a 1-0 win in Greece was followed by a 2-1 defeat in Spain – enough for them to progress on away goals. Cheered on by a vociferous support, Aris' 3-0 win over Red Star Belgrade in their opening group game extended their unbeaten run to 18 home matches in Europe, stretching back to 1968. Their away record was a real contrast, though, having lost 13 of their previous 18 European matches on their travels.

They arrived at the Reebok again fourth in the Greek top flight – behind only traditional powerhouses AEK Athens, Panathinaikos and Olympiakos. Their boss, the Bosnian Serb Dusan Bajevic, had taken charge at the start of the season but had gained a reputation as a somewhat temperamental character – having left not one but two managerial jobs DURING matches.

A former Yugoslavia international striker who had scored a hat-trick in the 9-0 win over the hopeless Zaire at the 1974 World Cup, he had success at the start of his managerial career with AEK Athens but then angered their supporters by joining fierce rivals Olympiakos. It was little surprise, perhaps, that when he returned for a second spell at AEK in 2002, his relationship with fans was difficult. Upset with the abuse he was receiving from a section of the club's support, Bajevic simply left the dugout and resigned during the first half of a match against Iraklis.

He returned to Olympiakos again, helping to lure Rivaldo to the club in 2004 after the Brazilian star's move to Bolton had infamously collapsed. From there Bajevic moved to Red Star Belgrade, but a slide in form resulted in fans putting a brick through his car window. Weeks later, as fans chanted for Bajevic's exit as they trailed 2-0 to Vojvodina, the manager again left the dugout midway through the match and quit.

Bajevic did not have to wait long before he was offered the Aris job and no doubt relished the 3-0 win over his old club Red Star. Aris did not have many well-known names and were missing injured striker Sakis Papazoglou, who had come off the bench to score twice in that game.

But the Greeks did have a number of talented technical players. Among them were former Barcelona B duo Javito and Toni Calvo as well as fellow Spaniard Koke, who had been on Marseille's books in 2006 but missed their UEFA Cup tie with Bolton after being loaned to Sporting Lisbon. Aris also had Brazilians Neto and Diogo Siston in their squad, as well as the impressive Bolivian midfielder Nacho Garcia.

In central defence was Avraam Papadopoulos, who would go on to star for Olympiakos and Greece, as well as the composed Brazilian Ronaldo Guiaro. In goal was Kostas Chalkias, a Greek international but a disaster in a brief spell at Portsmouth when he was maligned for his unpredictability – not an ideal quality for a keeper.

Bizarrely, Aris had to make the trip to Bolton without Albanian defender Kristi Vangjeli and Serbian midfielder Vladimir Ivic after it was discovered at the last minute that neither had the necessary visas to travel to England.

Bolton boss Megson made four changes from the side that had beaten Manchester United in their last league match to finally climb out of the relegation zone. Ivan Campo's omission was again enforced but Ricardo Gardner was rested, with Nicolas Anelka and El-Hadji Diouf starting on the bench. In came Gerald Cid, Gavin McCann, Christian Wilhelmsson and Stelios Giannakopoulos. The manager's priority remained the Premier League.

"When I took over it was stressed to me in no uncertain terms that the priority had to be to try and stay up," Megson said. "It was stressed that with the finance available in the Premier League, we had to make sure we were still there for the season afterwards. It would have been lovely to join a club who were in the top half of the Premier League and we'd be able to play the first team on a Thursday night in Europe and then compete on a Sunday in the Premier League, but that wasn't the case.

"When I first came into the club I also knew that Anelka was being sold in January. I wasn't particularly in on who he would be signing for, but it was made obvious to me, something I appreciated, that Nicolas would be leaving at the beginning of January. He was the top scorer, so we had to try and get as much done with Nic in the Premier League in that period up to January, because it was only going to get harder after that."

Despite Wanderers' poor start to the season, Anelka had surprisingly signed a new four-year contract with the club at the end of August. Looking frustrated at times in a team that could not match his own ability, speculation about his future continued and Chelsea completed a £15m deal early in the January transfer window.

The Aris match – shown live on Channel Five – would be Anelka's last UEFA Cup appearance for the club, but Wanderers were already trailing by the time he was introduced from the bench.

Megson had showed a certain amount of sentiment however, by handing a start to Stelios against a club from his home country. The Greek wide man had signed for Wanderers in 2003 after winning seven consecutive league titles with Olympiakos – three of which had come under the management of Bajevic.

Stelios was part of the Wanderers team that reached the Carling Cup final in his first season at the club. Then, against all the odds, in the summer of 2004 he helped Greece to win the European Championships, featuring in the starting line-up for the final victory over Portugal. After beating the Czech Republic in the semi finals, he had been joined on the pitch for the celebrations by his son who was wearing a Bolton shirt. In return, many Wanderers fans donned Greece shirts at the start of the new season. A bond had been formed between player and supporters.

"Even in my dreams I couldn't imagine that I would become a European Championship winner with my national team," Stelios says fondly. "It was something unbelievable, every word you can use is very poor, you cannot describe what the feelings were at that time.

"But the most unbelievable thing was the reception I received when I got back to the club. I had been given extra time off to have some rest and the fans, the players, the staff, the manager were all waiting for me to come back. I had an unbelievable reception and I will never forget it. I have very strong feelings for the club."

Briefly linked with a move to Liverpool, Stelios stayed and continued his knack of scoring important goals. Three times in his Wanderers career he netted in home wins over Arsenal. But by the first half of the 2007/08 season, now 33 years old, he had dropped down the pecking order to the disappointment of many fans. He had missed the beginning of the campaign through injury, returning to score the winner against Fulham in the League Cup. His only start of the season had been in the next round against Manchester City, and he was restricted to an occasional substitute's role in the league.

But Megson knew he was desperate to play against Aris, and hoped the motivation would be enough to spur an impressive performance from the Greek.

"Stelios hadn't been playing a huge amount because Dioufy had played most of the time," he said. "But looking at that game, I just thought that if ever there was a game where Stelios was guaranteed to play well and give it everything he'd got, it would be against a Greek team."

"When we got Aris in the draw I was hoping the game would be away," Stelios admits. "But it was a special game for me because it was a Greek team and I was playing against a couple of players like Avraam Papadopoulos and Kostas Chalkias the goalkeeper, who I played with in the national team.

"It was hard because I didn't have games in my legs, if you don't have games you feel a little bit out of form. But I wanted to show my manager that I deserved to get back into the team, so I had a very strong motivation. I gave everything."

Because of his affiliation with Olympiakos, Stelios was booed by the travelling Aris supporters who had virtually turned the match into a home game. Despite this being Wanderers' lowest attendance for a UEFA Cup match, the Greeks had brought more fans than any of the other eight European visitors to the Reebok.

Their 1,500 supporters, most clad in yellow, filled much of the lower tier of the South Stand and made their voices heard from well before kick-off, bouncing up and down to the rhythm of their chants. During the game, Wanderers possession was often met with whistles but their relentless singing livened up what could have been a pretty tepid atmosphere. The Aris fans made many friends that night, although that probably did not include the local stewards and police after their exuberance led to brief scuffles during the match.

Bolton started the game poorly, struggling to impose themselves on their opponents who were comfortable in possession and proving to be a better side than many Bolton fans expected.

Nicky Hunt said: "It seemed to me that the teams we got in our group stages were teams that you'd not necessarily heard of – obviously you'd heard of Bayern Munich, but Aris and Braga were really difficult teams to play against. Of course they must have beaten some teams to get to that stage but it just seemed to me that we got the most hard working, organised teams to play against in that group. It was a very tough game."

Wanderers also suffered an early blow when midfielder Gavin McCann was forced off following a clash of heads with Nacho.

"I'd cut my head in a game before that and then I headed it again and slashed my head right open in a different area," he said. "It was horrible, I had to come off. I was going to stay on but I remember the kit man saying, 'No, I wouldn't bother mate'. I think he could see the bone in my head. I had over 20 stitches."

On in McCann's place came Mikel Alonso, a starter in midfield in Munich. Koke and Siston put early efforts off target for Aris, but the visitors went ahead a minute before half time. Abdoulaye Meite could only half clear a cross from the left and the diminutive 20-year-old Toni Calvo superbly volleyed the loose ball past Jussi Jaaskelainen and into the bottom corner.

Now Wanderers were at serious risk of going out. If a draw would leave them with a lot of work to do in their last game in Belgrade, defeat would be all but certain elimination. Aris fans celebrated wildly at the other end of the stadium, knowing a shock victory would confirm their progression to the last 32 after only two group games.

But Wanderers almost levelled on the stroke of half time as Danny Guthrie's corner was flicked on by Kevin Davies at the near post and centre back Andy O'Brien somehow headed against the crossbar with the goal gaping.

Chalkias saved from Davies early in the second half as Wanderers switched to a 4-4-2, before Megson opted to call the big names off the bench – bringing on Anelka and Diouf. Meite soon headed just wide, before Nolan was similarly close to finding the target.

With Wanderers pushing forward, Aris almost caught them on the counter attack to make it 2-0 with eight minutes left. Nacho surged past Guthrie on halfway before looking up and attempting an audacious 45-yard chip to try to catch Jaaskelainen off his line. For a split second, it looked set to be one of the best and most inventive goals the Reebok Stadium had ever seen. But Jaaskelainen darted back and did just enough to claw the ball over the crossbar – just as the Aris fans were ready to celebrate their team's qualification for the next round.

Still the clock ticked down and no equaliser was forthcoming from Wanderers, who toiled away without the quality needed to really trouble Aris, for whom Ronaldo had impressed in defence.

That was until the third and final minute of injury time. Alonso launched a hopeful diagonal ball into the box and the Aris defence were left wrong-footed when Nolan failed to get a connection on the ball. Behind him was Stelios, cool as ever, to control on his chest and volley into the bottom corner in a flash. The visitors claimed offside but to no avail.

Stelios wheeled away in delight. Just as Ricardo Vaz Te had scored against Vitoria Guimaraes two years earlier, the script had been written for the Greek that night. Not only had he scored against his compatriots, but he had also bagged a crucial equaliser that saved his own club's hopes of progression.

"Whenever there was a cross I was always holding the back post position," Stelios says. "It was a cross from the right, I went to the back post, there was a gamble in the air from one player and the ball came to me. I had a touch and my second touch was the finish into the side of the net. That was one of my strengths I think, to be in the right place in the right moment. It was a very important goal and that goal threw Aris away from qualification."

For the first time, the Aris fans fell silent. Victory had been snatched away from them, and by the person they would least have wanted to score. Around 30 seconds from going through with two games to spare, now they knew they would have to go home with their fate still undecided. They never did qualify from that group, drawing at home to Braga before losing their final match at Bayern Munich. It was hard not to feel sorry for them. But without that equaliser from Stelios, Bolton's UEFA Cup adventure would have come to a meek end in the group stage.

"To score against a Greek club in the final minute of the game was a mixture of feelings for me," Stelios says. "I was very happy for my goal and my team, because we got the point from the game, but from the other side I was a little bit sad because I scored against a Greek team. But when you get your boots on you cannot think of those things, you have to do your job, you have to be professional and play for your team, and that's what I did.

"Olympiakos have a lot of enemies in Greece, so the boos at the start of the game from the Aris fans were what I expected. But I think the best thing was after the game when myself and Kostas Chalkias went to the fans of Aris, they clapped me. To be honest I didn't expect them to clap me but it was a pleasant surprise. When you get the applause of the fans, that's the best reward."

"Aris were a decent team, they were a bit of a surprise, but we were thankful that we got that goal," Megson said. "It was an important result for us."

"If we'd lost that game it would have been curtains for us really," Hunt admits. "It was just about getting the points on the board. It doesn't matter how you get them, scoring in the last minute, you've just got to get them."

As it was, a draw was still not a great result for Wanderers. In the other group game that night, Braga drew 1-1 at home to Bayern Munich, with Andreas Linz cancelling out Miroslav Klose's opener for Bayern. It left Wanderers sitting precariously in third place in the Group F table. Having drawn all of their first three group games, they now almost certainly needed to go to Red Star Belgrade and win. No British side had ever done that. But at least now there was hope.

Aris finished fourth again in the Greek top flight that season, going into the UEFA Cup once more. Having formed friendships on that trip to the Reebok, Wanderers travelled to Thessaloniki to face Aris in a pre-season match months later, as part of their tour of Greece. McCann scored in a 1-1 draw at the Kleanthis Vikelides Stadium. Around 50 Wanderers fans travelled – greeted warmly by their Aris counterparts, who seemed genuinely touched to be informed that of all the UEFA Cup visitors to the Reebok, it was the Greek supporters who had impressed many Bolton followers the most.

Aris' support was no less impressive on home soil, where thousands of fans gathered behind the goal to incessantly cheer on their team. The leaders of the ultras perched on the perimeter fence, backs turned to the match, choreographing every chant. If there has ever been a better atmosphere for a friendly match, I have yet to see it.

Wanderers and Aris had made a real connection that night in the UEFA Cup. In truth, Bolton knew they had got lucky. The European run could have been over there and then. Instead, further adventures were still in store.

Bolton: Jussi Jaaskelainen; Nicky Hunt, Andy O'Brien, Abdoulaye Meite, Gerald Cid; Kevin Nolan, Gavin McCann (Mikel Alonso 13), Danny Guthrie; Stelios Giannakopoulos, Kevin Davies (Nicolas Anelka 65), Christian Wilhelmsson (El-Hadji Diouf 65). Subs not used: Ali Al Habsi, Lubomir Michalik, Jlloyd Samuel, Andranik Teymourian.
Booked: Meite, Hunt, Giannakopoulos.
Goal: Giannakopoulos 90.

Aris: Kostas Chalkias; Neto, Avraam Papadopoulos, Ronaldo Guiaro, Nikos Karabelas; Sakis Prittas, Nacho Garcia (Spiridon Gogolos 83), Konstantinos Nebegleras; Toni Calvo (Javito 61), Koke (Anastasios Kyriakos 87), Diogo Siston. Subs not used: Marian Kelemen, Thymios Kouloucheris, Felipe, Marco Aurelio.
Booked: Papadopoulos, Gogolos.
Goal: Toni Calvo 44.

Attendance: 10,229.
Referee: Eduardo Iturralde Gonzalez (Spain).

Group F	P	W	D	L	F	A	Pts
B Munich	3	1	2	0	6	5	5
Aris	2	1	1	0	4	1	4
Bolton	3	0	3	0	4	4	3
Braga	2	0	2	0	2	2	2
Red Star	2	0	0	2	2	6	0

15

Welcome to Hellgrade

Red Star Belgrade 0 Bolton 1 – December 6, 2007

If anyone expected Wanderers' trip to Belgrade to be just like any other football match, the events of the weekend beforehand shattered those illusions.

As with Wanderers' very first European trip – to face a Lokomotiv Plovdiv team whose president had just been assassinated – Bolton knew before they departed for Belgrade that they were travelling to a place far removed from the sanitised experiences of English football. It was a place where all was not well, a place where serious violence could erupt at any moment.

The principal reason, if far from the only one, came from the internet reports that started to filter through from Red Star Belgrade's league match at home to minnows Hajduk Kula, four days before Wanderers' game in Serbia. The visiting side had just taken a shock 1-0 lead when a serious incident occurred in the home end involving a plain-clothes policeman. Nebojsa Trajkovic had been filming two groups of Red Star supporters, known as potential troublemakers, when hooligans recognised him and attacked him. They beat him with broken seats before appallingly attempting to force a lit flare down his throat.

Video footage of the attack, which soon became available on YouTube, was horrific. By now bruised, bloodied and burned, with his shirt ripped off in the attack, the middle-aged policeman fired several warning shots into the air, before his armed colleagues stepped in. Groups of fans then fought running battles with police inside the stadium, hurling seat after seat, flare after flare. Small fires burned as charging fans were pushed back. Think of the worst football riots of the 1970s in England, and this was up there.

Trajkovic's life was saved but his burns were significant after an attack that had taken place in the most public of places. Three fans were arrested over the incident and all later received prison sentences. One went to jail for 10 years for attempted murder.

The incident cast a shadow over Red Star, and it soon became clear that police were not only investigating the perpetrators of the violence but the club itself – believing more could have been done to prevent the incident from happening. Those investigations continued as Bolton arrived in Belgrade.

Hooliganism had long been endemic in Serbian football, and there were suspicions that the murky Balkan underworld was involved. Wider investigations in the country were looking at potential links between football and organised crime, with possible match fixing and transfer fraud other areas of concern. Red Star confirmed that week that they had made all of their transfer deals open for inspection by the tax authorities as part of the police's investigations.

The Hajduk Kula incident was far from the first time Red Star supporters had been involved in violence, in fact it paled into insignificance compared to what happened on May 13, 1990. Some still believe the events of that day played their part in starting war in the Balkans.

With communist Yugoslavia crumbling and nationalism taking hold in the region, Dinamo Zagreb met Red Star Belgrade in a top of the table league clash at the end of the 1989/90 season. Days earlier, in the Socialist Republic of Croatia, the first free elections had taken place since multi-party politics had been introduced. The new Croatian Democratic Union had defeated the communists – to the anger of the Socialist Republic of Serbia and their leader Slobodan Milosevic.

Around 3,000 members of Red Star's main ultras group – the Delije, or 'the Heroes' – travelled to Zagreb for the match. They were led by Zeljko Raznatovic, better known as Arkan, a Serbian nationalist who was wanted by Interpol and had considerable influence. He had escaped from jail in both Belgium and Holland during his days as a gangster and bank robber in western Europe – returning to Serbia to live in a mansion overlooking Red Star's stadium.

In Zagreb, fights took place in the streets before the game between the Delije and Dinamo's ultras, the Bad Blue Boys. Inside the stadium, the Delije tore down advertising hoardings and attacked their rivals with seats and knives, singing nationalist chants such as 'Zagreb is Serbian'. The Bad Blue Boys responded by storming the pitch, where running battles took place for some time, leaving more than 60 injured. Amid it all, Dinamo Zagreb captain Zvonimir Boban, a future star with Croatia and AC Milan, gained infamy for kicking a police officer.

The riots were the beginning of the end for the Yugoslav football league. In Croatia many still regard it as the symbolic start of the Croatian War of Independence, which began a year later. Then, Croats fought against Serb forces – including the Tigers, a paramilitary group that had been set up by Arkan. The group was later implicated in genocide in Vukovar, a Croatian town near the border with Serbia where hundreds were massacred in November 1991. Many of the Tigers had been recruited from Red Star's Delije.

Nationalism had reached such fervency by March 1992 that fierce Belgrade rivals Red Star and Partizan put football hatred to one side in a derby match between the two teams, when the Tigers made a surprise appearance inside the stadium holding up road signs. They said '20 miles to Vukovar', '10 miles to Vukovar' and 'welcome to Vukovar', before more signs were displayed of further Croatian towns that had fallen to the Serbian army. Arkan, the director of the Red Star supporters association, soon appeared to applause from both sets of fans. It was a chilling illustration of how powerful Serbia's football hooligans had become.

The war with Croatia ended in 1995, the same year in which the bloody conflict in Bosnia and Herzegovina also finally came to a halt. Arkan was assassinated in the lobby of a Belgrade hotel five years later.

In 1998, Yugoslav forces went to war with ethnic Albanians in Kosovo. A massacre in Racak prompted intervention from the United Nations. When peace talks failed, NATO were authorised to bomb Yugoslavia. For 78 days between March and June 1999 the bombs dropped – many over Belgrade.

The NATO bombing caused substantial damage to the city. Among the buildings hit were the huge Avala television tower, the Hotel Jugoslavija, the Central Committee building, several hospitals and a number of ministries.

When Bolton arrived in the city eight years later Belgrade still bore the scars of war, quite literally. Just a few hundred yards from the central square stood the RTS building, the home of the national television station, with one section still missing following the NATO operations. Sixteen technicians were killed when the bomb fell.

The scars were not just physical but psychological. Tension and nationalism still filled the air. This was a place where the hint of menace had never entirely gone away. The condemnation of much of the world for their wartime actions had produced an 'us and them' attitude, at least for some. Visitors could be treated with suspicion.

We touched down at Belgrade airport, via Munich, on the day before the game. It was the route Manchester United had taken almost exactly 50 years earlier for a European Cup tie at Red Star Belgrade, which had finished 3-3 before the trip ended in tragedy at Munich airport on the return journey.

From the airport we took the bus through the suburbs of Novi Beograd, or 'New Belgrade', an expansion area of the city with tower block after tower block, some from the Communist era, some more modern. Novi Beograd was separated from old Belgrade and the traditional centre by the River Sava, which flows into the River Danube a mile or two north of the city. Floating nightclubs on the Sava were a popular venue for locals in the evening.

Pleasant bridges spanned the river but traffic-filled roads polluted the air with fumes from cars, some of which looked like they belonged in the 1970s. Trams, looking no more modern, added to the congestion on the streets.

In the very centre of the city stood Republic Square, where the national theatre overlooked a statue of Prince Mihailo, a 19th century ruler of Serbia. The square had been the epicentre of major demonstrations in 1991 when tanks were deployed on the streets of Belgrade to restore order as up to 150,000 people protested against president Milosevic.

Wanderers arrived the day before the game too.

"The hotel was wonderful, it was like a brand new hotel," says Russell Byrne-Fraser. "But right next door was this shanty town, which was little more than holes in the ground with tin huts and people living virtually in cardboard boxes. The contrast between the two was hideous, but everybody there took it for granted."

That evening Wanderers trained at Red Star's stadium, but the session did not go well. Temperatures around the zero mark had been expected, but the weather had warmed a little and the snow had abated for now. Instead rain had made a mess of Red Star's pitch.

"We couldn't train on the pitch, they wouldn't let us because of the state of it," Byrne-Fraser said. "Instead they found us a patch of grass, which wasn't quite in the car park but was in the furthest extreme of the grounds around the stadium."

If that was not exactly ideal, worse was to follow in front of the watching media, who were allowed to film 15 minutes of training under UEFA regulations.

"We pitched up at Red Star and I had to go and do a press conference," says Gary Megson. "They were asking what I was most pleased with in the short time I had been at Bolton. I said it was the spirit among the players and the determination to do well in Europe, and not be relegated, and that the togetherness of the players would see us through.

"Then we started training and the press could watch it, and within five minutes a fight had broken out between Gary Speed and Abdoulaye Meite. I'd just been talking about the spirit and then that started."

"They were swearing and at each other's throats," recalls Nicky Hunt. "It got split up and they were all right after that, but I thought what's going on here?"

The build-up to the game was turning into a disaster for the players, who ended up having their evening meal at close to midnight. The experience would soon be miserable for many of the fans, too.

Bolton had sold around 500 tickets for the game, with most fans making the trip with the club's official travel, wary of Belgrade's reputation. They would arrive on the day of the match, and a plan was agreed between Wanderers and the Serbian authorities that they would spend some time in the city centre in the afternoon before being transported to the stadium for the match, as was the norm for such trips.

Unbeknown to Wanderers though, that plan was about to change. After the attack on the plain-clothes police officer at the weekend, the Serbian authorities had become rather twitchy about the possibility of further violence. Only four months earlier, Red Star's city rivals Partizan Belgrade had been thrown out of the UEFA Cup after fan violence in a qualifying round match at Bosnian club Zrinjski Mostar. Supporters clashed with riot police and UEFA decided enough was enough. Partizan had already been punished for some form of crowd trouble in 25 of their previous 36 European matches.

The Serbian authorities were becoming worried that any further issues could see Red Star also thrown out of European competition, possibly leading to a ban for all clubs from the country – as happened with English teams in the 1980s. For a country with ambitions to join the European Union, that would not look good.

As a result, the police decided they were taking no chances and Bolton fans bore the brunt of it. After arriving at the airport, supporters were put on to coaches as planned and taken to the nearby Hotel National, which was little more than a service station by the side of the road. Rangers supporters had been taken there when they faced Red Star in a Champions League qualifier four months previously, but kept there for only 40 minutes before being taken to the city centre.

This time Wanderers supporters soon discovered they were there to stay. All day. They would not be visiting the city centre at all, instead being taken straight to the stadium just before kick-off. The Serbian police had deemed it too risky to allow Bolton fans into the city, fearing it may attract Red Star supporters intent on violence. Even Wanderers fans travelling independently who had the misfortune to arrive in Belgrade that day found themselves herded to the same place. The Serbian police were not the sort of people you argued with.

These developments were met with bemusement by those of us who had travelled the day before and were freely wandering around Belgrade city centre with no issues at all. The news came through via text just as we were walking around the old fortress in Kalemegdan Park – a place that Wanderers fans had been warned to avoid at all costs at night, but where supporters travelling officially with the club had been due to spend time that afternoon.

If police had concerns about fans wandering around that area, it was difficult to fathom quite why. As we walked around the park, we were joined by other supporters openly wearing their white Wanderers home shirts. Contrary to fears, they weren't being set upon by rabid, knife-wielding Red Star fans but mooching around tourist style in what was one of the prettiest parts of the city – on a hill overlooking the Danube, where barges slowly carried their cargo in the direction of the Black Sea. It was all rather tranquil.

Meanwhile, back at the hotel, rumours spread that fans were being held because Wanderers supporters had been stabbed the night before, either in the city centre or at a basketball match. Neither was true. Fans would be kept at the hotel for around six hours and anger began to rise that – having travelled all the way to Belgrade, most for the first time – they would not be allowed to see any of the city.

"The official line was that it was for our own safety and they would monitor the situation," remembers Dave Blackburn, then the supporters club spokesman. "But fans were getting more and more frustrated. Drink was making some braver and they were demanding to be taken into Belgrade. I had a walk outside to have a look around, and there were plenty of police with machine guns surrounding the place."

"What they had said beforehand was that they would get everyone to this place, but then they would be chaperoned into Belgrade," said club secretary Simon Marland who had worked on the arrangements for the trip. "Obviously they changed their mind on that, but what can you do? You can't argue with the Serbian police, what do you say? All they need to say is for safety reasons we're not going to allow it. Unfortunately it is out of your hands. When you go to places you've just got to fall in line. When in Rome do what the Romans say, not what they do. If you start arguing with them, there's only going to be one winner.

"The way the fans were treated was disappointing. That's all part of the enjoyment when you're travelling to Europe. It's not just the 90 minutes of football, it's getting there, having a wander round, having a bite to eat, seeing the place, and then you can tick it off, you've been there. All right you're really going for the game, but it's everything else too. Belgrade wasn't Munich so they didn't miss a great deal, but you still want to be able to say you've been there."

While Marland was otherwise occupied at pre-match meetings with Red Star officials on the afternoon of the game, Wanderers chairman Phil Gartside travelled to the hotel in an attempt to resolve the issue. Police were adamant that the fans were staying, but Gartside bought some supporters a drink on a day he remembers for all sorts of reasons.

"I'd been told to go and meet a guy called Dan Tana for lunch," Gartside says. "He was one of the vice presidents of Red Star Belgrade. He was a film guru who lived in America and had a ribs restaurant in Hollywood. He got me so full of drink it wasn't true.

"After that we got this phone call saying there were a couple of hundred fans stuck in a hotel and would we go and try to help? People had gone out of their way to support us, and it wasn't their fault they had got shoved in a hotel like that so you've got to try to sort it out.

"So we jumped in Dan Tana's car and shot off to the hotel and spent the afternoon trying to sort that out with the police. After that Dan insisted on taking us out on the town. I don't remember the game!"

Tana had been a player for Red Star before defecting to Belgium and signing for Anderlecht. He later spent time living in London and had a spell on the board at Brentford, but his fame is perhaps greatest in Hollywood. A character in the recent American TV drama The Newsroom was named after him.

In the hotel, some fans were not prepared to accept no for an answer as they asked police to let them go to the city. This was not exactly Alcatraz, but some were determined to escape all the same.

One strategy, to walk out of the main entrance while the police were distracted, or to wander past them while pretending to talk on the phone, was flawed from the start and ultimately proved unsuccessful. The Serbian police were wise to such simplistic tactics.

Those who put a bit more effort into it had more joy. Some edged out of the back door and straight into a car dealers. From there they casually pretended to look at cars before making their escape. This was not foolproof, but worked for some.

Others decided they were really going to go for it. They climbed up to the first floor of the hotel and coaxed their way out of a padlocked fire escape. They then darted through muddy fields, clambered over a couple of fences and through an industrial estate to the dual carriageway. This was the sort of well thought-out plan that deserved the reward of freedom, and that was exactly what it brought. A bus or a taxi was flagged down, and took them to the city centre.

All except for one, that is, who managed to escape and flag down a taxi. Unfortunately queries over the fare to the city centre led to a communication breakdown, and the taxi driver decided he needed to ask at the nearest hotel. Yes, that hotel. At that point, the Wanderers fan in question was spotted by the police and hauled out of the taxi and back into the hotel. Even worse, the taxi driver still wanted a fare.

Around 20 people did manage to escape to freedom, if you can describe the city centre of Belgrade as that.

There were problems for others who had travelled independently and were staying in hotels in the city, with police ordering some to remain in their hotels in the afternoon. We had no such problems, although we were not dressed in Bolton colours and sensed it was probably best to stop speaking English as we passed police officers on the street.

By late afternoon the plight of the Wanderers fans still being kept at the Hotel National had started to make headlines back at home. Eventually the police gave the go-ahead for the supporters to be transported direct to Red Star's stadium, which was situated a mile south of the city centre – only a few hundred yards from the stadium of rivals Partizan.

We made our way independently to the stadium by taxi. As the winter darkness fell over Belgrade and the stadium drew nearer, the daunting presence of riot police lining the streets grew stronger. Hundreds of them, looking ready for battle should the need arise. It felt more like a road into a war zone than the approach to a football stadium.

The official coaches dropped Wanderers fans directly outside the entrance to the away section, ready for their hasty passage into the stadium before any trouble could erupt. Locals had set up stalls with scarves and Red Star merchandise outside the entrance, providing the only opportunity for souvenirs that some of the visiting supporters would get. But police were not in the mood for any delays.

"They just wanted to search us and herd us in, they wouldn't let anything get in their way," says supporter Blackburn. "A police officer just pushed the stall over and made fans go into the ground."

Arriving not long afterwards, our instructions to the taxi driver were to make sure at all costs that he dropped us directly outside the away entrance. We did not know what dangers lay in store elsewhere. The message fell on deaf ears, and we found ourselves on the wrong side of the stadium. We approached the nearest policeman for assistance, but were ignored. So from then on it was head down, walk swiftly, don't talk English and hope no-one figures out where we're from. Thankfully we made it to the away entrance without problems.

Red Star's home was the epitome of a sprawling Eastern European football stadium. It was a vast bowl with a capacity of 55,000, but basic in every sense. Less than luxurious toilets could be found at the back of the stand along with a tiny kiosk selling drinks, but the facilities pretty much began and ended there. Rows and rows of red seats descended down to pitchside, where fans were separated from the playing surface by a large fence, a wide moat and a running track.

The stadium was opened in 1963 and once drew a crowd of 108,000 for a derby against Partizan Belgrade. It soon became known unofficially as the Marakana after comparisons were made to the famous Maracana stadium in Rio de Janeiro.

The Belgrade version had played host to many great games over the years. Johan Cruyff's Ajax won the European Cup there in 1973, and three years later Antonin Panenka's famous dinked spot kick gave Czechoslovakia a penalty shoot-out victory over West Germany in the final of the European Championships.

In 1991 Red Star dramatically beat Bayern Munich at the Marakana to reach the European Cup final in front of a crowd of 100,000. This was the great Red Star team of Darko Pancev, Robert Prosinecki, Sinisa Mihajlovic, Dejan Savicevic, Vladimir Jugovic and Miodrag Belodedici, to name just a few. They would go on to beat Marseille on penalties in a goalless final in Bari to be crowned European champions for the only time in their history. The Marseille squad had included Dragan 'Piksi' Stojkovic, the star midfielder who had moved from Red Star the previous summer.

Red Star had previously reached the UEFA Cup final in 1979, and 2007/08 was their 46th campaign in European competition. They had missed out on qualification in only six seasons since the European Cup and the Fairs Cup started in 1955 – and three of those occasions were only because Yugoslavian clubs were banned from Europe for political reasons during the wars of the 1990s.

Red Star had long been the giants of Yugoslavian football, although they were formed only in 1945 at the end of World War II by members of the Serbian United Antifascist Youth League. Their formation came from the remains of SK Jugoslavija, a club who had been dissolved by Josip Broz Tito's communist authorities after being labelled collaborators with the Germans during the war. Red Star won the Yugoslav League on 19 occasions, eight more than Partizan and comfortably more than any other club in the socialist state.

Their status as a continental footballing power waned quickly after their European Cup victory of 1991, however. Just as Yugoslavia was beginning to break up, so too was the Yugoslav League and that famous Red Star team. Prosinecki left for Real Madrid and the club's defence of the newly renamed Champions League ended in the group stage. When Yugoslav clubs were subsequently banned from European competition, it sparked an exodus of Red Star talent to Serie A. Savicevic left for AC Milan, Pancev for Inter, Mihajlovic for Roma, Jugovic for Sampdoria. The club never recovered.

They returned to Europe in 1995 but incredibly – given what had gone before – they would never again even progress as far as the group stage of the Champions League. Indeed they won only one league title in the first seven seasons of the new Yugoslavia League, now shorn of clubs from Croatia, Bosnia, Slovenia and Macedonia.

After the turn of the millennium Red Star won five of the next eight titles, but this was a much weakened league in a country that was renamed from Yugoslavia to Serbia and Montenegro in 2003, before Montenegro became independent three years later.

Red Star continued to struggle in European competition – save for a notable home win over Roma in the UEFA Cup in 2005, when 6ft 7in striker Nikola Zigic scored twice on the way to big money moves to Spain with Racing Santander and Valencia, and then England with Birmingham City.

Famous former player Stojkovic had returned as club president in 2005 and Red Star won two successive league titles under his stewardship. The second title put Red Star into qualification for the Champions League in the 2007/08 season, but came amid rising discontent among fans over the sale of star players. Dusan Bajevic quit in March of the title-winning campaign after a dip in form upset the club's notoriously feisty supporters, before he later took charge of Aris.

In Champions League qualifying, Red Star scraped past Levadia Tallinn on away goals but their second leg defeat in Estonia prompted another change of coach with the sacking of Bosko Gjurovski. In came Milan Kosanovic as Red Star faced Rangers for a place in the group stage. Walter Smith's side progressed 1-0 on aggregate with a 0-0 second leg draw in Belgrade. Red

Star's consolation prize for missing out on the Champions League would be a place in the first round of the UEFA Cup, where they beat Polish club Groclin.

Already falling behind Partizan in the domestic league though, Stojkovic resigned as president, declaring that he was 'tired'. A month later, after Red Star's opening games in Wanderers' UEFA Cup group ended in defeat to Bayern Munich and Aris, Kosanovic stepped down in the latest in a long line of coaching changes at the club. Expectations were greater at Red Star, who were supported by close to 50 per cent of the Serbian population. Sasa Jankovic, an experienced assistant, was given his first managerial job and with it the task of somehow reviving Red Star's fortunes in the Serbian league and the UEFA Cup.

In truth, Red Star – referred to by UEFA as Crvena Zvezda, the Serbian translation of their name – just did not have a good enough squad to compete at any sort of level. While Partizan had future Manchester City striker Stevan Jovetic in their ranks, Red Star's last true star had left the building when Zigic departed more than a year earlier.

South Americans Mauricio Molina, Hernan Barcos, Franklin Salas and Segundo Castillo – the latter eventually joining Everton and Wolves on loan – were not particularly impressive. Red Star's brightest players were perhaps Dusan Basta, a scruffy blond-haired right back who would later join Udinese, and the creative midfield duo of Nenad Milijas and Ognjen Koroman. Koroman had returned to his native Serbia after a brief spell with Portsmouth, while Milijas was a talented left footer who would move to England with Wolves two years later.

But even if this was a poor Red Star team, Wanderers knew they still had their work cut out if they were to get the victory they surely needed to qualify from Group F. No British side had ever won at Red Star Belgrade, and plenty had tried.

Manchester United were the first to visit in 1958, drawing in the final game the Busby Babes ever played together before the air disaster in Munich. Wolves drew there too but Tottenham, Liverpool, Arsenal and West Bromwich Albion all lost in the 1970s. Scottish clubs had fared no better, with Celtic, Rangers, Hibernian and Hearts all failing to win.

Leicester had been due to play a UEFA Cup tie in Belgrade in 2000 but the match was switched to Vienna because of volatility in Serbia following elections, with protests leading to the overthrow of president Milosevic days later. Red Star fans had racially abused Leicester players in that game and months before Wanderers' visit to Belgrade there was a reminder that some football supporters in Serbia still carried such abhorrent attitudes, as England's Nedum Onuoha was targeted during a match at the European Under 21 Championships.

Even Red Star's striker on the night they faced Wanderers, Nenad Jestrovic, had form in that department. Jestrovic had been sent off during a

Champions League match for Anderlecht in 2005 after directing racist abuse towards Liverpool's Momo Sissoko.

Wanderers' task of becoming the first British side ever to win in Belgrade appeared all the harder when news emerged of the squad that Megson had taken to Serbia, and the players who had been left at home.

Among those who did not even travel were Kevin Nolan, Nicolas Anelka, Kevin Davies, Jussi Jaaskelainen and Ricardo Gardner. Wanderers had lost 4-0 at Liverpool days earlier and Megson had decided to prioritise the forthcoming home game against Wigan, despite the fact that Bolton would be out of Europe if they failed to secure the right result against Red Star. It may have been the safe option with regards to Premier League survival, but in terms of UEFA Cup progress it was a huge risk.

Ivan Campo was again ineligible and was another to stay at home. El-Hadji Diouf did make the trip but was not even named on the bench. Megson admits now that he never planned to select Diouf but wanted to make sure that the Senegal star, known for enjoying the high life away from football, was not enjoying himself a little too much.

"We took Dioufy with no intention of playing him, it was just to try to make sure that he behaved himself," Megson chuckled. "I thought if he was with me I could keep my eye on him and I knew where he was, rather than him being back in Bolton and not knowing what he was doing.

"Dioufy was tricky to handle but he was a great lad. I know he's done things in his past that he won't be pleased with, but when you actually meet him and you know him he's a terrific lad. He wasn't difficult to handle in that he loves his football, but he was difficult to handle off the pitch because he also loves that as well."

"Gary Megson was a very good guy, I know a lot of people didn't like him, but he is one of the nicest guys I've met in my life," Diouf says. "When he took me over there I thought maybe I was going to be on the bench. But he didn't put me on the bench, he put me in the stand to get ready for the next game. It was strange but it was a good trip because I know a lot of people over there and I had a good time. My agent (Aleksandar Krstic) lived there, he came with his family and after the game I went to have dinner with him."

Just as on Wanderers' previous UEFA Cup trip to Bayern Munich, Megson was forced into a late change to his planned line-up in Belgrade.

"Gerald Cid had a really small cut on his foot that required one stitch," the Bolton boss recalls. "He had a fitness test and said that he couldn't play. I was absolutely amazed and I told him that he could play with it as I'd had worse cuts shaving. But absolutely no way was he going to play with that little cut.

"Then on the other side of the coin was Gavin McCann, who had seven stitches in one head wound and six stitches in another head wound, and he played. They were both on his forehead and the first thing he did was head the ball and it all opened up again. He played the rest of the game with his head bandaged but managed to play all the way through and scored. It just shows you the different mentality."

Cid played only once more for Wanderers, in a January defeat to Sheffield United in the third round of the FA Cup, before departing the club by mutual consent and joining Nice. He retired for personal reasons in 2010 at the age of only 27.

With six changes to the side that had lost at Anfield, Wanderers' line-up was pretty much unrecognisable – in more ways than one. Cyrillic is often the alphabet of choice in Serbia and led to a phonetic transmogrification of the names of the entire Wanderers squad. This had bizarre results when the locals then attempted to translate the names back into the Latin alphabet.

So according to some Belgrade newspapers and the scoreboard at the Marakana on match night, this was Wanderers' team to face Red Star Belgrade: Ali Habsi, Niki Hant, Abdulaje Meite, Lubomir Mihalik, Lojd Samjuel, Andranik Tejmurijan, Gevin Mekken, Geri Spid, Stelios Janakopulos, Danijel Braten, Kristijan Vilhelmson. Substitutes: Ian Voker, Metju Kesidi, Robert Sizns, Deni Gatrije, Nejtan Vulf, Zoltan Harsanji, Dzejms Sinkler. Sadly, absences denied us such gems as Nikolas Anjelka, El Hadi Diuf, Kevin Dejvis, Zerald Sid and Dzoi O'Brajen.

While Wanderers supporters had not exactly been made to feel welcome in Belgrade, the squad were not enjoying their visit either. Preparations could hardly have gone worse the night before, and there were concerns among staff that the whole experience could catch up with them when the match started.

From their arrival at the stadium on match night, there was no doubt about the hostile environment they found themselves in.

"It was the worst and the best trip in my career, all mixed in," said Hunt. "We'd been warned about the violence in Belgrade, that there had been riots before we got there, so we took quite a bit of security with us. But we got to the game and outside they were chanting and there were flares going off. You've never seen as many police in your life and we were thinking, 'Oh my God, this game is going to get called off.'"

It never got to that stage, largely because of the massive police presence in situ.

"It was like Robocop," remembers Gartside.

"When we went to set up in the dressing rooms the police gave us a dog's life and started opening boot bags and skips, chucking stuff out," recalls Byrne-Fraser. "The stadium was prehistoric. It was decaying, falling apart and the changing rooms were on the outside of the stadium. We had to go to the pitch under about 200 yards of tunnel."

The walk from the dressing room is one of the abiding memories for

McCann and Megson.

"It was a really long tunnel and either side there were soldiers or policemen, whatever they were, with all the riot gear, and none of them were smiling!" Megson recalls.

"I just remember all these fellas with guns," McCann says. "You thought, 'Right then'. It was a bit different from normal."

"It was the most intimidating atmosphere I think I've ever been involved in," adds Megson. "We'd been told about what had happened in their league game, that they'd put the flare in a policeman's mouth. The ground just seemed like a war zone. There were police with guns and body armour all over and you could understand why. It was really threatening and intimidating for everybody.

"It was worrying but more so on behalf of other people because as footballers and the staff we were cosseted, the organisation for games in Europe was fantastic. We'd stay in good hotels, we always had security wherever we went. It was more when we heard what had happened to the supporters before the game. They never got to see anything of Belgrade, they hadn't been treated very well. Really that was not on, but you could understand that the last thing the police wanted was another incident."

By kick-off a vocal crowd had gathered at the Marakana. It was probably some way short of the 45,000 later reported as the official attendance, perhaps 25,000 would have been a better estimate, but the home fans were making themselves heard.

The players emerged from underground and on to the pitch at the home end of the stadium. There the huge letters DELIJE are painted into the seats but by now the stand was packed with Red Star's most fanatical supporters.

Another set of vocal fans situated themselves at the far end of the stadium, next to the 500 Wanderers supporters who had been placed in the corner of the ground. Opposite the Bolton fans was the slightly more sedate main stand, which was not full.

The Delije arrived not just to support their team but also to make a political point that night. Wanderers' arrival in Belgrade came at a time when Kosovo were preparing to declare independence, a move fiercely opposed by most Serbs. Still known as nationalists, many years after their role in war in the region, the Delije unveiled a banner during the Wanderers match stating their unequivocal stance. It said simply 'Kosovo je Srbija' – 'Kosovo is Serbia'.

Like Wanderers' first UEFA Cup match of the season at Rabotnicki, English television companies were not showing the match live. Strangely, the only way of watching the game back in England was via German satellite channel DSF, who were screening the match because Bayern Munich were not in action on matchday four. At home we still had an old satellite box with channels from various countries so we set it to record for posterity. The only copy of the match we have is with commentary entirely in German from Uwe

Morawe, whoever he is. It makes for a random evening's viewing.

When the game started, Wanderers quickly found that recent rain meant the playing surface was not exactly conducive to flowing football. "The pitch was like a turnip field, there was no grass on it," said Megson.

Hampered by the surface, the match was not a classic. Uwe Morawe probably didn't regard commentating on it as the highlight of his career.

Red Star still had one game left after the Bolton match, away to Braga. But having already lost to Bayern and Aris, they knew that victory would surely be required against Wanderers if they were going to find a way out of the group.

Wanderers also knew they almost certainly needed to win. Defeat and their exit from the UEFA Cup was confirmed. A draw would leave them in severe difficulties, while even three points would not guarantee their progress.

But Bolton were always going to need time to gel, such was the number of changes Megson had made. This was very much a shadow team, with the front three of Stelios Giannakopoulos, Daniel Braaten and Christian Wilhelmsson all short of match action. Meanwhile, Red Star – in their traditional red and white stripes – were simply poor.

McCann, meanwhile, was having issues with the head wound he had sustained against Aris.

"I had the headband on because of the big gash I had on my head from the week before," he said. "I wasn't really supposed to head the ball. It wasn't that I wasn't allowed to, but I knew it wouldn't do me any favours because the blood would start pouring. At corners I had a job where I marked on the post. When the first few balls came in during the game and I did the first few headers, the lads were all laughing. But it was worth it to play in a game like that. I've always tried to play, if you're a little bit injured always try to play."

Keeper Ali Al Habsi was making his first appearance since his heroics at Bayern Munich a month earlier and was on form again. He kept out a 25-yard strike from Joao Lucas before getting in the way of a header from Koroman. Dejan Milovanovic had earlier fired a free kick just off target. At the other end Stelios saw a shot deflected wide and Gary Speed – captain for the night – also missed the target.

Neither side were really building much pressure, but on the stroke of half time Wanderers crucially got their noses in front. It was perhaps the moment that McCann became best known for during his time at Bolton, the night he scored in the Marakana. Maybe it was not quite up there with John Barnes, but McCann's strike proved crucial. He would become the first player ever to score a winning goal for a British club at the famous stadium.

Wanderers won a corner – greeted by whistles from the Red Star fans who had chanted throughout the first half in support of their team. Andranik floated the ball into the box and Speed headed towards goal. Stelios tried to divert it into the net but saw his effort parried by keeper Ivan Randjelovic. The ball rebounded back to Stelios, now with his back to goal. The Greek looked up and picked out McCann on the edge of the box. McCann's strike into the net could not have been any sweeter.

"We'd had a couple of little chances and then I got the goal," McCann recalls. "I just hit it. I remember Stelios teeing it up for me, he knew what he was doing and just rolled it back. He rolled it and I smashed it. It might have gone through someone's legs, then off the post and it went in. I didn't get many goals so when I did score I enjoyed it!"

Wanderers fans celebrated a goal they knew could be their lifeline in the UEFA Cup. They did not want to go feebly out of Europe at the group stage that night. Such was the club's league form, qualifying for the UEFA Cup again seemed a distant dream. If they went out now, that could be it.

Red Star supporters barely reacted to the goal. They just carried on with their song, hardly pausing for a split-second, almost as if nothing had happened.

Their side leading 1-0 at half time, Bolton fans came under aerial bombardment during the interval. Thankfully the objects concerned were nothing more serious than snowballs. Red Star supporters situated to the left of the away section gathered snow from the front of the stand, which had not melted after the recent cold snap. They lobbed their missiles over the fence separating the two sets of fans, but the incident brought humour rather than hostility from the Wanderers fans.

Given the undoubted edge to the whole evening, some Bolton supporters were perhaps rather brave to respond with a chant of 'I'd rather be a Croat than a Serb'. When travel advice was handed out for the trip to Belgrade, don't mention the war was probably pretty high on the list. But I think they got away with it.

Early in the second half Wanderers came close to making it 2-0 when Stelios headed into the side-netting. Red Star toiled away in search of an equaliser but frankly never looked particularly like getting it. Lubomir Michalik, who had played in the draw at Bayern Munich, was defending well to shut out the irritable Jestrovic and the forward was eventually substituted.

Right back Hunt was happy to use all the tricks in the book to frustrate the home side. "I love winding people up on the pitch and I was winding up their striker and their winger, and they were getting really annoyed," he remembers. "If I was kicking the ball out of play, I kicked it into their dugout purposely to really rile them. I love anything like that, although maybe Belgrade wasn't the best place to do it.

"The crowd were worse than Marseille, they were chanting and they could be intimidating. There were things thrown but I don't think it was anywhere near us. I think they were just doing it in protest because they couldn't believe they were 1-0 down."

The atmosphere was becoming increasingly flat though, with the Red Star fans losing faith that their team could get back into the game. Stelios and Wilhelmsson were using all their experience to wind the clock down by retaining possession in wide areas. Wilhelmsson perhaps had the best game of his brief and otherwise unsuccessful Wanderers career that night.

With three minutes left Megson brought on 20-year-old James Sinclair in place of Braaten for only his third Wanderers appearance and his first in Europe. In injury time, Sinclair nearly scored a stunning goal on the counter attack – darting past three defenders from halfway, before seeing his shot blocked. That really would have been a fairytale moment for a player who never represented Wanderers' first team again.

Bolton had already done enough to win though. The final whistle was greeted by jeers from the disgruntled home supporters. Wanderers had become the first British side ever to win at Red Star Belgrade. Not only that, but they had knocked the 1991 European champions out of the UEFA Cup. Wanderers fans bounced in joy before players darted over to them to celebrate.

"They were great scenes after the game," Hunt says. "We loved winning there. It was a great way to end a horrible trip."

"We had to win that game," McCann adds. "I don't think anyone backed us or thought we'd get anything, and I read after the game that no British team had ever won there. It was a good achievement.

"I think the game was pretty comfortable. I don't think Red Star Belgrade were in good shape at the time. They weren't obviously the great team then that they'd had in the past with Prosinecki and all of those players."

For Megson, this time the gamble of leaving several star players at home had paid off. Three months later in Lisbon that would not be the case, but the manager was proud of the performance his makeshift side produced in Belgrade.

"To go there in an atmosphere as intimidating as that and play as well as we did and win was great testament to the players," he says. "I was well aware that no British team had ever won there.

"I remember afterwards we were watching the video of the end of the game, when all the players went across to the Bolton supporters. They'd segregated the supporters and either side of the Bolton supporters in the corner there were about 50 yards with nobody in it. Abdou Meite still had the matchball and he had this massive terracing to aim at, to kick it to one of the Bolton supporters. But he sliced the arse out of it and put it into the empty section, where there was no-one to get the ball! The terracing was about 80 yards wide and he missed it. He got a bit of stick for that."

Wanderers fans were kept in the away section for some time after the game. Some minutes after the final whistle, Gartside made his way across the stadium to applaud them for their support, mindful of the experience many of them had endured earlier in the day. Another to emerge to celebrate with supporters was Diouf, a player who always knew how to win the affection of the fans. Often he would be the last off the field after an away victory, milking the applause and throwing his shirt to the crowd. This time he had not even been on the bench, and he was still being hailed as if he had scored the winning goal. Classic Diouf. He would be the subject of some banter as Wanderers left Belgrade, though.

"When we first arrived at Belgrade airport, as usual Dioufy had the big glasses on and I won't say he was being mobbed but he had a little bit of fuss around him and he was making the most of it," Byrne-Fraser chuckles. "We got to the hotel and he was saying how he was twice African player for the year and everyone knew him, banging on about it.

"In the end Gavin McCann scored the winning goal and on the way out of Belgrade all you could hear was these Serbian people shouting, 'McCann, McCann'. You'd never even realise Gavin was a player half of the time, he just hides at the back and tries to get on with it. But they were making a big fuss of him and I remember as he was signing autographs for everyone he was caning Dioufy, telling him, 'Not so famous now!'"

The celebrations of players and fans were slightly dampened by news from Greece. Victory for Wanderers in Belgrade left them with six points, having won one and drawn three of their four matches – exactly the same record as they had when they progressed from the group stage two years earlier. Having been in grave danger of going out, they now actually topped the group ahead of Bayern Munich. Bolton's win would be enough to confirm their qualification there and then, unless Aris' home match against Braga that night ended in a draw. Unfortunately, it did. Ronaldo Guiaro's equaliser cancelled out Andreas Linz's goal for Braga and the game finished 1-1.

Wanderers would have to wait until the final matchday of the group, when they were not in action, to find out if they would qualify. Only an unlikely set of results – a draw for Aris at Bayern Munich, combined with a win for Braga at home to Red Star – would eliminate Wanderers. But fans still travelled back to England not knowing whether they may be returning home from Europe for the last time.

Before the squad left the day after the game, they had a special visitor. Serbian playmaker Sasa Curcic became a hero with Wanderers fans during his one and only season with the club in the 1995/96 campaign. Although Bolton were relegated from the Premier League that year, his skills and stunning solo goals dazzled supporters before he left for Aston Villa.

Curcic remained a follower of Wanderers' progress and would have enjoyed their victory over Red Star, having played for their rivals Partizan during his younger days.

He returned to his native Belgrade in 2000 and retired at the age of 29, having fallen out of love with the game, but his colourful personality kept him in the public eye. Like Diouf, he enjoyed the nightlife.

Curcic once said – possibly only partially in jest – that he would not return to football even if he was offered 15 million dollars, but would consider it if he was offered 15 women from all around the world.

Months before Wanderers' visit to Belgrade, Curcic had been crowned the winner of the Serbian Celebrity Big Brother programme, Veliki Brat.

"Sasa Curcic turned up at the hotel before we went home," McCann remembers. "He was buzzing and he was speaking to the lads. He'd just won the Serbian Big Brother so he was famous over there! I'd never met him before but he was laughing and joking and a bit of a character."

While Wanderers received a visit from Curcic on the morning after the game, Red Star officials received a visit from the police in connection with the riots at the match against Hajduk Kula days earlier. The club's headquarters were raided and Red Star's secretary general, security commissioner and stadium director were all detained, together with the match delegate from the Kula fixture, as police looked at whether more could have been done to stop the violence. The quartet were questioned for several days before eventually being released.

Wider political issues also rumbled on. Four days after the Wanderers match, a UN deadline expired for an agreement to be reached on the future of Kosovo. Two months later, Kosovo declared independence, sparking widescale demonstrations and rioting in Belgrade. The US embassy was set ablaze, while a McDonald's restaurant just yards from the hotel where we had been staying was trashed, together with a number of shops.

In 2009, the dangers posed to football fans visiting Belgrade were spelled out in the worst possible way. Immediately after Wanderers' experience in the city, the Football Supporters Federation had issued a statement questioning whether UEFA should ask teams to play in Belgrade if the safety of fans could not be guaranteed in the city. Those fears were borne out when Toulouse travelled to play a Europa League match against Partizan Belgrade, and a French supporter was attacked in an Irish pub in the city centre by a 30-strong group armed with iron bars and baseball bats. Days later, he died from his injuries in hospital. Two other Toulouse fans were injured in the attack. Many Wanderers supporters may have been unhappy to have been kept out of the centre of Belgrade, but Toulouse's experience was far worse.

A month after their defeat to Bolton, Red Star signed Ivan Trickovski – the striker who had terrorised Wanderers at Rabotnicki – in a bid to turn around their fortunes. It made little difference and Partizan won the league as they started a long run of consecutive titles. Jankovic, Red Star's coach, was sacked at the end of the season.

Bolton: Ali Al Habsi; Nicky Hunt, Abdoulaye Meite, Lubomir Michalik, Jlloyd Samuel; Andranik Teymourian, Gavin McCann, Gary Speed; Stelios

Giannakopoulos, Daniel Braaten (James Sinclair 87), Christian Wilhelmsson. Subs not used: Ian Walker, Matthew Cassidy, Robert Sissons, Nathan Woolfe, Danny Guthrie, Zoltan Harsanyi.
Booked: McCann.
Goal: McCann 45.

Red Star Belgrade: Ivan Randjelovic; Dusan Basta, Djordje Tutoric, Milos Bajalica, Grzegorz Bronowicki (Dusan Andjelkovic 80); Dejan Milovanovic, Joao Lucas, Nenad Milijas (Igor Burzanovic 73); Mauricio Molina; Ognjen Koroman; Nenad Jestrovic (Filip Djordjevic 64). Subs not used: Zoran Banovic, Vladimir Djordjevic, Milanko Raskovic, Segundo Castillo.
Booked: Koroman.

Official attendance: 45,000.
Referee: Paul Allaerts (Belgium).

Group F	P	W	D	L	F	A	Pts
Bolton	4	1	3	0	5	4	6
B Munich	3	1	2	0	6	5	5
Aris	3	1	2	0	5	2	5
Braga	3	0	3	0	3	3	3
Red Star	3	0	0	3	2	7	0

Wanderers learned their qualification fate two weeks later, when other sides in Group F played their final matches. Bolton fans could only watch and wait at home, trying to follow events via the internet.

When Braga took an 11th-minute lead at home to the already eliminated Red Star thanks to a goal from Roland Linz, Wanderers were briefly looking at the nightmare scenario. As things stood, Bolton would slip from first to fourth in the group, and go out on goal difference.

Wanderers had drawn at Bayern, so could Aris do the same? In the end, thankfully the answer was emphatically no. A full-strength Bayern were in no mood to risk the home defeat that would have signalled an embarrassing exit for the tournament favourites, and they were ahead at the Allianz after 25 minutes through Luca Toni. The Italian scored twice more to complete his hat-trick just after the hour mark, and Wanderers could start to celebrate a place in the last 32. Aris would not be getting the point they needed. Toni scored his fourth before Christian Lell and Philipp Lahm made the final score 6-0.

As Wender added a second goal for Braga against Red Star, Aris were out

– three weeks after they had been seconds away from qualifying with two games to spare at the Reebok.

Bayern's victory saw them take top spot in the final group table, with Braga's 2-0 win enough for them to finish second. Wanderers would take third place, where they had finished in their group in 2005. It would mean another potentially tricky last 32 clash when the draw was made at UEFA headquarters. But Wanderers would worry about that later. They were through, still in Europe after Christmas for a second time. Fans could start planning yet another UEFA Cup away day. The European tour lived on.

Group F	P	W	D	L	F	A	Pts
B Munich	4	2	2	0	12	5	8
Braga	4	1	3	0	5	3	6
Bolton	4	1	3	0	5	4	6
Aris	4	1	2	1	5	8	5
Red Star	4	0	0	4	2	9	0

16

The Forgotten Triumph

Bolton 1 Atletico Madrid 0 – February 14, 2008

Norwich beating Bayern Munich. Fulham defeating Juventus. Ipswich beating Inter Milan. Middlesbrough overcoming Roma. Not often in recent years has an English club gone into a European match as a genuine underdog. Rarer still has that underdog actually won against any of the most famous names of European football.

Wanderers' victory over Atletico Madrid deserves to be mentioned on that list. Atletico have long been one of the giants of the Spanish game – reminding everyone of that in 2014 by beating Barcelona and Real Madrid to the La Liga title and then coming within two minutes of winning the Champions League. For Bolton, just being in Europe was an achievement. What happened at the Reebok Stadium in February 2008 should be regarded as one of the greatest nights in the club's history, and one of the biggest giant-killing acts by an English club for many years.

But try to find video footage of the match and you'll struggle. It is virtually inconceivable in an era when football's every move is documented in the minutest detail. Bolton really did beat Atletico Madrid, and hardly anyone outside of the town noticed – mainly due to the fact that incredibly, the game was not shown live on television. Wanderers' matches against such European greats as Lokomotiv Plovdiv and Rabotnicki had been screened live to an often slightly puzzled nation, but Bolton versus Atletico Madrid did not make the cut. Television viewers could watch Atletico live on Sky in La Liga that weekend, but when they faced an actual English team the TV companies decided they had bigger fish to fry.

Channel Five instead screened Tottenham, who secured a routine 2-1 win at Slavia Prague that may just edge into 372nd place when they go through the list of Spurs' greatest ever European games. The Bolton match was shown live on Spanish television station laSexta, but this was not a great help to the average armchair football fan in England. Footage of the game in this country was limited to little more than a minute of highlights later in the evening.

But those who were at the Reebok that evening understood the magnitude of the achievement they had witnessed. It may still be the stadium's greatest night.

Wanderers' third-placed finish in Group F had left them having to face a group winner in the last 32, as had been the case two years earlier when they were drawn against Marseille – the side that knocked them out of the UEFA Cup.

When club officials travelled to Nyon for the draw, Wanderers' potential opponents were the Spanish trio of Villarreal, Atletico Madrid and Getafe, German clubs Hamburg and Bayer Leverkusen, or Bordeaux from France. Everton had also won their group, but English sides could not be drawn against each other in the last 32.

When Wanderers' opponents were selected, the card said 'CLUB ATLETICO DE MADRID'. The draw for the last 16 was made at the same time, with the winners of Wanderers' clash with Atletico facing Sporting Lisbon or Basel.

There were mixed emotions about being drawn against Atletico in the last 32. The Spaniards looked possibly the hardest of the options. They were not far behind Bayern Munich in the list of favourites to win the UEFA Cup. Wanderers' chances of progressing, and bettering the club's UEFA Cup run of two years earlier, seemed slim. But Bolton fans could hardly complain about the opportunity to see their team play Atletico Madrid, or a trip to the easily accessible Spanish capital.

As with Marseille during the 2005/06 season, Atletico had actually qualified for the UEFA Cup via the Intertoto Cup. They had almost gone out at the very first hurdle in late July, after a weakened side suffered an embarrassing first leg defeat to minnows Gloria Bistrita on a sunny Saturday afternoon in deepest Romania. Future Wanderers winger Martin Petrov was part of the beaten line-up in his last appearance for Atletico before joining Manchester City. Atletico had been 2-0 down in that first leg but Giourkas Seitaridis pulled a goal back and the Spanish side were forced to wheel out more of their stars for the second leg in Madrid, which they won 1-0 thanks to a strike from Diego Forlan. Atletico were through, but only on away goals.

From there Atletico went into the UEFA Cup second qualifying round, easing past Serbian side Vojvodina 5-1 on aggregate. By the first round they were in full flow, hammering Turkish side Erciyesspor 4-0 at home and 5-0 away. They made light work of the group stage too. After a 3-3 draw at Lokomotiv Moscow, they beat Aberdeen 2-0 in Madrid and then defeated FC Copenhagen and Panathinaikos to top the group.

While Marseille had Franck Ribery in 2006, Atletico's star player was also the next big thing. Sergio 'Kun' Aguero was little known in England at that stage but was already starting to make a big name for himself in Spain. Known as Kun because of a resemblance to Japanese cartoon character Kum-Kum from his favourite television programme as a child, Aguero had made his debut for Independiente in his native Argentina just days after his 15th birthday. It saw him break Diego Maradona's record as the youngest player ever to play in Argentina's top division and he quickly excelled, scoring some astonishing solo goals before earning a move to Atletico Madrid for a club record €23m. Such was his popularity, the Argentinian band Los Leales had written a song about him.

Aguero was still only 19 when the match with Wanderers arrived and his talent was obvious just by watching clips of him in action. Lethal in front of goal, when he picked up the ball he seemed to glide effortlessly past defenders. With a low centre of gravity, his dribbling style reminded some of the Brazilian Romario, others of Maradona. Aguero would later marry Maradona's daughter Giannina.

But the forward was just one of several star names in the Atletico squad. His strike partner Forlan had flopped badly at Manchester United, but returned to prolific goalscoring form after moving to Spain with Villarreal, and then Atletico.

On one flank was ex-Barcelona man Simao, one of the stars of the Portuguese national team who had also helped knock Liverpool out of the Champions League with Benfica in 2006 when he scored a stunning long-range goal at Anfield. On the other wing was Jose Antonio Reyes, once a big money buy for Arsenal in a deal worth up to a club record £17.5m.

The list went on. Atletico's captain was Argentinian Maxi Rodriguez, scorer of a goal of the tournament contender at the 2006 World Cup and a midfielder who would later join Liverpool. The Anfield link continued with Luis Garcia, who had returned for a second spell at Atletico after winning the Champions League with Liverpool in 2005. Goalkeeper Christian Abbiati was an Italian international on loan from AC Milan. Add in former Barcelona playmaker Thiago Motta and talented Spaniard Raul Garcia, and it was quite a formidable squad – although the latter would miss both legs of the Wanderers clash through suspension after being sent off for violent conduct during the group stage.

Atletico could even afford to loan out Portuguese star Maniche, the former Champions League winner with Porto, for the rest of the season to Inter Milan.

"When we were drawn against Atletico Madrid we were all thinking 'Wow', with the team they had," admits Nicky Hunt.

"It was a tough draw," says Gary Megson.

Atletico's history was impressive enough too, having won La Liga on nine occasions. Los Rojiblancos (the red and whites) actually started their existence in 1903 in blue and white kits bought from Blackburn Rovers, before a board member returned from England with the red and white striped shirts of Southampton eight years later. Atletico retained Blackburn's blue shorts.

They were originally known as Athletic Club de Madrid and then Athletic Aviacion de Madrid after a merger with a team involved with the Spanish air force. Two years later, after Francisco Franco had taken power in Spain, the dictator issued a decree banning football clubs from having foreign names, so 'Athletic' became 'Atletico'. The club dropped the Aviacion part of its name in 1947.

After league titles in 1950 and 1951, Atletico trailed behind Real Madrid and Barcelona for a period. But they became the biggest challengers to the great Real's dominance of the 1960s and 1970s, winning the league on four occasions.

In 1962 they beat Fiorentina to win the European Cup Winners' Cup before losing 5-1 to Tottenham in the final of the same competition a year later. In 1974 they reached the European Cup final, despite having three men sent off in the first leg of the semi final against Celtic.

They would lose the final to Bayern Munich in heartbreaking fashion – an experience that would be cruelly repeated 40 years later when they eventually reached the final again. In 1974 a goal from Luis Aragones, who would later coach Spain to glory at Euro 2008, put them ahead. But Bayern equalised in the last minute after a mistake from goalkeeper Miguel Reina, father of Pepe Reina, and the Germans won the replay 4-0. Atletico did actually win the Intercontinental Cup months later after Bayern opted not to take part, and reached the Cup Winners' Cup final in 1986 only to lose to Dynamo Kiev.

Controversial politician Jesus Gil took over as club president in 1987 and became known for ruthlessly hiring and firing coaches – among them Argentina's 1978 World Cup winning coach Cesar Luis Menotti and Ron Atkinson, who lasted only three months and was replaced by his assistant Colin Addison. Gil also closed down the club's youth academy in 1992, a move that resulted in Atletico prospect Raul switching to city rivals Real. The rest was history.

After narrowly avoiding relegation in 1995, Gil brought in former Luton player Raddy Antic as boss and spent big on the likes of Jose Luis Caminero and Diego Simeone. Incredibly, within 12 months the new look team had won the league title – a feat Simeone would achieve again as manager in 2014. The signings of Christian Vieri, Juninho and Jimmy Floyd Hasselbaink followed Atletico's title win in 1996, but they were relegated in 2000.

They returned to La Liga two years later, just as Fernando Torres was starting to break into the first team. Wanderers and Atletico did business in 2004, when Sam Allardyce brought in striker Javi Moreno for a brief and unsuccessful loan spell. Salva Ballesta and Quinton Fortune were among others to have played for both clubs.

A seventh-placed finish in 2007 was enough to earn Atletico a place in the Intertoto Cup before they reached the UEFA Cup to return to European competition proper for the first time in eight seasons. They had been rocked that summer though when fans' favourite Torres asked to leave and join Liverpool, departing for £26.5m. Forlan was quickly brought in as a replacement.

Under grey-haired Mexican boss Javier Aguirre, who had coached his country at the 2002 World Cup, Atletico had risen into fourth place in La Liga by the time they arrived at the Reebok for the first leg of their last 32 clash with Wanderers – putting them in contention to qualify for the Champions League for the first time in 12 years.

Wanderers, meanwhile, were still adjusting to life without star striker Nicolas Anelka. As Megson had been warned months earlier, Anelka was sold to Chelsea for £15m early in the January transfer window. His destination though, could have been very different.

"A couple of days before Nico went he said he wanted to tell me that he was probably on his way," remembers Russell Byrne-Fraser. "I asked if he had somewhere in mind, and he thought it was probably Manchester United. We kept it quiet, we didn't say anything, but he just wanted me to know in case he was gone, because when it happens it happens like that. I said to him, 'You can't get a better move than that'.

"Then the morning he left, Gary Megson called me into his office and said Nico was going. I said, 'Oh, is he?', doing my best to sound surprised. Gary said he was off to Chelsea and I had to bite my lip and stop myself from saying, 'You mean United?'. I think Chelsea just came in with something firm and concrete, but maybe United were a bit slow in getting the deal done, who knows."

Anelka had helped Wanderers climb away from the Premier League relegation zone before his exit, though. Three days after Bolton's victory with a weakened team at Red Star Belgrade, a full-strength Wanderers side had won 4-1 at home to Wigan. Anelka scored in that game and then added two more in a 3-0 home triumph over Birmingham. The Frenchman's last game for Wanderers saw bottom club Derby defeated 1-0, thanks to an injury time goal from substitute Stelios Giannakopoulos.

Also leaving the club in January were Gerald Cid and Lubomir Michalik, while Gary Speed departed for Sheffield United and Christian Wilhelmsson's season-long loan from Nantes was cut short. But Megson did add to his squad with right back Gretar Steinsson coming in from AZ Alkmaar and Matt Taylor from Portsmouth, each for £3.5m, while Israeli midfielder Tamir Cohen was brought in from Maccabi Netanya. Controversially, Wanderers' only signing up front following Anelka's exit was the arrival of Polish striker Grzegorz Rasiak on loan from Southampton. Sadly, Rasiak lacked the poise, speed, finishing ability or pretty much anything else that Anelka had possessed. Ever willing but much derided by fans, he played seven games for Wanderers and scored no goals.

Shortly before the window closed, however, Wanderers did significantly swoop to sign centre back Gary Cahill from Aston Villa for £5m. On his debut, Cahill helped Wanderers to a crucial 2-0 win at Reading but the club went into the first leg of the Atletico tie on the back of a 1-0 home defeat to Portsmouth. It left them in 15th place, but still only three points clear of the relegation zone.

Wanderers' UEFA Cup hopes were aided by the fact that an early FA Cup exit at home to Sheffield United meant they would have a blank weekend between the two legs of the Atletico tie, which were played within seven days of each other.

Megson admits that allowed him to field a stronger side in the first leg at the Reebok than he otherwise might have done.

"We could play the first team near enough because it was a blank weekend and that made it a lot easier," he said.

Wanderers were close to full strength, with the likes of Kevin Davies, Kevin Nolan and El-Hadji Diouf all starting. Diouf had recently returned from representing Senegal at the Africa Cup of Nations. Abdoulaye Meite was on the bench after also returning from the tournament. Cohen and Steinsson were cup tied for the UEFA Cup because they had already played in the competition that season for their previous clubs, while Ricardo Gardner was out with a virus and Heidar Helguson was again injured – having failed to feature in a single European match so far that season.

Steinsson's absence meant that Nicky Hunt returned at right back for his first appearance since early January, after the Icelander's arrival had seen him drop to second choice. Hunt's next four appearances would all come in the UEFA Cup.

"It was very hard for me as I'd been playing for three or four years," Hunt says. "The thing was I'd only just signed a four-year deal when he got Steinsson in. Although Sammy Lee gave me my contract, I thought surely the chairman must know that he's given these contracts out? But Gary Megson had a different direction for the club and wanted to bring his own players in. Managers either rate you or don't, and unluckily for me Megson didn't.

"But it spurred me on to want to be the best in every game I played. I was on the bench in every Premier League game and never came on, but I knew that if I kept myself fit and did myself justice then nobody could ever say to me, 'That's why you don't play in the Premier League'.

"I think I did myself justice in my European games. The results were good and my own performance was good, I thought. I thoroughly enjoyed playing in those games. I think Gretar might have been a bit gutted that he couldn't play in the big European games to show what he could do."

While Steinsson and Cohen missed out, there were European debuts for Cahill and Taylor. Under competition rules Wanderers were allowed to add three players to their UEFA Cup squad from the first half of the season. Deciding his third addition to the squad, Megson opted to overlook Rasiak and instead register Ivan Campo, after the Spaniard's shock omission by Sammy Lee in September.

Campo had missed six UEFA Cup games, but this was the perfect game for the midfielder to return in. As a former Real Madrid player, a match against their city rivals Atletico was always going to mean a lot to him.

"Before I got to the club they hadn't registered him, I don't know why, that was other people's choice," Megson says. "He was a little bit upset about it, as you could understand. But I really liked Ivan and Atletico Madrid was his first game back."

Atletico were missing Luis Garcia for the first leg, with the former Liverpool man serving a one-match ban for yellow cards picked up earlier in the competition. Motta was also absent with persistent injury problems. Most significantly, Atletico boss Aguirre decided to start with Aguero on the bench, to give the striker some rest after recent international duty with Argentina. It was a gamble, and a message that Atletico felt they could still beat Wanderers without their best player. In his place there was a start for Mista, with the former Valencia forward playing in midfield to allow Maxi a more advanced role.

Despite Aguero's absence from the starting line-up, Atletico still had more than enough talent in their team to make Wanderers' task daunting, with the likes of Forlan, Simao and Reyes all starting.

Hunt said: "When you're warming up and their team comes up on the scoreboard, you're thinking, 'My God'. Obviously it was a bonus when their best player didn't start the game but we knew they had world class players other than him. Reyes and Forlan, the keeper was an Italian international, they had an unbelievable team. But we'd experienced it with Marseille, Bayern Munich and Zenit. They had some good players when we played them too."

Wanderers had reduced ticket prices dramatically for the game, with season ticket holders gaining admission for only £5, while a child's ticket cost just £1. It was a smart move, following low attendances in the group stage, and it worked perfectly. While the Marseille home game at the same stage two years earlier had attracted an attendance of 19,000, this time the gate was 26,000 – the biggest crowd of the season and the highest for a UEFA Cup match at the Reebok. Most of the South Stand was opened to Bolton fans for the first time in the UEFA Cup, and a 'singing section' was created in the North Stand.

The atmosphere that night was electric. When clubs around the country speak about the unique atmosphere of European night matches under the lights, this was exactly what they meant. For the visiting Atletico team it was partisan and hostile – everything that Wanderers would need if they were going to get a result from this game. Bolton fans knew they may not get many more chances to see a match like this. Every attack was roared on vociferously. Inflatable 'clappers' had also been handed out to fans, who banged them together to deafening noise.

"There was a fantastic atmosphere that night," Megson remembers. "They'd given these things out to the supporters, I don't know what they were but they made this noise and the atmosphere was crackling."

"There haven't been many nights like that at the Reebok," said Davies. "We used to love that. The night games under the floodlights, you ask a lot of football players, it's just a different atmosphere. Those European nights, it was something new that the fans hadn't seen. We generally had a pre-season game, the last one, against a European team but that was a friendly game, it wasn't where there was something on it. This was a knock-out game as well.

"It's just the buzz, you finish the game at the weekend and look forward to playing Atletico Madrid. It's just something different inside you and you can feel it going to the ground. Playing in front of a full house is a fantastic experience. The atmosphere was amazing that night."

Atletico were well supported too, with around 1,000 fans making the trip to England. A little strangely, they were joined in the away section by around 40 Polish supporters wearing the blue and white colours of their own club Ruch Chorzow. Ultras from Atletico – known as the Frente – and Chorzow's 'Psycho Fans' group had been friends for several years.

But the visiting support was drowned out by the home fans from the opening whistle. Wanderers players had promised to throw everything at Atletico and they stayed true to their word. If the Spaniards thought they would be allowed time on the ball, within seconds of kick-off they found out that they were mistaken. Davies, who had set the tone right at the very start of the draw at Bayern Munich with a tackle on Marcell Jansen, did the same again. This time he charged in to win the ball from Atletico's Pablo Ibanez, an accomplished centre back who had played for Spain at the 2006 World Cup and would later move to West Bromwich Albion and Birmingham.

Davies' tackle nearly led to a goal inside the first minute, as Abbiati saved from Taylor. It was a sign of things to come for Atletico as Wanderers hustled and harried their opponents, who were starting to look shell-shocked, not knowing quite what had hit them. Cleber Santana, their plodding Brazilian holding midfielder, was dispossessed time and again. Wanderers also looked to expose defender Antonio Lopez, a Spanish international left back but playing out of position on the right, with natural right backs Seitaridis and Juan Valera both injured.

Campo was in his element, popping up all over the pitch, even on the left wing, with a strut and confidence in possession that suggested he was loving every second of being back in UEFA Cup action.

Wanderers forced countless set pieces, many of which were delivered dangerously by Taylor and prompted Atletico keeper Abbiati to do his best Superman impression. The shaven-headed Italian, with a hint of Uncle Fester about him, charged off his line at every opportunity to punch the ball clear in comically dramatic fashion. He looked like he had a disaster in him, but he managed to avoid it on this occasion.

Taylor, known for his long-range shooting, was still seeking his first goal since joining Wanderers and had three more attempts saved by Abbiati before the interval. Davies, too, was denied by the keeper. Bolton's pressure deserved a lead, but they could not quite find the breakthrough.

Atletico attacked rarely and when they did Forlan, booed by Wanderers fans because of his Manchester United connections, looked like he had reverted to the sort of form he had shown during his nightmare spell in the Premier League. The visitors might have wished they still had Torres at their disposal, with the former Atletico star cheering on his former club from the stands.

Atletico did produce one chance before the interval, with Jussi Jaaskelainen having to save well to keep out Lopez's header from a Reyes free kick. But undoubtedly the visitors had been rattled, as displayed when a first-half challenge from Diouf on Simao briefly sparked a melee. An obviously angry Diouf was quickly squaring up with Atletico's Mista. There were accusations of spitting, with Mista under suspicion, but it was later confirmed that no such incident had been included in the report lodged to UEFA by Danish referee Peter Rasmussen. Diouf says that it was words that had riled him as much as anything.

"We had a little argument and he called me something that I don't want to say," Diouf remembers. "But it's better to talk about the good things that happened in that game."

"We really got into them and they couldn't handle it," says Megson. "Some of the stuff that the manager and the coaching staff were doing was outrageous. They wanted Davo booked for just standing there, they weren't happy with what he was doing. Whether you like it or not, when you've got Kevin Davies in the team you've got to play to his strengths. He's big, he's strong and he's a handful. They just couldn't handle it at all."

Davies said: "We didn't hold any sort of fear towards them. We had confidence in ourselves, particularly at the Reebok where we'd been quite hard to beat over the years."

"The game was really fiery," said Hunt. "There were tackles flying in and off-the-ball incidents. There weren't as many cameras as you have now, so you could half get away it – stamping on people's toes and their Achilles, elbowing in the box, it was all happening, it was just one of those games.

"I think the focus we had in that game was fantastic, we were tough tackling, we were in their faces, which was what we should have been in the Premier League, especially at home. It just used to come out of us in the European nights, which made them extra special.

"It was just the pressing and the shutting down, they weren't used to it because in the Spanish league they get that much time on the ball it's frightening. They weren't used to people being in their face, the referee was giving free kicks here, there and everywhere and they weren't used to stop-start football, they were used to free-flowing play. We never let them breathe."

In the second half, Wanderers knew that they really needed a goal to show for their display. They had only been able to draw 0-0 at home to Marseille in the last 32 two years earlier, and ultimately it had cost them. Until Wanderers got their noses in front, Atletico would remain firm favourites to progress. Like Marseille in 2006, would this be another night when Wanderers had most of the chances, but just could not score?

In actual fact, the second period started in more worrying fashion for Wanderers. In the 53rd minute, Forlan fired in a snapshot that clipped the outside of the post. The last thing Bolton could afford to do was fall behind, killing all the momentum they had built up.

In the 59th minute, Atletico summoned Aguero off the bench, sending him on in place of the ineffective Reyes.

"At the time he was not really that known to us, but look at him since then," Davies said of Aguero, who would later move to Manchester City for £38m and score the dramatic late goal that won the Premier League title in 2012.

"He was a fantastic talent and they brought him on to try to change the game," Megson says.

Aguero did just that, and with Atletico's star now on the field, Wanderers must have started to wonder whether their chance had gone. The visitors were now starting to look dangerous going forward, finding Aguero and letting his dancing feet create magic. The teenager weaved his way across the edge of the penalty area before teeing up Maxi, who sliced wide.

Aguero's cameo would only last 14 minutes though, before probably the crucial moment of the tie. The Argentinian chased down Taylor, who was attempting to clear the ball near the touchline but was tripped by Aguero. Inexplicably, the Atletico star then spat in Taylor's direction. Whether it was actually aimed at the Wanderers player, only Aguero will ever know. The quick apology in the direction of the linesman suggested he was a little worried about what he had done. But it was too late. The linesman had already decided that Aguero had spat deliberately at Taylor. The referee was summoned and a red card was shown, to the delight of the home crowd. Arms aloft, Aguero reacted in disbelief, quickly joined by his team-mates. He could only trudge disconsolately to the tunnel, pausing for a second before being ushered to the dressing room by stewards.

"When Aguero got sent off we knew that was a massive thing for us," says Nolan.

In that moment the crowd, who had been quietened a little for a period during the second half, audibly lifted. They knew the momentum had swung back in Wanderers' favour. Atletico were down to 10 men and their star player would now be suspended for the second leg in Madrid. But Bolton still needed a goal, and they had only 17 minutes to make the most of their one-man advantage.

As it turned out, they needed just 19 seconds after play restarted. The home fans roared with extra fervour now as Jaaskelainen punted the free kick downfield to set Wanderers on the attack. Davies won the header and as Bolton pressed the loose ball a now panicked Atletico defence failed to clear sufficiently. Hunt picked the ball up on the right and found Stelios, on as a substitute minutes earlier. The Greek swung in a cross that Taylor headed towards goal. Pablo blocked the header but it rebounded to Diouf, who lashed an angled shot into the bottom corner from 10 yards.

The goal that never came against Marseille at the Reebok, and was starting to look like it would not come on this occasion, had arrived. Wanderers were beating Atletico Madrid. Atletico Madrid! Joy was unconfined inside the stadium, both on and off the pitch, as Diouf raced away and down the touchline to celebrate with assistant manager Archie Knox.

"There were a lot of people in the box and I just put it into the net," Diouf says. "Atletico Madrid were a tough team to play, they were one of the teams that no-one wanted to play at that time. To score against them was fantastic."

"The whole place went crazy," Davies remembers. "I don't know what the expectation was, probably over two legs that it would be difficult for us to get through, but Dioufy was one of those players who could win you a game with a bit of brilliance. He was pleased with that one and more than happy in the dressing room afterwards, he was going around saying he was the man and stuff like that."

Against 10 men, Wanderers even looked for a second goal. Atletico tried in vain to secure an equaliser, but they created little and substitute Jose Manuel Jurado's off target effort was pretty much as close as they came.

The final whistle was greeted by cheers around the Reebok. A 1-0 victory at home was close to the ideal result, and had given Wanderers a real chance of going through. Now they could set up for a draw in Madrid, knowing that an away goal would put Atletico in all sorts of trouble.

"The feeling afterwards in the changing room, you never forget that, all the lads were buzzing," Hunt said. "It's a great, great feeling. It was an absolutely brilliant night."

"We played ever so well on the night, I can't remember them having too many chances and Dioufy scored a terrific goal," Megson remembers. "It was a really good night. It was Atletico Madrid and they were in the north west, but they weren't playing Liverpool or Manchester United, they were playing Bolton and they were expected to walk over us. But I can't remember them getting near us."

Buoyed by the victory, Megson even made a cheeky attempt to sign Atletico front man Forlan after the final whistle.

"I remember speaking afterwards to Forlan because there had been a lot of talk about him and I was asking him whether he wanted to come back to the north west," Megson says. "He was a terrific talent, although he didn't really do anything that night. I did ask him whether he wanted to come to Bolton, but it was more tongue in cheek!"

Even for some in Bolton, the achievements of that night were quickly forgotten, overshadowed in part by the controversial events to follow at Sporting Lisbon.

"I agree, it's one that was perhaps overshadowed," Davies admits. "It was brilliant, what a result for us. It was one of the great nights at the Reebok."

Megson, too, feels sad that the result that night did not live long in the memory for some, including the national media.

"That was the only downside of my time at Bolton because I loved the club, it was a great club," he said. "But the focus was always on myself and the fact that the supporters didn't like me, the focus wasn't on that night because we were doing okay at that time.

"We were doing well in Europe but it wasn't on television and nobody seemed to show a great deal of interest in it apart from the people who were local to it, and yet it was a great occasion."

The rest of the country may not have cared, but Wanderers had beaten Atletico Madrid. Whatever followed, both that season and in the years to come, it was a result that could not be taken away from Bolton. It was in the history books. In 140 years of existence, perhaps one of the club's finest results.

Bolton: Jussi Jaaskelainen; Nicky Hunt, Gary Cahill, Andy O'Brien, Jlloyd Samuel; Kevin Nolan, Ivan Campo, Danny Guthrie (Stelios Giannakopoulos 59); El-Hadji Diouf, Kevin Davies, Matt Taylor. Subs not used: Ali Al Habsi, Abdoulaye Meite, Joey O'Brien, James Sinclair, Ricardo Vaz Te.
Booked: Diouf.
Goal: Diouf 74.

Atletico Madrid: Christian Abbiati; Antonio Lopez, Luis Perea, Pablo Ibanez, Mariano Pernia; Simao (Jose Manuel Jurado 72), Cleber Santana, Mista (Miguel de las Cuevas 88), Jose Antonio Reyes (Sergio Aguero 59); Maxi Rodriguez; Diego Forlan. Subs not used: Ismael Falcon, Fabiano Eller, Alex Quillo, Alvaro Dominguez.
Sent off: Aguero 73.
Booked: Reyes, Cleber Santana.

Attendance: 26,163.
Referee: Peter Rasmussen (Denmark).

17

Pain in Spain, but Wanderers Reign

Atletico Madrid 0 Bolton 0 – February 21, 2008

On the pitch, Wanderers' trip to Atletico Madrid was one of the best experiences during their two seasons in Europe. Off the pitch, it was maybe the worst.

With glamorous opposition and an attractive location, Wanderers' following in Madrid was sizeable. Even before they had defeated Atletico 1-0 in the first leg at the Reebok, they had already sold out of tickets for the second leg in Madrid. An initial allocation of 2,900 had been extended to 3,100 in the 55,000-capacity Estadio Vicente Calderon.

Travelling to one of the biggest clubs in one of the biggest leagues in the world, it was perhaps reasonable to expect no problems. Many travelled as families, keen to savour what could be Wanderers' last UEFA Cup trip, if the result went against them. Expats arrived from as far afield as Los Angeles.

There were early signs though that this may not be the modern enlightened football experience that most anticipated, and indeed had enjoyed at Bayern Munich. Bolton's chief superintendent Dave Lea warned before the trip that the Madrid police were 'very robust', 'not the most friendly' and 'do not take dissent very well'. By the end of the trip, we could certainly see what he meant.

The Spanish police were gaining a reputation for being rather unforgiving to football supporters after riot cops charged Tottenham fans during a UEFA Cup tie at Sevilla a year earlier. Spurs criticised the police for overreacting and also hitting a disabled fan with a baton, knocking him out of his wheelchair. Sevilla backed their protests, but the Spanish government blamed the incident on drunken Tottenham supporters. There were similar accusations of heavy-handed policing as problems erupted when Rangers visited Osasuna during the same season.

When Aberdeen made the trip to Atletico Madrid three months before Bolton – taking 6,000 fans with them, only 3,000 with tickets for the away section – 17 people had been injured in appalling scenes of rioting outside the stadium. Around 20 skinheads from Atletico's Frente ultras group, their faces hidden by scarves and balaclavas, were said to have started the violence by attacking Aberdeen fans outside a bar before throwing flares. Aberdeen complained that riot police had responded to the incident by attacking innocent Scottish fans with batons. One supporter was beaten unconscious and spent the night in intensive care.

There had been issues of racist chanting in Madrid, too, when England played a friendly at the Bernabeu in 2004 and Shaun Wright-Phillips was among those targeted with monkey chants. Spain may be a regular holiday destination for Brits, but their football stadiums were rather less welcoming than their beaches.

After an acrimonious first leg at the Reebok, Wanderers were left furious by Spanish antics even before they arrived in Madrid. A day before Bolton's flight into the capital, Atletico published Wanderers' entire travel itinerary on their official website – flight number, arrival time, training schedule and hotel location. Individual room numbers, supposedly the ones due to be used by the players, were posted elsewhere on the internet. Wanderers, keen to prepare for the match as privately as possible, regarded it as a serious security breach and made an official protest to UEFA as well as raising the issue with the British Embassy in Madrid.

Given their travel plans were now public knowledge, perhaps it was no surprise then that when Wanderers arrived at Madrid's Barajas Airport it was bedlam – particularly around one man. Ivan Campo was returning to play a competitive game in Spain for the first time since he had left Real Madrid for Bolton in 2002. As a Champions League winner and former Spanish international now facing Real's fierce rivals Atletico, he was always going to attract attention.

Campo had also been at the centre of controversy after the first leg against Atletico, after he had reportedly branded Sergio Aguero 'a fool' for being sent off for spitting at the Reebok. Atletico captain Maxi Rodriguez responded by demanding an apology from Campo, saying the supposed comments 'lacked respect' and had upset the La Liga team.

The Wanderers midfielder's distinctive hairstyle meant he never exactly blended into the background wherever he went, but he was a shy man and did not always like the attention. At the airport he was keen to escape the media as quickly as possible.

"When we arrived at Madrid airport, Campo just set off, weaving through people," remembers Gary Megson. "He'd been brought up with that and knew what was happening I think.

"Suddenly all these cameras and journalists were just trying to get to Campo – they weren't particularly interested in anyone else. I don't mean half a dozen either, there were loads of them. Ivan got on the bus and these journalists were trying to cram on to the bus at either end. We had to sling them off.

"Then one of them, I don't know who she was, I think she was something to do with a television station, said, 'Can I go and get Campo to do an interview?' I asked Ivan if he wanted to do it and he said no, so I told her no and she went ballistic with me. We just drove off but it was an amazing reaction to Ivan in Madrid."

Wanderers fans began to arrive in Madrid gradually throughout the week, with the Bolton presence becoming strong in the city centre as early as a day before the game. Some optimistically arrived in shorts as if they were on their way to the Costa del Sol in the height of summer, only to find that Madrid was a rather cooler 15 degrees in late February.

An impressive city with a population of six million, Madrid was the third biggest metropolitan area in the European Union behind London and Paris – and the fourth most visited city in Europe by tourists. There was plenty to see and do for Wanderers fans. The Royal Palace was a short walk from the centre in one direction, while in the other direction by the picturesque Buen Retiro Park stood the Prado, one of the world's most famous art museums. Nearby was another art museum, the Reina Sofia, which housed Pablo Picasso's famous Guernica painting.

For those supporters not big on culture, there were many bars around the Puerta del Sol, a pedestrianised area where stood a slightly odd statue of a bear and a madrono tree, an image that features on Atletico Madrid's club crest. In the afternoon a Mexican mariachi band, complete with sombreros and guitars, arrived to entertain passers-by. A few hundred yards down the road was another gathering point, the imperious and expansive Plaza Mayor, also lined with bars and restaurants.

The square had been constructed in the 17th century by the ruling Habsburg Empire. In more recent history Madrid had been the subject of a siege between 1936 and 1939, during the Spanish civil war, and had been the first European city to be bombed by planes. Madrid expanded rapidly during the economic boom years of the 1960s under the nationalist regime of dictator Francisco Franco, and consolidated its status as one of Europe's finest cities in the years after his death in 1975.

The night before Wanderers' match against Atletico, many travelling supporters gathered in bars to watch Champions League action – some joined by former Bolton cult hero Tony Kelly who had made the trip to Madrid with fans. Nicknamed Zico during his playing days, Kelly had been a sometimes bulky but skilful midfielder who had earned popularity as part of Bruce Rioch's successful Bolton team of the early 1990s. Back then Wanderers were fighting their way out of the Third Division, with Kelly scoring a notable solo goal at Wigan's particularly uninviting former Springfield Park ground, where away fans were housed on an old-fashioned grass verge.

It was scarcely believable that 15 years later Wanderers were now in Madrid to face the famous Atletico in the last 32 of European competition. Despite that obvious discrepancy in standard, Kelly was still being feted by fans, regarded as a hero in just the same way as Wanderers' UEFA Cup team. Supporters had not forgotten the players who had started the club's long and winding road to Madrid. Never shy of enjoying a pint and a chat, the continuing rapport he shared with Wanderers supporters saw him appointed as the club's official fans' liaison officer months later.

Many fans again arrived on the day of the game as part of the club's official travel package. Unlike in Belgrade, they were free to spend the day wandering wherever they liked in the city.

On matchday a large number of Wanderers supporters spent the afternoon taking a tour of the Bernabeu, the home of Real Madrid, a few stops north of the city centre on the metro. There they passed the time wandering around the club museum, which housed picture upon picture of Real Madrid greats – including past and present Bolton stars Nicolas Anelka, Fernando Hierro, Campo and, er, Julio Cesar.

By 2008 Hierro had become sporting director of the Spanish Football Federation and was in Madrid when Wanderers visited to face Atletico. Before the match he turned up at the team hotel to say hello.

"Fernando came to the hotel, I'm sure primarily to see Ivan," remembers Russell Byrne-Fraser. "But he said, 'Come on we're going to have a beer, I can have a beer now.'"

There were other visitors to the team hotel before the game, too, including one of the canine variety.

"Although he's not from Madrid, Ivan asked if he could bring his family down to Madrid to see him in the hotel," Megson said of Campo, who hails originally from the Basque region. "Ordinarily we wouldn't do that but because we were abroad and he was sub for the game, we said it was okay.

"Then he came up to me and said if it was okay to bring his dog into the hotel? I told him it was all right with me. I think if anybody was asked at that time to have a guess at what kind of dog Ivan had, you wouldn't have been too far away! If you say that dogs look like their owners, he was walking around this five-star hotel in the middle of Madrid with this big Chow dog, and it just looked like him with his barnet."

Greek supporters of AEK Athens were also in the city that day to see their side play a UEFA Cup tie at Getafe, who were based on the outskirts of Madrid. AEK fans were heavily outnumbered in the capital by Bolton supporters though, and would see their side lose 3-0 to go out of the competition.

As night began to fall, Wanderers fans started to make the short journey of little more than a mile south west of the city centre to the home of Atletico Madrid, the Vicente Calderon. Some travelled by metro, trying to avoid the pickpockets for which Madrid is notorious.

"When we first got to Madrid there were a lot of pickpockets and within 20 minutes one lad's wallet was gone," remembers Carl Crook, who had travelled with friends to support Bolton in the Spanish capital.

Those not travelling by metro made the trip to the stadium on foot, following a main road that dropped down a hill towards the not particularly attractive River Manzanares, next to which the Vicente Calderon was situated.

Bizarrely, a riverside highway actually passes underneath the main stand of the stadium, in a tunnel reminiscent of one you might see at the Monaco Grand Prix.

Anyone expecting a state of the art stadium was left sorely disappointed. The Vicente Calderon was basic, short on facilities and with uncovered two-tier stands on three sides of the pitch. The main stand had a roof and was a little smarter. Built in 1966, and soon named after the club's own particularly modest president, it was a venue not designed for comfort. Quite how it had been categorised as a 'five-star UEFA elite stadium' was a mystery. By 2008 Atletico were already talking of leaving the Vicente Calderon and moving into a renovated home at La Peineta, a stadium on the other side of the city.

The Vicente Calderon had hosted three games at the 1982 World Cup and over the years had seen visits from British clubs such as Leicester, Derby, Aston Villa, Manchester United, Celtic, Hearts and Bangor City. None had won there. Neither had Aberdeen, who had lost 2-0 in the group stage.

Problems started before many Wanderers fans had even got into the stadium. Many visited the myriad of stalls outside the away entrance selling souvenirs, drinks and food. Strangely, the matchday food of choice in Madrid was corn on the cob and sunflower seeds, the latter seemingly giving Spanish football fans the same diet as the average English gerbil.

Even gerbils probably would have received better treatment from the Spanish police, though. With large numbers of Bolton fans queueing to get through the old-fashioned turnstiles, the area around the away entrance started to turn into a crush in the minutes before kick-off. Supporters began to become agitated that they might miss the start of the game.

The Spanish police, who had been a growing and ominous presence in the city during the day, responded in less than helpful manner – wading in with horses and batons, aiming indiscriminately. It was a scary experience for fans unused to such a reaction. Supporters filming with their phones were ordered to stop by police.

"It started before the beginning of the game with the police horses," remembers Crook. "It was hard work getting into the ground because there were that many Bolton fans. You had to scan the ticket and go through, but it was hard work and then the police horses came running in. I think it might have all stemmed from a lad dropping his keks at the police. The horses went flying through the Bolton fans, so they just opened the gates.

"Even though we had tickets everyone just piled in and I lost my mates, I was on my own. First they put us in the bottom tier where all the Madrid fans were. That's where it all stemmed from, they opened the gates and everyone just steamed in close to kick-off."

When Wanderers fans did eventually get inside the Vicente Calderon, the large majority were situated in a strip of seats along the length of the pitch, at the very top of the upper tier of the stand opposite the main stand.

Segregation on either side was rudimentary, a small barrier and a line of riot police, with Spanish stadiums not accustomed to large numbers of away fans at matches. On the concourse underneath the stand there was no segregation at all, with home and away fans sharing the same facilities.

"The segregation was awful," remembers Dave Blackburn, then spokesman for Wanderers' supporters association. "I went down to the toilet, got a tap on the shoulder and was asked if I was from Bolton. This man proceeded to tell me, 'Don't worry, we don't fight'. But I went back to my seat and sat with my legs crossed for the rest of the game."

Those Bolton supporters who had bought the extra allocation of 200 tickets were strangely placed right on the opposite side of the ground, at one end of the main stand. Deep beneath the main stand, the Wanderers squad were preparing for the chance to make history, and reach the last 16 of the UEFA Cup for the first time.

"The atmosphere in that dressing room before that game was one of the best atmospheres I've ever known," Megson remembers. "It was a strange dressing room, you were in like a dungeon, in among all the offices. It was too warm in there, I don't know if they'd done that on purpose, but we had the music going, Dioufy was on form and everybody was just bang up for the game. It was a fantastic atmosphere in the hour and a half before we went out for the match."

With a Premier League game at Blackburn three days later, Megson made three changes to the side that had won the first leg a week earlier. Joey O'Brien replaced the injured Danny Guthrie in midfield, while El-Hadji Diouf and Campo were rested to the bench – replaced by Stelios Giannakopoulos and Gavin McCann.

"I'd been out injured for a couple of weeks but you want to play in a game like that," McCann says. "It was good because my cousin lived over in Madrid so she was there at the game."

Atletico had learned only a day before the game that their appeal against Sergio Aguero's suspension, following his red card in the first leg, had been rejected. Their star striker was out, replaced in the line-up by Luis Garcia, who had returned from a ban. Talented young midfielder Jose Manuel Jurado came in for Simao, who had gone off injured late in the first leg.

Wanderers emerged on to the pitch for the 8.45pm kick-off to strains of 'Atleti, Atleti, Atletico de Madrid', the Spanish club's official hymn.

Bolton knew what they had to do. A draw would be sufficient, and even an Atletico goal would only be enough to force extra time. Better still, an away goal from Wanderers and Atletico would have to score three. The likelihood was the winners would face Sporting Lisbon, who went into their second leg in Switzerland 2-0 up over Basel thanks to a double from Simon Vukcevic in the first leg.

The Atletico match was again not being shown live on television in

England, despite Wanderers' victory in the first leg at the Reebok. The home sections of the stadium were around half full.

"The stadium wasn't full but it was a really tense, tight atmosphere," says Nicky Hunt.

The home end became a little emptier after a worrying incident early in the game. Wanderers fans watched on in bemusement as violence erupted in the lower tier of the Fondo Sur – where Atletico's ultras, the Frente, based themselves.

The Frente often received economic support from the club, but had also been involved in violence in the past. In 1998, a Real Sociedad fan was stabbed to death outside the Vicente Calderon. Before a derby against Real Madrid in 2007, Atletico fans had destroyed at least 30 cars outside the stadium with baseball bats and fire extinguishers.

It was not entirely clear what started the incident early in the Wanderers match. There were suggestions that a flare had been thrown, or that it was simply due to long-running disputes between different factions of Atletico's hardcore support. Whatever the reason, Bolton fans found themselves distracted from a quiet start to the match as they watched the sort of scenes that were banished from the English game long ago.

Atletico fans fought with each other before large numbers of riot police moved in with batons, clearly in no mood to mess around. They charged supporters to the back of the stand, chasing some out of the ground altogether. For the rest of the game, the area of seating immediately behind the goal was left completely unoccupied, with the ultras who still remained pushed to each end of the stand. It was hard to believe that, in a city as civilised as Madrid, this was what the football experience was still like.

There was a more comical moment in the away section.

"At one point Tony Kelly stepped in to stop a fight between a couple of Bolton fans," says supporters club representative Blackburn. "One fan had been complaining he had a restricted view because there was someone sat in front of him with a huge Campo wig on."

The most significant moment on the pitch early in the game was a chance for Bolton, when Stelios fired in an angled effort that had to be smartly tipped over the bar by Christian Abbiati. Apart from that, very little was happening, which was perfect for Wanderers. Perhaps it was just as well the game was not on television, because in truth it was not one to entertain the neutral – not that any Bolton fan cared.

A 0-0 draw would do Wanderers just fine, and they had set up in solid fashion to protect their aggregate lead. Bolton were playing with a hard-working midfield trio and were well marshalled at the back by Gary Cahill. Without Aguero, Atletico were struggling badly to break Bolton down.

"They probably couldn't because we were so deep," laughs Joey O'Brien, one of the midfield three that night. "We had the goal to hang on to and I think we got hardly out of our half for 90 minutes."

"It was backs to the wall stuff, but hoping you could get a counter and hit them on the break," says Kevin Nolan. "We knew that a 0-0 would be enough, or if we got one goal they had to score three. It was as simple as that."

"We just dug in, it was a hard working performance," says Kevin Davies. "They found it incredibly frustrating, the fans and everyone."

"We said what we would do, that we would just sit and let them come on to us," Megson reflects. "We were doing okay and I can't remember them having too many chances. We were throwing our bodies in the way and making decent blocks."

If there was not much in terms of entertainment on the pitch in the first half, there was some on the sidelines involving assistant manager Archie Knox and goalkeeping coach Fred Barber.

"At Atletico the dugout was down below ground level," Megson remembers. "Archie wanted to get up and make a point but he didn't want to go to the end of the dugout and climb up the stairs so he tried to lift his leg up high enough to get some leverage. Bless him he was struggling, because he wasn't the youngest any more. His big fat backside was there so Fred got two feet and booted him! He shot out of this dugout like he'd been shot out of a cannon. We had a bit of a giggle about that."

Before the half was over Atletico did create a couple of openings. Diego Forlan headed wide from a good position before Luis Garcia missed the best chance of the game and a golden opportunity to level the tie. Forlan squared the ball into the danger area and Garcia looked all set to fire into the net, only to somehow blaze the ball over the bar. It was a real let-off, and a moment from which Atletico never recovered.

The home fans had been quietened, frustrated by their side's inability to cause Wanderers enough problems, although they were awakened by the presence of a former Real Madrid player on the touchline, prompting jeers and whistles from the stands.

"We put Campo on the bench that night and I told him to go and get warmed up," said Megson. "But he got out of the dugout and the noise... I thought, 'Jesus, come and sit down again because you're waking the game up a little bit too much'. Ivan warming up started to build the atmosphere up, after we'd managed to go and kill it. That was only going to help them so we sat him back down again."

By the hour mark, though, Megson decided to introduce Campo for McCann, tiring on his return from injury. Diouf also came on for Stelios. Both substitutes were greeted by a rapturous reception from the away section – but boos from the rest of the ground. Their arrivals helped Bolton keep the ball in the final half hour of the game as Wanderers became even more comfortable than they had been before.

Despite all the talent at their disposal, Atletico looked like a side who had lost belief that they could score even the one goal they needed to force extra time. Jussi Jaaskelainen had virtually nothing to do.

Just as all was looking great for Wanderers on the pitch, there was trouble off it. At the far end of the long strip of Bolton fans in the upper tier, there were some exchanges with the adjacent Atletico supporters. That quickly spiralled out of control as riot police inexplicably decided to intervene with batons, targeting only the Wanderers fans.

Crook was one of many blameless supporters caught up in the thick of it.

"It was right near the end of the game and I just think the Atletico Madrid fans had had enough," Crook says. "They were chucking stuff, bottles and things like that, and our fans were chucking things back. There were some idiot Bolton fans chucking seats but they were just young kids, there were only a few of them.

"I looked to the lad at the side of me and asked him if he was thinking what I was thinking. He replied that he was so I said 'Come on, we've got to go.' But as we said that the police just charged and everyone was panicking. There was a fence on one side and everyone was up against that, being crushed, but they just waded in. As they ran towards us there was an opening where we could run away and they blocked it off so they knew what they were doing.

"There were so many fans running that I tripped. I was on my back and I got bashed by the police. They had big batons and they had shinpads on and big boots. I was in the paratroopers when I was younger but this was horrible, it was frightening. I was on the floor, people were on top of me, and everyone was getting crushed because we couldn't go anywhere. The police just laid in and they were putting the boot in as well.

"Bolton fans shouldn't have been chucking seats but the police shouldn't be doing things like that. They were hitting a woman, and one of the guys who was in our hotel and was in his late 50s, you should have seen the cut on his head. You can see on YouTube where they were bashing him."

Megson said: "We could see it all happening from where we were in the dug-out, we were facing it and it wasn't very nice to see. The behaviour of the police that night to Bolton supporters was really shocking. I don't know what had gone on that had caused them to do that but the reaction was just way over the top. Whatever had caused it had stopped and they just made it 10 times worse.

"Their behaviour was bang out of order. We had good support and the fans hopefully had a decent time in Madrid but for the police to react like they did was bordering on brutal from what I could see."

Some supporters who had been in that area left the stadium because of injury, fear or simply disgust. Others who stayed found it hard to pay much attention to the final minutes of the game.

Many Wanderers fans seated elsewhere in the stand had not seen what had happened though, and cheered their team on as vocally as ever in the closing stages of the match. Atletico pressed forward urgently, knowing they were out if they did not score.

Polish referee Jacek Granat waved away a penalty appeal for handball when Forlan's cross struck Jlloyd Samuel, while Reyes lashed a 25-yard shot comfortably over the bar. In injury time, Atletico sent giant goalkeeper Abbiati forward for a corner and then a free kick. It made no difference.

As Wanderers cleared the danger and Abbiati raced back towards his goal, the final whistle sounded. Arms were raised aloft both on the pitch and in the stands. Bolton had drawn 0-0 and knocked the famous Atletico Madrid out of the UEFA Cup, 1-0 on aggregate.

It had been one of the worst matches any Bolton fan had seen, in terms of the actual football on show, but also one of the best. Two years after the bitter disappointment of Wanderers' unlucky last 32 exit in Marseille, now supporters were ecstatic with joy – celebrating progress to the last 16, possibly one of the biggest achievements in the club's history.

"To beat Atletico Madrid and to qualify for the next round really was a great result," says O'Brien. "My mam and dad had come over to watch the match, so it was a fantastic night."

"Atletico were flying in the Spanish league and they had great players but we stopped them," said Hunt. "We played really well. It just showed us how far we'd come as a club. Fans and people outside the club were saying, 'Why can't you perform like that on a Saturday and win games in the league?' But you can't pinpoint it, the whole European occasion benefited us because we all loved it and relished playing in it."

As incredible as the 2-2 draw at Bayern Munich was, there was an argument to say that overcoming Atletico Madrid was a bigger feat. Bayern qualified anyway, this time Atletico had been eliminated. One of the favourites to win the competition had gone, to the surprise of many around Europe.

"I think it was a bigger achievement because it was over two legs," Megson said. "You've got one of the biggest clubs in Europe and I suppose it can happen that you get a poor result. But they had another 90 minutes to put it right on their home patch.

"I don't know what it was but there just seemed an unwritten thing that 'well, they've lost 1-0 at the Reebok but they'll put it right at their place'. But that never happened and they didn't really get close to us. A lot of people played really well that night."

Players celebrated with fans before returning to the dressing room. Wanderers supporters continued to party, after being kept inside the stadium for more than half an hour. Such was the feelgood factor, after showering and changing the players returned to the field to applaud the fans again. It was a special moment, at a high point in the club's history. Stelios and other players recorded the celebrations on their mobile phones for posterity.

"I was impressed but not surprised by how many fans were there, because the English fans follow their team everywhere," Stelios says. "Always when you have the fans on your back supporting you it's like you have an extra player on the pitch. They helped a lot and even now I have to say a big thank you to all of those who came and supported us away. Wherever we played, they were there. It's a little bit late, but now I have the chance to say thanks."

As ever when post-match celebrations were involved, it was the larger than life Diouf who stole the show when the players came back on the pitch. Diouf was last to emerge and Campo jokingly signalled to team-mates to form a guard of honour for the Senegal star, all bowing down to him as if he was a king. Diouf darted past them all, doing some sort of bizarre African dance in front of the Wanderers fans while the rest of the players burst out laughing.

"That was Dioufy all over, since he left I've still seen him around and he's never changed even a little bit," Davies laughed. "It was a good feeling to knock Atletico out. You don't get much sleep after games like that, you're on such a high.

"The fans always supported us. Living in the town people would say to me, 'I've got a lads' trip booked, we're all off to Madrid'. You wanted to do it for them."

News filtered through that Wanderers would be off to Lisbon in the last 16, after Sporting won 3-0 in their second leg in Basel thanks to a goal from Bruno Pereirinha and two from Liedson – securing a comfortable 5-0 aggregate triumph.

Fans eventually departed the stadium, many making their way back to the city centre. Some encountered more problems on the way.

"My wife was there and I was scared for her safety outside afterwards because it was kicking off a bit," says Davies.

"When we came out of the ground I was on my own, because we'd all got separated before the match," remembers Crook. "We were on the phone saying, 'Where are you?' We walked up the road to a massive roundabout and there were Atletico fans there wading in to anybody. They kept saying, 'We're Millwall'.

"The police waded into my mate Kev. He got hit because he was squaring up to this lad, but he got attacked and the Spanish boy didn't.

"We sat in a pub at the top of the hill and even though Bolton had gone through we were devastated, all of us, because my mate had just been attacked and I'd been hit by these coppers for no reason in the ground. It did put a dampener on it for us. Kev's not like that and I'm not. What I saw was bad. It had never happened to me before, I'd never seen the police do that to any football fans."

For some fans, it was a case of agony and ecstasy. Seventeen supporters were officially reported as injured and the Spanish police were heavily criticised, both by those who were there and others who saw the widespread reports about what had happened. Former Wanderers boss Sam Allardyce spoke out, saying that some of his friends had been hurt in Madrid and that one had required two brain scans in hospital before being given the all clear. With fans still nursing wounds as they returned from Spain, the departure lounge at the airport resembled the waiting room at A and E.

"I remember during the game seeing the trouble going on," said O'Brien. "Then the next day when we were flying back we met the fans at the airport and a few of them were in a bad way. They'd taken a bit of a hiding."

Wanderers were furious about what had happened, making an official complaint to UEFA over the 'disproportionate' treatment of their supporters by police. The club liaised with Greater Manchester Police and the British Embassy in an attempt to obtain an explanation from the Spanish authorities.

"It was a sad incident and it wasn't our fans' fault, they didn't cause any trouble," said chairman Phil Gartside. "We made great representations about it but obviously Atletico Madrid were trying to cover things up because of the overreaction to what happened."

"I had a big line right across my back from where I'd been hit, so when I got back I went to my MP Lindsay Hoyle and told him about it," said Crook.

"I think he wrote a letter. I knew nothing would happen, but I just wanted to make a point that if it was in the news, that it wasn't all down to Bolton fans. I think English fans just get stuck with that stigma of hooligans.

"You try telling people about what happened in Madrid and they say, 'You must have done something' – not me personally but the Bolton fans in general. But they didn't. There were a few young idiots but there was nothing serious."

UEFA responded to Wanderers' complaints by opening disciplinary proceedings against both clubs. A month later Wanderers were fined £5,000 for crowd disturbances, while Atletico had to pay £15,000 after their fans threw missiles and flares during the match.

"What happened was out of order because we'd taken a greater number of people to Portugal before that without any major issues whatsoever," said Wanderers secretary Simon Marland. "But for whatever reason the Spanish police decided to do what they wanted to do and that was it. We can put complaints into UEFA but unfortunately what had happened had happened.

"To go to their place and get a 0-0 draw, Atletico Madrid were steeped in European football. They weren't an Atletico Madrid who were struggling, you looked at their team and you thought this is going to be a real tough one.

"To get that result, it was sad that it was overshadowed because of everything that went on off the pitch."

Indeed Wanderers fans still euphoric from the result at the Vicente Calderon returned to England to be greeted by headlines about the police violence rather than the historic achievement of the team. "Bolton win marred by overzealous police," was how one national newspaper summed it up.

Sadly, as with the first leg, for most around the country the significance of what Wanderers had actually done on the field was lost. Nine days after going out of the UEFA Cup to Bolton, Atletico beat Barcelona 4-2 at the Vicente Calderon. They finished the season in fourth place in La Liga, to qualify for the Champions League.

They went from strength to strength after that, beating Fulham to win the Europa League in 2010 thanks to two goals from Forlan. Despite selling Aguero a year later, Atletico won the competition again in 2012.

Add in the feats of Sevilla and Zenit, and in six of the last nine years the UEFA Cup or the rebranded Europa League has been won by a club that Wanderers played and held their own against in Europe.

In 2014, under Diego Simeone, Atletico progressed even further – shocking everyone by clinching the Spanish title, albeit with a team that contained none of the players who had lost to Wanderers.

Atletico almost won the Champions League too, only for the demons of 1974 to return to haunt them. Leading in injury time against Real Madrid in the final, their city rivals levelled and then romped to a 4-1 victory in extra time.

Atletico's achievements in 2013/14 put Wanderers' feat against the Spanish side into context. The police ensured that Bolton's trip to Madrid was not as perfect as it could have been. But what Wanderers did over two legs should never be forgotten. Little old Bolton, as some used to call them, had eliminated the mighty Atletico Madrid.

Bolton: Jussi Jaaskelainen; Nicky Hunt, Gary Cahill, Andy O'Brien, Jlloyd Samuel; Joey O'Brien (Abdoulaye Meite 85), Gavin McCann (Ivan Campo 59), Kevin Nolan; Stelios Giannakopoulos (El-Hadji Diouf 59), Kevin Davies, Matt Taylor. Subs not used: Ali Al Habsi, Mikel Alonso, Andranik Teymourian, Ricardo Vaz Te.
Booked: Joey O'Brien, Nolan, Diouf, Davies.

Atletico Madrid: Christian Abbiati; Antonio Lopez, Luis Perea, Pablo Ibanez (Mista 67), Mariano Pernia; Jose Manuel Jurado, Cleber Santana, Maxi Rodriguez, Luis Garcia (Miguel de las Cuevas 54); Jose Antonio Reyes; Diego Forlan. Subs not used: Ismael Falcon, Fabiano Eller, Ze Castro, Alex Quillo, Alvaro Dominguez.
Booked: Maxi.

Attendance: 30,000.
Referee: Jacek Granat (Poland).

18

The Beginning of the End

Bolton 1 Sporting Lisbon 1 – March 6, 2008

Having defeated Atletico Madrid, one of the favourites to win the UEFA Cup, Wanderers were suddenly starting to dream. Just how far could they actually go in this competition?

Like Atletico, Sporting Lisbon were one of the most famous clubs in Europe. But Wanderers now had the belief that they could beat anyone. If they could knock out Atletico, why not Sporting too?

The final that season was to be held at Manchester City's Eastlands stadium, just 20 miles from the Reebok. Players and fans began to wonder whether maybe they were destined to be in that final. Maybe they could even win the UEFA Cup. It would have been quite a fairytale, a chance to write Bolton's name into the history of European football.

"We were confident in ourselves having just knocked Atletico Madrid out," says Kevin Davies." We started to get a real bit of belief, thinking that maybe we could go on here and do something in this competition.

"The previous season in the UEFA Cup was about enjoying the experience. This time we got to that stage and thought, 'We've knocked Atletico Madrid out, and they were probably one of the favourites.' We started to get a sense that we could go and do it."

"You beat Atletico Madrid and get Sporting Lisbon in the next round and you think that if we beat them we're in the quarter finals, we can have a right go," said Kevin Nolan.

The first leg of the last 16 against Sporting would take place at the Reebok, only a fortnight after Wanderers' trip to Madrid in the previous round. The second leg would be a week later.

Bolton faced a Sporting side who were not having a great season in the Portuguese Primeira Liga by their standards. In a game shown live on Setanta in England, they had drawn 1-1 at home to Benfica in the Lisbon derby on the weekend before their trip to Reebok. It left them fourth in the table and a massive 17 points behind runaway leaders Porto, with Vitoria Guimaraes above them in third.

Expectations were so much higher at Sporting, who at the absolute minimum were supposed to finish in the top three along with Porto and Benfica. Those were the three stand-out clubs in Portuguese football, having dwarfed the rest of the league for decades.

With 18 league titles to their name, Sporting fans expected their team to beat Porto and Benfica too. Recent times had been leaner and they had won the league only twice since 1982, but trailing their rivals yet again meant there was pressure on boss Paulo Bento, a former Sporting player and once a dogged holding midfielder in the Portuguese national team.

Bento stayed at Sporting after his retirement in 2004, joining the coaching set-up before being promoted to manager a year later at the age of 36. He helped the club recover to second in the league in his first season in charge before they won the Taca de Portugal, the Portuguese version of the FA Cup, a year later. They missed out on the title by one point to Porto.

Sporting's struggles in the league during the 2007/08 campaign made the cup competitions all the more important for them. They had already reached the final of the Taca da Liga, the Portuguese League Cup, and would go on to retain the Taca de Portugal that season.

They were expected to do well in Europe too, as regulars in continental competitions. They had traditions to behold.

"Bolton are a great team but our goal is to reach the final," said Sporting defender Anderson Polga.

Sporting had won the European Cup Winners' Cup as far back as 1964, when they defeated MTK Hungaria. In the first leg of the last 16 that season, they had remarkably beaten APOEL Nicosia 16-1, a record in any European competition. In the quarter finals they thrashed Manchester United 9-1 over two legs.

The last time they had failed to qualify for Europe was in 1976 – an incredible run of 31 consecutive seasons in European competition. They knew they were favourites against Wanderers, and Bento more or less admitted he was happy to be facing Bolton instead of Atletico Madrid.

"Theoretically it is better to face Bolton," he said. "But they are the side that won the tie."

In 2004/05 Sporting had overcome English opposition in the form of Middlesbrough and Newcastle on the way to the UEFA Cup final. Firm favourites to win the final – coincidentally being played at their home stadium, the Estadio Jose Alvalade, that season – they suffered a surprise defeat to CSKA Moscow. The club still carried the scars, determined to right that wrong.

Sporting's second place finish in the league in 2007 had earned them qualification for the Champions League group stage for a second season in a row. As was the case a year earlier, they were unable to make it out of the group. Cristiano Ronaldo scored the winner for Manchester United on his emotional return to the Alvalade. Sporting then won at Dynamo Kiev but took only one point from two games against Roma before defeat at Old Trafford confirmed their exit from the Champions League. Ending the group with a 3-0 home win over Kiev, however, they did take third place to earn a spot in the last 32 of the UEFA Cup. There they made light work of Basel to book their meeting with Bolton.

This was the first time that Wanderers had played a Champions League drop-out in their two seasons in the UEFA Cup, but the third time that they had faced Portuguese opposition – after 1-1 draws with Vitoria Guimaraes and Braga.

Wanderers had played Sporting before, during a pre-season tour of Portugal in 2004. A small group of Wanderers fans had flown to Lisbon before travelling 50 miles north to the sleepy town of Rio Maior, where the match was held in a tidy 8,500-capacity stadium on a pleasant summer's evening.

Wanderers won 2-1 thanks to goals from Henrik Pedersen and trialist Hassan Kachloul, the Moroccan former Southampton midfielder who did not end up signing for Bolton. Wanderers new boy Michael Bridges had been sent off for violent conduct and his Bolton career went downhill from there, as he failed to make a single competitive appearance for the club.

Few players remained from that game – particularly on the Sporting side. Bento had made many changes to his squad, with signings complementing an emerging group of young talent. Winger Nani had been a revelation but joined Manchester United at the start of the 2007/08 season for €25m. The creative Joao Moutinho had broken into the Portugal national team, where he would earn many caps.

Behind him in midfield was deep-lying playmaker Miguel Veloso, a stylish left footer with hair wrapped into a ponytail and a deadly delivery from set pieces. Even before Sporting faced Wanderers in the UEFA Cup, Bolton boss Gary Megson was a big admirer and was monitoring whether he could one day sign Veloso, then only 21.

"Veloso was certainly one that we were aware of before we played against Sporting," Megson says. "I went across and watched him a couple of times, I thought he was a talented lad who would do well in English football. You're around in Europe all the time, or we were when Bolton were in the Premier League, because you're looking at those kinds of players.

"I tried to bring Blaise Matuidi to Bolton and he seems to have been doing okay for himself since then."

Playing for Saint-Etienne, Matuidi was a talented young midfielder like Veloso and has since gone on to star for France and Paris Saint-Germain.

Sporting had more talent at their disposal during the 2007/08 season, too. Pacy Brazilian striker Liedson was a prolific goalscorer who had caused Middlesbrough all sorts of problems in the UEFA Cup three years earlier. Goalkeeper Rui Patricio was still only 20 but had broken into the first team following the sale of Portuguese international Ricardo – England's penalty shoot-out nemesis at both Euro 2004 and the 2006 World Cup. Patricio would later succeed Ricardo as Portugal's regular keeper.

The current Sporting crop knew they had big boots to fill as they lived in the shadows of past legends. Youth team product Ronaldo stood out in recent history but before that were Joao Pinto, Paulo Sousa, Simao, the great Luis Figo and Ricardo Sa Pinto, a fine striker whose career was marred when he received a lengthy ban for punching Portugal manager Artur Jorge.

Another club legend was Mario Jardel, who scored 67 goals in 62 games for Sporting between 2001 and 2003 – winning the European golden boot with a stunning 55 goals in his first season with the club. Jardel had won the honour once before while with Porto. Sadly, when the Brazilian moved from Sporting to Bolton in 2003 he had lost form and shape after a spell on the sidelines because of depression, partly related to marital issues. He scored in a Carling Cup triumph for Wanderers at Liverpool but was otherwise often mocked by opposing fans for his more rotund figure. He later moved from country to country with little success, from Italy to Argentina to Spain to Brazil to Portugal to Cyprus to Australia to Bulgaria to Saudi Arabia before retiring in 2011.

Sporting had also gone through a more curious period at the turn of the millennium when they signed Phil Babb and Alan Mahon. Respecters of the game on these shores, earlier they had been managed by a string of British coaches – Bobby Robson, Keith Burkinshaw, Malcolm Allison, Jimmy Hagan, Ronnie Allen, Randolph Galloway, Bob Kelly, Arthur John and Scotsman Charlie Bell, who first took charge in 1919.

The club were founded as Sporting Clube de Portugal and that is the name by which they are still known today, with no mention of Lisbon in their official title. To their irritation, though, they have always been commonly referred to in England as Sporting Lisbon, in Germany as Sporting Lissabon, in Spain as Sporting de Lisboa and so forth.

As they had done against Atletico Madrid, Wanderers again reduced ticket prices in a bid to recreate the special atmosphere from the previous round.

The match was again not being shown live on television. Wanderers chairman Phil Gartside revealed that the club had turned down an offer from Channel Five and a more substantial deal with a Portuguese broadcaster to screen the game because both would have meant moving the kick-off time – either to 7pm or 8.45pm. A less lucrative deal was agreed to show the game live on Portuguese television at the scheduled 8pm kick-off time, which Wanderers were keen to retain to attract the biggest crowd possible.

The atmosphere was perhaps not quite as electric as it had been against Atletico, but still 25,664 packed into the Reebok to cheer on Wanderers. Sporting had only 300 or 400 in the away section.

Wanderers came into the game having been dragged back into Premier League relegation trouble in the two weeks since eliminating Atletico Madrid in Europe. Fans still on a high on their return from Spain had been brought crashing back down to earth with a 4-1 defeat at Blackburn, before Liverpool won 3-1 at the Reebok. Bolton had dropped back to 17th in the table, level on points with the drop zone.

Despite the euphoria of the win over Atletico, and the fact that Wanderers were now in the last 16 of European competition, Megson's focus was starting to turn away from the UEFA Cup. At the pre-match press conference, Portuguese journalists voiced their puzzlement as they sensed the Sporting match was not high on his list of priorities. "You sound as though it would be a relief if you lost?" one visiting reporter asked Megson.

Wanderers made only four changes for the home leg, all of them enforced. Their scheduled Premier League opponents that weekend, Manchester United, were in FA Cup action instead so Bolton would again have the luxury of a blank weekend – meaning they had no reason to rest players.

They were without El-Hadji Diouf, serving a one-match ban for picking up his third booking of the competition against Atletico Madrid, and Gretar Steinsson was again ineligible. Nolan failed a late fitness test on a back injury and there was an even later selection issue when Jussi Jaaskelainen sustained an injury during the warm-up. It meant another UEFA Cup start for reserve keeper Ali Al Habsi. Unlike at Bayern Munich, his short-notice selection meant this time he was feeling the nerves.

"We had just started the first 10 or 15 minutes of the warm-up and then Jussi got injured," he remembers. "I started to warm up. To be honest it was a really big pressure and I was nervous, I felt myself feeling heavy."

Also coming into the side were Nicky Hunt, Gavin McCann and Heidar Helguson – the latter playing his first game for Wanderers in the UEFA Cup. Injuries had restricted the striker to only five appearances since he had arrived at the start of the season.

Helguson's selection allowed Wanderers to take a direct approach when required, with Kevin Davies and the Icelander both strong in the air. They had linked up only once before from the start of a match, a 2-0 win at Reading when Wanderers not only had Davies to flick on balls into the box, but Helguson behind him to flick it on again for the likes of Nolan and Matt Taylor. It was perhaps the first step towards a full team of 11 players flicking the ball back and forth to their heart's content.

Sporting were dealt the blow of going into the game without leading scorer Liedson because of injury, and they were short of options up front with Yannick Djalo and Derlei – scorer of two goals in Porto's UEFA Cup final win over Celtic in 2003 – also sidelined. In their absence, Bento fielded the makeshift forward line of the inexperienced Rodrigo Tiui, a Brazilian livewire with a similar style to Ricardo Vaz Te, and Montenegrin international Simon Vukcevic – often used in a more withdrawn role in midfield.

The match started in cagey fashion but the physical presence of Helguson and Davies in forward areas was unsettling Sporting, playing in their famous green and white hoops. Patricio was rattled when he came charging off his line and collided with his own defender Polga. The goalkeeper received a bloody nose but things could have been more serious soon afterwards.

Wanderers thought their opponents would be reduced to 10 men – like Atletico had been in the previous round when Sergio Aguero was sent off – as Patricio came off his line again to intercept McCann's long pass towards Helguson. The keeper appeared to not only pole-axe Helguson, but also handle the ball outside of the area. Incredibly, Israeli referee Alon Yefet did not even show Patricio a yellow card.

Megson says: "The main thing I remember about that game was we put a ball over the top, the goalkeeper came running out and handled it but nothing happened, the referee just gave a free kick.

"You were looking at it and thinking, 'Right, what shall we do when he gets sent off?' It wasn't a case of if he gets sent off. In my mind I wasn't even thinking if he was going to get a yellow or a red. I was thinking what should we do with the advantage of an extra man because he's got to go. But nothing happened to him, it was ridiculous."

The setback did not affect Wanderers for long, though. In the 25th minute they were ahead. Hunt floated a deep free kick into the box and Davies flicked the ball on to Helguson. The Icelander controlled the ball and poked it to Taylor, whose shot was blocked. But the ball fell invitingly to McCann, in space in the penalty area. The midfielder calmly fired an angled shot low into the bottom corner from 15 yards with Patricio wrong-footed.

The trademark headband that he had worn when scoring the winner at Red Star Belgrade had long gone, but McCann's UEFA Cup goalscoring feats were continuing. At that stage they were the midfielder's only two goals for the club. It is a quirk that McCann can only partially explain.

"I don't know why that was, I probably found it easier than playing in the Premier League," he says. "The tempo of the games might have been a bit slower than I was used to during my career. I quite enjoyed it.

"For the goal I just side-footed it into the corner, there was a gap and I just rolled it in."

The goal had put Wanderers in control against top European opposition once more, reasserting their belief that they could do to Sporting what they had done to Atletico Madrid. The quarter finals and beyond were starting to feel like a very real possibility.

Sporting were not completely succumbing, with Veloso impressively composed in midfield. Bruno Pereirinha lofted an effort just over the bar before forcing a save from Ali Al Habsi with a 30-yard shot.

But Wanderers were close to going 2-0 in front and putting Sporting in real trouble, when Taylor's right-foot shot went just wide five minutes before the interval. They came closer still to a second goal early in the second half. Ivan Campo crossed into the box and Davies flicked on for Helguson to head goalwards, only to see his attempt from six yards strike the crossbar.

"We should have been about 3-0 up," McCann says.

Sadly, Helguson's header against the woodwork proved to be the turning point in the tie. Sporting had made a tactical change at half time, bringing on Argentinian midfielder Leandro Romagnoli for right back Abel and pushing Pereirinha back into defence. The visitors began to work their way back into the game and keep possession, before Romagnoli's fine angled effort came back off the bar.

If that was a let-off, Wanderers' lead did not last much longer. With home fans growing audibly uneasy about the turning tide of the match, Polga played a pass into front man Vukcevic. The Montenegrin laid the ball off instantly to strike partner Tiui, who completed a quickfire one-two. It was a smart piece of play, and was enough to allow Vukcevic to escape Gary Cahill. Now in the clear, he took aim with his stronger left foot from the edge of the box and hammered the bouncing ball thunderously past Al Habsi into the net. Bang. There was no saving that.

"It was a great finish," Al Habsi admits.

It was a ruthless strike that fitted in perfectly with the character of a man who did not suffer fools gladly on or off the pitch. You could tell as much just by looking at him. Moody and brooding, his default facial expression suggested he was not someone to be messed with.

Some had tried. After being criticised for excessive solo play during his early days at Partizan Belgrade he had moved to Russian club Saturn for big money, only to publicly fall out with coach Vladimir Weiss – father of the former Bolton player of the same name. After his time at Sporting he moved to Blackburn, but made little impact in England before moving on to Ukrainian side Karpaty Lviv.

That night at the Reebok though, he looked a top player. The goal was a moment of quality that Wanderers could do little about. The stadium fell silent, save for the roars of the travelling Sporting fans, who knew how important Vukcevic's strike could be.

Just one goal had shifted the balance of the tie so much. A 1-0 home win would have given Wanderers a massive chance of progressing, as it had done against Atletico. But now Sporting had the away goal. If a 0-0 draw at home to Marseille two years ago had been a bad result, this was worse. Bolton would travel to Sporting Lisbon – not an easy task at the best of times – knowing they had to score or they were out.

In the closing stages there were chances for either side to win it but the game finished 1-1. While Sporting celebrated the result with their supporters, Wanderers players trudged off – fearing they were now in real danger of going out. There was a sense that this could be the beginning of the end for Wanderers in Europe. Unless Bolton could pull off something pretty special in Lisbon, it would be their last game in the UEFA Cup.

"We were a little bit disappointed with the draw at home," said Davies. "It's kind of weird saying it against Sporting Lisbon but you always feel you need to take something away, because we knew it was going to be a difficult game over there. They came and played some good stuff at times. It was probably a fair result in the end, but we maybe felt we needed a lead."

Megson concurred, believing an opportunity had been missed to secure victory that night.

"They had some good players and they were one of the strongest teams in Portugal so they probably were expected to go through, but I thought we deserved more than we got in the first game," he said. "I didn't think they were as strong as Atletico and I didn't think they were as strong as Bayern. But the away goal made a big difference."

"They probably came over for a draw and it gave them something to hang on to," says McCann. "They had a couple of decent lads, Moutinho, Veloso, lads that went for good money."

Moutinho would switch to Porto in 2010 for €11m before his value doubled when he signed for Monaco in 2013.

Veloso became a regular with Portugal and moved to Serie A with Genoa in 2010, before joining Dynamo Kiev two years later. A year before he left Sporting, though, Bolton made a firm attempt to sign him. Veloso's performance against Wanderers had strengthened Megson's admiration, and the manager was looking for a new midfield general on the last day of the 2009 January transfer window following the surprise sale of Nolan to Newcastle.

Reports suggested Bolton were trying to seal a £13.5m deal for Veloso, an astonishing figure that would have shattered the club's transfer record. The midfielder's agent, however, insisted Veloso was staying at Sporting and that was what happened. Unable to secure their prime target, the window shut without any replacement for Nolan.

Megson later hinted that Sporting had wanted to keep Veloso and had priced them out of a move, appearing to play down the £13.5m figure. He was also quoted by Sky Sports as offering a comment that was both intriguing and perplexing in equal measures.

"If we'd have bought a certain player that would have cost us absolutely millions, I don't think we're ready for that," he was quoted as saying, seemingly referring to Veloso. "It would have been like putting a tiara on a big shire horse."

It was a turn of phrase that conjured up quite an image, perhaps of Megson down at the stables, armed with a step ladder and only the finest tiaras. There was a feature idea for Sky Sports News if ever there was one. The quote was the source of much amusement and bemusement, although Megson admits he cannot remember ever uttering the phrase. "No, I wouldn't say anything like that," he laughed.

As well as the disappointment of the draw at home to Sporting, McCann also knew he was out of the second leg in Lisbon.

"You got suspended if you got three bookings in that competition and I got my third booking in the home leg," he says. "When the referee showed me the yellow card I knew that I was suspended. I was gutted. If I hadn't been suspended I'd have probably played in Lisbon."

As it turned out, McCann would be far from the only one to miss that second leg, as Megson pondered his selection options for the trip to Lisbon. They did not know it at the time, but for many of Wanderers' first team the 1-1 draw with Sporting at the Reebok had been their last game in Europe.

Bolton: Ali Al Habsi; Nicky Hunt, Gary Cahill, Andy O'Brien, Ricardo Gardner; Joey O'Brien (Danny Guthrie 67), Ivan Campo (Andranik Teymourian 84), Gavin McCann; Kevin Davies, Heidar Helguson (Stelios Giannakopoulos 55), Matt Taylor. Subs not used: Ian Walker, Jlloyd Samuel, Abdoulaye Meite, Ricardo Vaz Te.
Booked: Joey O'Brien, McCann.
Goal: McCann 25.

Sporting: Rui Patricio; Abel (Leandro Romagnoli 46), Tonel, Anderson Polga, Leandro Grimi; Bruno Pereirinha, Joao Moutinho, Miguel Veloso, Marat Izmailov (Gladstone 85); Simon Vukcevic, Rodrigo Tiui (Adrien Silva 79). Subs not used: Vladimir Stojkovic, Pedro Silva, Pontus Farnerud, Milan Purovic.
Booked: Grimi.
Goal: Vukcevic 69.

Attendance: 25,664.
Referee: Alon Yefet (Israel).

19

The Lisbon Decision

Sporting Lisbon 1 Bolton 0 – March 13, 2008

It remains possibly one of the most controversial moments in Bolton Wanderers' long history. Years later, the subject of the away game at Sporting Lisbon still conjures up strong opinions.

"Until right now the fans are still talking about it," says El-Hadji Diouf.

"It was the biggest dilemma I had," says Gary Megson, looking back over his turbulent time as Bolton manager. There were plenty who disagreed with the choice he made.

If Megson wasn't exactly popular before, many fans never forgot the decision he took to leave almost his entire first team at home when Wanderers travelled to Sporting Lisbon for the second leg of their last 16 tie. The match brought a sad end to Bolton's two wonderful seasons in the UEFA Cup and drove an irreparable wedge between supporters and manager.

"We were gutted," is how Kevin Davies sums up the feelings of those players who were left in England.

The Premier League fixture list was the reason why Megson felt he had a decision to make. With Wanderers not in action on the weekend after the first leg, Reading won to push Bolton back into the bottom three for the first time since November.

Three days after the second leg against Sporting Lisbon, Wanderers were due to travel to face Wigan, who sat in 13th place but just three points above Bolton in the table. Megson viewed the game as a vital six-pointer, knowing that victory would see them leapfrog their local rivals.

"It was a huge, huge game against Wigan and as much as it stuck in my throat, I had to put all my eggs in the Wigan basket to try to make sure we got a result there," he says. "We didn't want to do it, we wanted to play the strongest team we could against Sporting. But we were starting to struggle in the league and that Wigan game was just massive for us.

"We near enough picked the team for Wigan before we picked the team for Sporting. I knew that we couldn't go to Lisbon and draw, we had to look for a result. But I looked at it and if I played the first team against Sporting – the team that was going to play against Wigan – I thought we would get a result, but the Wigan game was more important because they were down there with us."

Megson selected his squad for Sporting and informed Davies, Diouf, Ivan

Campo, Matt Taylor, Andy O'Brien and Ricardo Gardner that they would not be travelling. Instead they would remain at the club's Euxton training ground to prepare for the Wigan game.

"I wanted to play," Diouf says. "But with Gary Megson you couldn't say anything. If he got something in his head he was going to do it."

"He just said you're going to stay behind and rest up for the weekend," Davies remembers. "Sporting were another big club, a well known club in Europe, and you want to be involved in those games. But it's out of your hands sometimes, the decision was up to the manager. He knows the players, he has to look at things like age and the amount of games you've played.

"He makes the decisions, it's not really up for discussion. As players you don't know the conversations that are going on between the manager and the chairman. Staying in the Premier League was a huge priority for the club financially. Maybe if you'd gone and said, 'Look, I want to play', he might have thought about it. But you leave it to him, he's the manager.

"He was always up front with us and I think he did a good job for the club overall. We proved with Bayern Munich that we could get a result with a weakened team. I think at the time he would have taken a good performance in Lisbon and a win against Wigan. That would have been what he wanted."

Jussi Jaaskelainen and Kevin Nolan had been nursing back injuries. The latter faced Wigan three days later and confirms now that he would have been fit enough to travel to Portugal. But Megson decided not to risk his skipper, leaving him at home.

"A lot of lads were carrying knocks, we'd had a long season with a lot of games," Nolan says. "The manager thinks, 'If we take them, it's a risk for the weekend.' In the end he decided that everyone who had little niggles, he wanted them for Sunday and they weren't going. He's the manager and you have to accept his decision."

Gavin McCann had already known he would miss the game through suspension, while Gretar Steinsson, Tamir Cohen and Grzegorz Rasiak were again ineligible for the UEFA Cup. It left Wanderers with very few experienced players remaining for the trip to Lisbon.

Wanderers fans would not find out about the squad Megson had picked until later, but their reaction would not be good.

Many Bolton supporters were struggling to afford the trip to Lisbon, after spending large sums travelling to Madrid in the previous round. It had been far from certain that Wanderers would reach the last 16, so some fans had not budgeted for what was effectively a bonus away match in Europe – one more than they had enjoyed in their previous season in the UEFA Cup. While supporters had two months to plan their trip to Madrid after the draw was made in December, this time there were only three weeks between

Wanderers reaching the last 16 and their match in Lisbon. Such short notice made it difficult to organise travel and accommodation, and book time off work.

Despite all of that, Wanderers fans regarded this as one of the biggest and most prestigious games in the club's recent history – the last 16 of the UEFA Cup. Desperate not to miss it, they pushed the boat out financially to make their way to Lisbon. Some travelled independently, others snapped up £259 official travel club packages for the game.

Wanderers were allocated just short of 3,000 tickets in the away section at Sporting's Estadio Jose Alvalade. Just over 1,500 were sold – still a highly respectable figure for the second trip to Europe in the space of 21 days. Fifteen or 16 years earlier, Bolton's average attendances for home fixtures in their own town were only 6,000.

Everyone knew this could be Bolton's last European trip – probably for many years. They were determined to relish every second of it. On matchday, many supporters gathered in the central Rossio square, an expansive area surrounded by bars and historic buildings. The towering Column of Pedro IV, a former king of Portugal, dominated the square.

It was an almost idyllic place in which to pass the time, as the spring sun shone over the city. With locals playing accordions and guitars, fans put washing powder in the fountain for old time's sake, proudly sung Bolton songs and kicked footballs and beach balls around. Occasionally they landed on the roof of a car, to some laughter but no ill-feeling. On several occasions fans had to scale their way into the centre of the ornate fountain to retrieve balls, a precarious task that entertained onlookers.

Many fans took the opportunity to wander further afield and see more of Lisbon, known as 'The City Of Seven Hills', with winding cobbled streets climbing steeply on either side of the square. On one side stood the Castle of Sao Jorge, a Moorish castle on a hilltop which offered stunning views of the city and the vast River Tagus estuary, marking the eastern and southern edges of the city – as the river flows west towards the Atlantic Ocean.

Two huge bridges span the river. The Vasco da Gama Bridge, opened in 1998, is the longest in Europe and travels 10.7 miles to the eastern bank of the Tagus. The 25 de Abril Bridge, bearing a resemblance to the Golden Gate Bridge in San Francisco, connects Lisbon with the south and the huge Cristo Rei monument on the other side of the river. Arms outstretched, the giant figure of Christ stands atop an 80m high pedestal and looks towards the centre of Lisbon. It was inspired by the famous Christ the Redeemer monument in Rio de Janeiro.

Some supporters also ventured to the west of the city to the district of Belem to see the spectacular Jeronimos Monastery and the Belem Tower on the bank of the river. Both were completed in the 16th century and are UNESCO heritage sites, situated in a picturesque area visited by coachload upon coachload of tourists from around the world. Lisbon truly deserves its standing as one of the finest cities in Europe.

The oldest city in western Europe, it was invaded by Napoleon in the early 19th century and was the site of three revolutions during the 20th century. The second saw a right-wing authoritarian dictatorship come to power in 1926, eventually led by Antonio Salazar. In 1974 that culminated in the Carnation Revolution, when a military coup ousted the country's unpopular rulers. People took to the streets of Lisbon in joy, celebrating by putting carnations into the muzzles of soldiers' rifles. 'Freedom Day' is still marked each year with a national holiday across Portugal.

Football is a big part of the identity of Lisbon, a city of three million people. In the west of the city still stood the Estadio Nacional, where Celtic's players became Lisbon Lions with victory over Inter Milan in the 1967 European Cup final. The stadium was decaying and isolated in an overgrown area, but still traditionally hosted the Portuguese cup final each year.

Belenenses had entertained Bayern Munich in their 30,000 Estadio Restelo earlier that season. But they are very much the third club in Lisbon behind the giants of Sporting and Benfica, whose stadiums are separated by only a mile and the highway on the northern edge of the city.

A statue of the great Eusebio stood outside Benfica's spectacular 65,000-capacity Estadio da Luz, where Wanderers wide man Stelios Giannakopoulos had helped Greece to victory in the European Championships final over Portugal in 2004. Now he was back in the city, hoping for a win with Bolton.

Tours of Benfica's stadium were on offer. On the way round, we exchanged views with the tour guide about Portuguese under 21 international Ricardo Vaz Te. He wasn't a fan. Then came the opportunity at the end of the tour to pose with the famous Benfica eagle, which swoops down on to the pitch before every home match as part of a club tradition. 'Come, come, see the eagle, have your picture taken with the eagle!' staff shouted over-excitedly, as if English people had never seen birds before. They seemed most disappointed at our indifference. Even the eagle looked indignant. No-one snubs the Benfica eagle and gets away with it.

A museum inside the stadium paid homage to legends of the past. The new Estadio da Luz was opened in 2003 to replace the old venue on the same site. Vast but dilapidated, the previous Estadio da Luz had attracted a crowd of 135,000 for a match between Benfica and Porto in 1987.

Sporting had similarly moved from their old 60,000-capacity open bowl of a stadium into the modern version of the Estadio Jose Alvalade on an adjacent site, in time for Euro 2004. The new stadium hosted five games at the championships, including Greece's quarter final win over France and Portugal's semi final victory over the Netherlands – achieved with the aid of a stunning long-range goal from Maniche. The new venue, with a capacity of

50,000, had also hosted the 2005 UEFA Cup final as CSKA Moscow shocked Sporting in their own home.

The new Alvalade was an impressive, plush venue bedecked in green and yellow. It also housed a mall complex with a 12-screen cinema, the official Sporting museum and a health club.

As is the case with a number of clubs around Europe, Sporting have teams in a whole host of sports. The Sporting Clube de Portugal billiards team have won the Portuguese Three-Cushion Men's Billiard League on 16 occasions, they'll have you know. The club even had a motor racing team in the Superleague Formula series.

At the Alvalade, a moat-like structure separated the pitch from the seats, which were oddly coloured in all sorts of random hues. The colour scheme was a deliberate trick on the eye to make it look like the stadium was packed with fans even when it was completely empty, perhaps a sign that Sporting were a little sensitive about dipping crowds for home games. Even on match night, fans blended into the camouflage seats to such an extent that it was hard to tell exactly how many supporters were in the stadium. It was a little disconcerting to be honest.

Organised ultra groups waved giant flags and banners in peaceful fashion. The Torcida Verde based themselves to the left of the Wanderers supporters, at the same end of the stadium. The biggest Sporting fans' group was the Juventude Leonina, so named because the club's nickname was the Leoes, or the Lions.

Many Wanderers supporters arriving at the Alvalade for the game, some via the smart metro system, had started to hear news earlier in the day and the night before that many of the club's stars had been left at home – much to their bemusement and annoyance. For any who still did not know, the arrival of the players at the stadium told the story.

"When the players came out on to the pitch to have a look around, I've never noticed audible disappointment like that from the fans," remembers Russell Byrne-Fraser. "You could see all the punters – these people who had spent whatever they'd spent to get there – saying 'What on earth?' The players came out in dribs and drabs, in twos and threes, and it didn't take long for the penny to drop that nobody was there."

The club made some attempts to point out that there were six full internationals in the starting line-up to face Sporting that night – Ali Al Habsi, Abdoulaye Meite, Andranik Teymourian, Joey O'Brien, Heidar Helguson and Stelios Giannakopoulos. But everyone, even the players on the field themselves, knew it was a virtual reserve team cobbled together at short notice – seemingly with the primary aim of merely fulfilling the fixture. Megson's team selection in league matches told them as much.

Each and every one of them had very respectable careers in the game, but the large majority were short of match practice. Al Habsi had never made a league appearance for Wanderers. Nicky Hunt had not started a Premier League game since December and neither had Jlloyd Samuel. Meite had not featured in the league since his return from the Africa Cup of Nations.

In midfield, Andranik's only start in any competition since Megson took over was when a similarly weakened team was fielded at Red Star Belgrade. Danny Guthrie had been in and out of the side and although Joey O'Brien had been playing regularly, he was sometimes being used in an unfamiliar right wing position in the league and did not make the starting line-up at Wigan three days later.

In the front three, Stelios and Helguson had each made only one league start during Megson's tenure. Vaz Te had made none, having been out for months with a serious knee injury sustained on the opening day of the season. Sporting was his first game back, with some wondering whether he could make another fairytale return to his native Portugal, having scored at Vitoria Guimaraes two years earlier. Megson selected the forward in the hope that he could do against Sporting what Stelios had done against Greek team Aris.

"Vaz Te was playing up front because again I thought if ever he was going to really turn out, it would be in Portugal," Megson says.

It was a return for Vaz Te to the city where he was born, and to his boyhood club, the club he had represented briefly as a child.

"It was very emotional for me because it was the club I supported," he says. "When I was 12 I played there for a few months but my mum took me out because I wasn't getting good grades. I was so young and she was working so hard and she had no way out. So it was either find my way to training alone or she had to take me and she couldn't do it, she couldn't do the two things. Plus I wasn't doing so well at school so she wanted me to focus more on school. I thank her for it, because school is more important."

The only player featuring that night to start the league games immediately before and after the two legs of the Sporting tie was Gary Cahill, although Al Habsi also played three days later at Wigan. The Oman keeper would be a regular for the rest of the season after Jaaskelainen was ruled out for several weeks with injury.

On occasions in the past, Wanderers had taken some of their stars and placed them on the bench in case of an emergency. Megson had done that with Campo and Diouf at Atletico Madrid. But the bench that night in Lisbon was significantly weaker than the starting line-up. Ian Walker and Daniel Braaten were experienced but well out of the first-team picture. The other substitutes were all youngsters – Robert Sissons, Nathan Woolfe, James Sinclair, Zoltan Harsanyi and Scott Jamieson, who was later capped by Australia but never played for Wanderers' first team.

"We probably didn't have the players to come on and change the game for us," says Joey O'Brien. "I think in some of the games we had a lot of the lads on the bench who had been playing in the Premier League, and if needed they'd come on. But in that game I don't think we had a lot of options on the bench with senior players. I know the manager was thinking of the Sunday but for a selfish personal reason I was thinking if you'd had Nobby (Kevin Nolan) or Kevin Davies, you could bring them on, we might have thrown one in the box and one of them would have scored.

"But it was a great chance for certain lads who hadn't been in the team. They were getting the run-outs on the European nights. It was a fantastic stadium, and it was another game that my mam and dad went to. You treasure those games now. My dad has passed away now and that was probably one of the last games he saw me play live in the stadium. That game is always something that will stay with me."

Hunt was another of those relishing the chance to start – again knowing he had a point to prove if he wanted to play more regularly in the Premier League.

"Obviously you're doing it for the team as well, but you're doing it for yourself and your career," he said. "The pitch was slick, it was fast, I loved playing in that game."

The match was being shown live on Channel Five, with commentary from former Bolton School pupil Dave Woods. Back in England, a number of first-team regulars were sat in front of the television, powerless to aid Wanderers' UEFA Cup cause.

"I just watched it at home with the kids," says Davies.

The stadium was around half full by kick-off, with Wanderers fans cheering on their side from the corner of the lower tier. Bolton were the last English side left in the UEFA Cup by that stage, after Everton and Tottenham had gone out the night before.

For the second leg Sporting welcomed back star striker Liedson from injury, but key midfielder Miguel Veloso was absent.

Wanderers knew that first and foremost they had to score. A 0-0 draw after 90 minutes would put Sporting through on away goals. It was the home side who came close to scoring within a minute, though, as Al Habsi had to save a 25-yard free kick from Simon Vukcevic.

Despite Wanderers' weakened team, for much of the first half they more than held their own. Players keen to impress were creating some attractive passages of play, with Andranik and O'Brien influential in midfield, finding the raiding full back Hunt time and again on the right flank. Sporting were labouring, unimpressive and wasteful with their final delivery. Shots from distance were comfortably off target. The home team could play much better than this. They were there for the taking.

"I didn't think that there was a massive difference between Sporting Lisbon's first team and our reserve team to be perfectly honest," says

Megson. "They were a strong enough team but I didn't think they were a terrific team."

For a brief second it looked like Vaz Te would have another magic moment in Portugal, as he was released into space. Destiny seemed to beckon again for him, but his shot hit the side-netting. The first half would get worse for the forward.

"That game was very dramatic for me because after 30 minutes I damaged the meniscus of my knee and I didn't come off, I tried to play on," said Vaz Te, who completed the 90 minutes, desperate to shine against the club he had always followed.

"But after that game I had to have an operation right away. Then I had another operation which put me out for about 18 to 20 months straight and it was kind of a career-ending injury. Sporting Lisbon was the last 16, the furthest Bolton had ever been in Europe. But for me it was very sad, because I took so long to come back from injury and then in the first game back I got injured again."

Vaz Te made only two more fleeting appearances for Wanderers in two seasons before being released – moving on to Greek club Panionios, before rebuilding his career with Hibernian and Barnsley. It earned him a move to West Ham, where he scored in their Championship play-off final victory over Blackpool in 2012.

Given the injury problems he had after that Sporting game, does he regret playing on? "No, I don't regret anything I've done," he insisted.

At the other end in the first half at the Alvalade, Russian midfielder Marat Izmailov steered over after a Bruno Pereirinha cross had been flicked on, then Romagnoli shot straight at Al Habsi.

As the game moved into the second half, Sporting were starting to look more comfortable in possession but without creating much. They knew the onus was on Wanderers to score, not them, and Bolton were creating even less. As much effort as Wanderers were putting in and as well as they had acquitted themselves, they never totally looked like they had the quality to get the goal they needed.

"It was probably one of my better games in a Bolton shirt, but we maybe just didn't have a goal threat," O'Brien says. "We were well in the game but I don't think we had the firepower."

Al Habsi saved from Pereirinha and Liedson, while Megson turned to his bench for the closing stages. He brought on Braaten for Andranik, before surprisingly handing a first-team debut to Woolfe, introduced on the left wing after replacing Helguson. It was a massive ask for the 19-year-old to make an impact in a game like this.

Woolfe actually did surprisingly well, beating his man and lofting in a couple of dangerous crosses. He could be proud of his brief contribution in what would be his only appearance for Wanderers. After a loan spell with

Wrexham he moved to Spain with the Glenn Hoddle Academy, joining local side Jerez before returning to England with non-league clubs Northwich and Hednesford.

By now, Wanderers were trying to push men forward, but the golden opportunity they needed never came. With five minutes left, Sporting countered and broke the deadlock. Bolton fans knew the game was up.

Izmailov darted forward on the left before finding Joao Moutinho infield. In space, the midfielder looked up and calmly switched the play to raiding right winger Pereirinha. The 5ft 8in right winger advanced into the box, turned inside Meite on to his weaker left foot and curled a perfect shot into the top corner beyond Al Habsi, right in front of the Bolton fans.

In some senses, Pereirinha's strike changed nothing. Wanderers still needed only one goal to save themselves, even if now it would only be to force extra time rather than win the tie.

But psychologically it was the killer blow. On a night when Bolton had started at a distinct disadvantage, now most sensed that the UEFA Cup run was over. Hunt and Al Habsi looked devastated. Wanderers fans held heads in hands, disconsolate that their incredible adventure was coming to an end.

"It was a real sucker punch," Hunt says. "We'd given our absolute all and we just had nothing left."

Wanderers again pressed forward in the final five minutes, but a goal was never close to coming. The final whistle signalled the end of a dream. Players trudged towards the away fans, heartbroken but knowing they should acknowledge the supporters who had followed them around Europe for so long.

The fans did not blame the players. They knew those who had been selected had given everything and gave them a standing ovation, singing 'We love you Bolton, we do' at the top of their voices. It was a touching and emotional moment.

Supporters were sad, but they were bursting with pride too. It was all over, but Bolton had achieved so much in two seasons on the European stage. The club had moved into uncharted territory, gaining respect across the continent. Wanderers had lost only two of their 18 games in the UEFA Cup, both on the nights they were eliminated from the competition. Include the matches in the Anglo-Italian Cup, and it was two defeats in 24.

"It was sad to go out but on the other hand you had to be proud, to go all that way to the last 16," says Al Habsi.

Some, like Stelios, lingered on the pitch as if trying to soak up the final few seconds of Wanderers' European experience, before following the rest of the team back to the dressing room.

"It's always disappointing when you don't have the result that you want and I knew it was a big chance to go even further than the club had ever gone before," says Stelios of what proved to be the final European game of his career. "It was the end of the story but it was like a dream come true, this run that we had in the UEFA Cup."

Hunt says: "It was mind boggling in a way when you were sat back in the changing room and you were thinking to yourself, 'It's gone now, that's it, it's over.' It was really, really sad. It was a long way back. We were down there in the Premier League, it was all doom and gloom."

Some were not happy with Megson's response to the result.

Byrne-Fraser says: "Going back in that dressing room afterwards was the lowest place I think any of us had ever been. I was sat with Jlloyd Samuel and Gary walked into the room and said, 'What's the matter with you two?' I really couldn't get my head around that. I said, 'It's taken some of us 18 months to get to this stage'. He clapped his hands and said, 'Come on, let's get packed up and let's go, we've got an important game at Wigan on Sunday'."

Back in England, it had been a difficult night in front of the television for Nolan. Never a good watcher at the best of times, he admitted his evening's viewing had been like torture.

"Even when I watch any game now it is torture, especially watching on TV knowing if we'd had a full strength side out we would have given them a really good game and we would have had a really good chance of winning," he says. "I'm not a good watcher and never have been, especially for nights like that when you really want to be a part of it, special nights.

"No disrespect to the lads who stepped in but having our first XI out I think we would have upset them and probably come away with a result. It was upsetting. You get upset because you lose and you get upset because you're not able to have a go.

"But I think that season really got overshadowed in Europe because of the season we were having in the Premier League. We did really well in Europe, but if we'd have been safe I think we would have had a real chance and a proper good go at it, because I think we had a decent enough side.

"If the second campaign had been like the first campaign when we had Sam, I think we definitely would have been in a better place in the league, and we would have been able to kick on in the second year of the European adventure.

"It was just the start of that season that absolutely killed us, it rocked the camp a lot, and the main priority went towards the Premier League which was really unfortunate. That's why in the end Europe disintegrated really. It was such a shame looking back now."

Even those players who had been given the opportunity to play were left wondering what would have happened had a stronger squad been taken to Lisbon.

"The whole thing was to stay up in the league, that's the way the manager saw fit and I think he did a good job when he was at the club," says O'Brien.

"Probably if I was the manager I would have done the same thing, made sure the players didn't travel and had the extra bit of recovery. But maybe as a selfish player, I was thinking what might have been."

"Gary Megson had a thing for doing that, I don't know why, he took Europe really lightly," says Hunt. "We're in Europe, take your strongest squad, do the best that the club can do, because people are paying God knows how much money to come and watch. As players everyone wanted to play in the European games, no-one wanted to sit at home knowing that the other lads were away. They wanted to have that satisfaction of saying, 'Yes, I played in Europe and it was great'.

"Obviously the press were right on it saying he didn't take it seriously. It looked to us like he didn't take it seriously. Nothing against the players who played that day because they couldn't have played any better and they were fantastic, but as a football club as a whole, you want to take your best 11 and your best subs, you don't want to leave anything to chance.

"If we'd gone there and lost 6-0 with our best 11 then he's taken everyone and they've let themselves down. But the fact that he didn't and we still performed to the level that we did, I think that says a great deal about the players that he did take. They didn't let anything get on top of them, whatever was said, they never lost their focus."

If the UEFA Cup exit was bitterly disappointing, things were about to get a whole lot worse when fans ruefully returned to England from Europe for the final time.

Three days later, around 4,000 supporters packed the away end for the crucial league match at Wigan. To many, only victory could go even close to justifying the decision that had been taken to rest almost the entire team for the trip to Lisbon.

Victory looked fairly likely when Wigan had Jason Koumas sent off for a rash tackle after only five minutes. But despite playing against 10 men for 85 minutes, Wanderers lost 1-0 to a goal from Emile Heskey. The UEFA Cup dream had been sacrificed for nothing.

The atmosphere in the away end was toxic, and it was no better in the dressing room after the game.

"Nobody could have been more angry than I was at Wigan," Megson says. "I can remember going absolutely ballistic because Koumas got sent off really early on and you thought that everything was right for us. All the players had a rest but we got beat 1-0 to a long throw which really stuck in my throat because the team that we played at Sporting Lisbon was a squad team, a reserve team.

"I remember losing it big style in the dressing room afterwards at Wigan because that was the big game of that season. Everyone was fresh and all the big hitters didn't have to travel across to Portugal, then we didn't turn up against Wigan. It was a real disappointment. We probably got an expected result in Lisbon but we really didn't perform against Wigan, which negated both games."

Hunt was not selected in the squad to face Wigan but believes the sadness of the club's UEFA Cup elimination, and the disappointment of those left at home, may have contributed in part to the poor performance.

"Possibly, yes," he said. "Players want to play every game, but what do you do if the manager says you're not in the squad? There's nothing you can do other than accept it and those players who did stay at home would have been wanting to prove something to the manager at Wigan.

"But obviously that went belly up and it all came out in the press about this and that, second team, first XI and all that. It was a bit demeaning to everyone involved. The players that played in Lisbon were just axed for the Wigan game, apart from Gary Cahill and Ali Al Habsi.

"Everyone he left at home played at Wigan, supposedly fresh and ready to go, but it didn't happen like that. It could have happened, we could have beaten Wigan 4-0 or 5-0, then it was a great move from the manager. But it didn't.

"Yes, the players were upset because it was the last 16 of the UEFA Cup. We knew we might never get to play in that again."

"It was a real anti-climax to the UEFA Cup and obviously we didn't perform well at the weekend on the back of that, so it wasn't a great few days to be around to be honest," Davies admits.

For many supporters, the draw for the quarter finals of the UEFA Cup added to their disgruntlement, as Sporting Lisbon were handed a tie against Rangers. How Wanderers fans would have loved to have played the Scottish giants in a real Battle of Britain.

Rangers would beat Sporting, drawing 0-0 at home before winning 2-0 in Lisbon. They went on to defeat Fiorentina on penalties to reach the UEFA Cup final, where they lost to Zenit St Petersburg in Manchester – on a night marred when Scottish fans, who had travelled down in incredible numbers without tickets, rioted in Manchester city centre. Rangers' run to the final was based on grit and hard work, however, rather than incredible ability.

"If we'd beaten Lisbon we'd have played Rangers and I think we would have had a chance to beat them," said McCann. "I think we could have played in the final at Eastlands, but it's easier said than done now.

"If we'd taken Nolan and Davies, those two lads and maybe one more, I think we would have maybe turned Lisbon over. I just felt a little let down. You're only a few games away from the final. Obviously the priority was the Premier League but if we'd won in Lisbon, the game on the Sunday would have taken care of itself. The lads would have been buzzing."

Some office staff at the club were also disappointed by the manner of Wanderers' UEFA Cup exit.

"You look back on it and just think maybe was that a bit of a lost opportunity," says club secretary Simon Marland. "Personally I thought we could have at least got to the final. Fulham are an example, Middlesbrough are too, of clubs who got to the final and had good runs. It would have been nice to have on the honours board UEFA Cup winner or finalist, rather than going out the way we did, which was frustrating more than anything."

Sam Allardyce had quit as Wanderers manager almost a year earlier, but was still keeping a close eye on his old side. He says had he been in the same situation, he would not have selected the squad Megson did for the Sporting game.

"They could have gone all the way," Allardyce says. "It was only because they didn't manage that season as well as we managed the first season we were in Europe, which was critical. What became more important was staying in the Premier League and that never was the case when we got there in year one.

"In that season we always wanted to build a big enough and strong enough squad to have two teams to play in the space of a week. We could have one team that could play on a Thursday in the UEFA Cup and win, and yet we wouldn't have to play too many players from that team on the Sunday in the Premier League. Because we did it like that, we were successful in both.

"The next time around, the last 16 against Sporting, unfortunately I think Gary couldn't go for it because he was having to leave out top class players to try and make sure that they stayed in the Premier League. Well there's nothing worse than that for me. I would have probably sacrificed the Premier League to try to get to the final because Steve McClaren had done it at Middlesbrough and I think that gives you great kudos across Europe, not just in your own country.

"It gives you coaching status across Europe that your small team has got through to the final of the UEFA Cup. It was a shame that they had to sacrifice the opportunity of going farther to try to secure their Premier League status, which was obviously the most important to the club at the time."

Megson, though, doubts the claim that Allardyce would have sacrificed the Premier League in search of personal glory in the UEFA Cup.

"You don't do that as a manager," he said. "It's happened in the past where it's gone okay for the manager but the club has got relegated. I could have picked a team to try to do better in Europe, and then Bolton get relegated.

"I don't think Sam thinks that anyway because when I was at Sheffield Wednesday after that, we played West Ham in the FA Cup when they were to trying to get promoted. He put out a weakened team at Hillsborough and we beat them. Your bread and butter has always got to be the league.

"Before I joined the club the chairman had made it perfectly clear to me that it had to be about surviving in the Premier League. If you look at it just from a financial point of view – and I know you don't, none of us do because you want to do well in every facet – if we win the UEFA Cup we might make £1m. If we finish fourth bottom in the Premier League we'll make £80m next year and be able to stabilise the club and take it forward."

Chairman Phil Gartside stresses that he never had any conversations with Megson advising him on a squad to select for Lisbon, with the manager acknowledging that he made the decision alone. "I don't pick the football team, I've always said that, there's no way," Gartside said.

But the chairman still looks back supportively on the decision that the manager took. He said: "It was done for the right reasons. It was difficult because we had a big game on the Sunday, it was important to us that we won the game on the Sunday. All right, we didn't and it backfired on us something rotten, but we weren't that far off winning in Lisbon. He made that decision, he stuck by it, he chose to put the team out that he did. The fact that we didn't do very well, you can put any team out on the day and if they don't do well they don't do well. It's not a gimme that you put a different team out and you win, there's no such thing as a best team.

"It was a bit of a blow because it sort of spoiled what was a great campaign, remembering that we got through to the last 16. It just soured it that fans didn't appreciate it at the end. The last 16 is an achievement when you look at the teams we were playing. We weren't playing dummies. When you list the teams we played in Europe – Marseille, Red Star Belgrade, Bayern Munich, Zenit St Petersburg – it was better than going to Darlington and Peterborough."

Despite the criticism Megson received and the fact Wanderers lost at Wigan, he insists he would make the same decision again. He has no regrets.

"No, I'd have done exactly the same thing again, but I expected us to beat Wigan," he says. "Hindsight's wonderful but I was determined, I didn't want to be the manager who ended up taking Bolton into the Championship because I knew all the other stuff, how much the club owed, although we were so fortunate to have Eddie Davies. Since then you've seen Wigan and Birmingham who have done ever so well in cups but been relegated. That was something that couldn't happen to Bolton and certainly wasn't going to happen on my watch.

"You can look at the Wigan game as a one-off, but there were other times when we did exactly the same thing and then we came back and beat Wigan at home 4-1 having played on the Thursday night (in Belgrade). We finished the season well and managed to stay up, but those results were the ones that kept us up as well.

"Everybody looks back and thinks if he'd have played a stronger team against Sporting we'd have won and we'd have gone on even further. That might be, that might not be, but you could also say the same thing when we came back and beat Wigan at home. When I left it, the club was in the Premier League because of the decisions we made in Europe, with an eye on the Premier League games."

Megson also disputes the assertion that what became known as 'the Lisbon decision' was the point when his relationship with the fans was critically damaged. Believing that they disliked him anyway, he insists the reaction of the supporters to that and the Wigan defeat did not bother him.

"That was like water off a duck's back in the end," he says. "Whenever we got results, it was very difficult for me personally to the point where I knew what was happening all the time, and after a while it didn't matter. It was just one of those things, they didn't seem to want me as the manager, however well or badly they thought it was going. There was always something to criticise me for.

"But overall when I look at where we were when we joined and the fact that we took Bolton further than they'd ever been in Europe and we stayed up from the worst start, I don't think it was too bad. We'd have cruised staying up and possibly done better if Anelka hadn't been sold in January."

For Byrne-Fraser, the Lisbon experience was the beginning of the end of his own time at the club. He survived sweeping changes to the backroom staff that summer, but differences in opinion with Megson led to his resignation not long afterwards.

"The Sporting Lisbon game was when I started to question what I was doing," he says. "It gets back to the thought of why or what are you doing it for? If you boil sport down to a very basic level, you're in it to compete and win if possible, aren't you? Did I really want to be involved in football? You're involved in the second most prestigious club competition in Europe and you're fielding a weakened team because you're playing Wigan in the Premier League on Sunday?

"The lads who played that night gave their best, it wasn't their fault. Going out of Europe that season was very sad but in a completely different way to the Marseille experience. Marseille was everybody giving their best and we fell short. For Sporting Lisbon, there was basically a starting XI sat at home, all wanting to be there."

Sporting's win over Bolton lifted the pressure on boss Bento and they would recover in the Portuguese league to finish second that season, qualifying for the Champions League once more. Pereirinha, the goalscorer at the Alvalade, would later move to Lazio. Bento eventually resigned in 2009 and became manager of Portugal a year later. After his exit, financial problems saw Sporting slip to seventh in the domestic league by 2012/13 – the lowest finish in the club's entire history.

After that defeat at Wigan, Wanderers slipped deeper into relegation trouble – failing to win any of their next four league games. They lost 3-2 at home to Arsenal after leading 2-0, in a game that saw Hunt make his last appearance for the club. The defender came on as a substitute but went off again three minutes later after the latest in a long line of shoulder dislocations. Falling down the pecking order, after loans at Birmingham and Derby he cut short his Bolton contract in 2010 with a year remaining on his deal. He would move on to Bristol City, Preston, Rotherham and Accrington.

"I dislocated my shoulder about six times at Bolton, it was so frustrating," he says. "It was sad for me to leave, but I couldn't do another year just sat on the bench. It was pointless for me."

Wanderers' 4-0 defeat at Aston Villa in early April left them four points adrift of safety with only five games left. Such was their form, they looked virtually down. But a home win over West Ham was followed by a 1-0 triumph at Middlesbrough, when Al Habsi miraculously kept Bolton in the game and McCann scored the winner in the second half.

"That season I think I made a great name for myself at Bolton Wanderers, with the European run and the way I finished the season in the last 10 games in the league," Al Habsi says.

"I remember the Middlesbrough game, when I made three saves in the first 15 minutes and then we won 1-0. You can't imagine how much pressure there was to perform because Jussi Jaaskelainen had been fantastic for the club and to come with no experience into those 10 games and having to win every one, it was a big pressure. But thanks to god for helping me so I could perform and help keep Bolton Wanderers in the Premier League."

After the Middlesbrough win, all of a sudden Wanderers were out of the relegation zone. They then secured a surprise draw at Spurs thanks to substitute Stelios, who netted what would be his last goal for the club before being released that summer at the end of his contract. He represented Greece at Euro 2008 before moving to Hull and then back to his homeland with Larissa. He later retired and had a spell as the president of the Greek Professional Footballers Association, before his first managerial role at Paniliakos.

"I had so many good moments at Bolton and these things are always going to be in my head," he says. "I will never forget it. I had a great time."

A turbulent and unforgettable season, for all sorts of reasons, ended on a high note after Wanderers effectively secured their survival in the Premier League with a game to spare, to huge relief. Diouf was the man who scored the crucial goal that put them on course for a 2-0 home win over Sunderland in the Reebok sun.

Diouf still regards it as his favourite Wanderers goal, but it came in his last game for Bolton at the Reebok. That summer he joined Sunderland, having voiced his desire for a new challenge. Later he moved on to Blackburn, Rangers, Doncaster and Leeds, but perhaps never reached the heights he had achieved with Bolton, where he remained a cult hero long after his departure. Looking back on his decision to leave, he admits part of him does regret it.

"A little bit, for the fans," Diouf says. "I'm so proud to have played for Bolton, so proud to have done what I did for the club because of the fans. They gave me everything. I know they loved me so much and that's why I never wanted to disappoint them.

"In England I can say it was the best time of my career because I played great football with wonderful players."

Also departing that summer was Campo, who moved to Ipswich and then Cypriot club AEK Larnaca before retiring. Meite joined West Bromwich Albion and eventually ended up in Finland with Honka Espoo, before returning to England with Doncaster. Guthrie and Mikel Alonso returned to their parent clubs after season-long loans, while Braaten left for Toulouse but would later represent FC Copenhagen in the Champions League. Andranik switched to Fulham and then went back to play in his native Iran. In 2011 he was surprisingly joined at Esteghlal by former Wanderers team-mate Samuel.

Megson stabilised things during the 2008/09 season, as Wanderers finished 13th – despite selling Nolan to Newcastle. But the manager had still not won the fans back after Lisbon, and the tension between supporters and boss persisted as the long-running theme of his tenure.

Days after Christmas in the following season, Wanderers were third bottom – albeit with games in hand – going into a home match against fellow strugglers Hull. Wanderers led 2-0 but the visitors pulled a goal back and Megson then infuriated fans by bringing on midfielder McCann in place of striker Ivan Klasnic, in a bid to protect the lead. It backfired spectacularly, as Hull equalised to boos from the home supporters.

"I'd had a knock in a game just before that, and my ankle wasn't right," McCann says. "Even I was wondering why he was putting me on. I was the same as all the people who were booing, I was thinking the same thing."

Deciding the caustic relationship between fans and manager could not go on, Gartside relieved Megson of his duties the morning afterwards. Megson still thinks it was the wrong decision.

"We kept the club up, we did okay in Europe, the year after that we stabilised it and finished mid-table and then I got the boot," he says. "We still had three games in hand and we were three points off 12th. The club was starting to repair from what had gone on. Now I look at it and what has happened since, and it's a crying shame."

Wanderers had good times initially after Megson was replaced as boss by Owen Coyle. Bolton ended that season in 14th and a year later were surprisingly challenging for Europe again, both in the league and the FA Cup. A quarter final victory at Birmingham set up an FA Cup semi final against Stoke at Wembley, with the winners going into the Europa League – the competition previously known as the UEFA Cup.

Sitting eighth in the table at the time, Wanderers were the favourites for that semi final, but incredibly lost 5-0, in one of the most shocking games in the club's recent history. That, and a serious knee injury sustained by midfielder Stuart Holden weeks earlier, proved to be a real turning point. Bolton slid to 14th in the final table and were relegated from the Premier League a year later on the last day of the season.

The UEFA Cup days were long gone and so were many of the remaining players from that era. Surgery on McCann's ankle injury did not have the desired effect and he was forced to retire, joining Wanderers' youth set-up as well as having a spell as assistant manager at Hyde.

Both O'Briens left in 2011, with Andy joining Leeds and Joey released after more knee problems meant he did not make a single appearance for Wanderers for two-and-a-half seasons. He would later rejoin Allardyce at West Ham, where he got his career back on track in the Premier League. He still treasures those days in the UEFA Cup.

"I have some great memories of the two European campaigns that will be with me forever," he says. "I look back and it's one of the highlights of my career."

That summer Taylor also moved to West Ham and Al Habsi signed for Wigan, where he would win the FA Cup with a shock victory over Manchester City in 2013. Cahill joined Chelsea for £7m midway through Wanderers' relegation season, and helped the Blues win the Champions League with victory over Bayern Munich in the final at the Allianz Arena months later, before lining up for England at the 2014 World Cup.

After the club dropped into the Championship, Gardner was not offered a new contract and Jaaskelainen left to join the former Wanderers contingent at West Ham after failing to agree terms on a deal. Davies, the last player remaining from the club's UEFA Cup days, was released after one season in the Championship, joining Preston at the age of 36.

The contribution of Davies and all his team-mates from the UEFA Cup years will always be remembered by Wanderers fans. It was a remarkable era when greats of the game played for Bolton, and helped the club compete with the greats of European football. Wanderers became known as a top half Premier League team and a team that no-one in Europe wanted to face. Ask Atletico Madrid, Arsenal, Liverpool, Manchester United, even Bayern Munich.

By the end of their second season in Europe, Wanderers had climbed to 47th in the UEFA rankings – up from 78th after their first campaign. Bolton Wanderers really were officially the 47th best team in Europe – better than famous names such as Galatasaray, Borussia Dortmund, Paris Saint-Germain, Lazio, Dynamo Kiev, Anderlecht, Besiktas, Deportivo La Coruna, Feyenoord, Atletico Madrid and Manchester City.

After their 4-0 defeat at Scarborough in 1987, they stood 83rd in England, let alone Europe – behind the likes of Hereford, Halifax and Darlington.

That, perhaps more than anything, told you how far Bolton had come. The ending may not have been perfect but it had been quite a journey – a journey that in two seasons in the UEFA Cup had taken them to Lokomotiv Plovdiv, to Besiktas, to Vitoria Guimaraes, to Marseille, to Rabotnicki, to Bayern Munich, to Red Star Belgrade, to Atletico Madrid and to Sporting Lisbon.

Yes, it really did happen. No-one who was there will ever forget it.

Bolton: Ali Al Habsi; Nicky Hunt, Gary Cahill, Abdoulaye Meite, Jlloyd Samuel; Andranik Teymourian (Daniel Braaten 71), Joey O'Brien, Danny Guthrie; Ricardo Vaz Te, Heidar Helguson (Nathan Woolfe 76), Stelios Giannakopoulos. Subs not used: Ian Walker, Scott Jamieson, Robert Sissons, James Sinclair, Zoltan Harsanyi.
Booked: Teymourian, Guthrie.

Sporting: Rui Patricio; Abel, Tonel, Anderson Polga, Leandro Grimi; Bruno Pereirinha, Joao Moutinho, Marat Izmailov (Gladstone 87), Leandro Romagnoli (Adrien Silva 75); Simon Vukcevic (Rodrigo Tiui 66), Liedson. Subs not used: Vladimir Stojkovic, Ronny, Pontus Farnerud, Yannick Djalo.
Booked: Moutinho.
Goal: Pereirinha 85.

Attendance: 22,031.
Referee: Bertrand Layec (France).

About the Author

Chris Flanagan has been a journalist for 10 years and was present at all 18 of Bolton Wanderers' matches in the UEFA Cup as a lifelong supporter of the club.

He graduated from Oxford University and has since spent many years travelling to more than 30 countries watching sport. He has reported on Amir Khan fights in the United States and rugby league in Australia, as well as writing about his experiences of Champions League football in the depths of the Russian winter and the World Cup in Brazil.

In 2014 he was nominated for the daily sports journalist of the year at the British Regional Press Awards, for his work at the Lancashire Telegraph.